M000210816

OPENING THE SEVEN SEALS

OPENING THE SEVEN SEALS

THE VISIONS OF
JOHN THE REVELATOR

RICHARD D. DRAPER

Deseret Book Company
Salt Lake City, Utah

To Barbara,
in appreciation for
years of support

Library of Congress Cataloging-in-Publication Data

Draper, Richard D.
    Opening the seven seals : the visions of John the Revelator /
Richard D. Draper.
        p. cm.
    Includes bibliographical references and index.
    ISBN 0-87579-547-1
    1. Bible N.T. Revelation—Criticism, interpretation, etc.
I. Title.
BS2825.2.D73   1991
228'.06—dc20   91-26254
                                                                 CIP

Printed in the United States of America

10   9   8   7   6   5   4

CONTENTS

PREFACE

For thus saith the Lord, in the spirit of truth,
I am merciful, gracious, and good unto those
That fear me, and live for the life that's to come;
My delight is to honor the saints with repose;
That serve me in righteousness true to the end;
Eternal's their glory, and great their reward;
I'll surely reveal all my myst'ries to them, —
The great hidden myst'ries in my kingdom stor'd —
From the council in Kolob, to time on the earth,
And for ages to come unto them I will show
My pleasure & will, what my kingdom will do:
Eternity's wonders they truly shall know.
Great things of the future I'll show unto them,
Yea, things of the vast generations to rise;
For their wisdom and glory shall be very great,
And their pure understanding extend to the skies.
Joseph Smith[1]

Joseph Smith counseled the brethren to preach both repentance and the warning that the kingdom of God was at hand. He instructed further, "Never meddle with the visions of beasts and subjects you do not understand."[2] That counsel is good. So what am I doing writing an analysis of a book in which some of the fiercest and most mysterious beasts in the whole Bible are found?

I have asked myself that question quite a number of times both before undertaking the task and as I was in the process of research and writing. I must admit that the book engrosses me as it has other quacks and cranks through all ages up to the present. But I am also impressed that it has haunted the greatest poets from Dante and Spenser through Milton to Blake and Shelley. But most importantly, the work is one of only three biblical texts endorsed in the Book of Mormon.

The greatest commendation went to Isaiah. Of his writing the Lord said to the Book of Mormon people, "A commandment I give unto you that ye search these things diligently; for great are the words of Isaiah" (3 Ne. 23:1). He also revealed large sections of the writings of Malachi (see 3 Ne. 24–25), explaining that "these scriptures, which ye had not with you, the Father commanded that I should give unto you; for it was wisdom in him that they should be given unto future generations" (3 Ne. 26:2).

Concerning the writings of John, as will be amplified in the next chapter, the Lord has promised that "when ye shall rend that veil of unbelief . . . then shall the great and marvelous things which have been hid up from the foundation of the world from you [be revealed]. . . . Then shall my revelations which I have caused to be written by my servant John be unfolded in the eyes of all the people. Remember, when ye see these things, ye shall know that the time is at hand that they shall be made manifest in very deed" (Ether 4:15–16). I believe that the Saints have come to that era. Through the revelations given to the Church, much of John's master work can be understood. As we do so, we truly see that "the time is at hand."

Those who get into the book can't seem to leave it alone. In Western literature the apocalyptic genre always returns to Revelation rather than to Zechariah, Ezekiel, or Daniel. I believe the book grasps and holds because of the hope that weaves itself throughout the work. Those who understand the message of Revelation want the end to come out as the vision shows. Good must triumph over evil. The cosmos must be swept clean of malevolence, and love must overmaster all. Any other outcome would be tragedy.

But the message is not all that holds a reader. The method

in which John saw the vision, wrote it, and magnified it holds the imagination. He used the most graphic of images — images drawn from the most sublime of dreams, and the most tortured of nightmares. Few works depict the depth of evil or the height of good better than Revelation.

Two needs kept pestering me to write. The first was for a clear analysis, using insights from modern scripture and prophetic utterance, of one of the greatest prophecies ever recorded. The second was to identify and point out those portions for which we must yet await further enlightenment.

Two other factors contributed. The first is the whelming enthusiasm I found for the book in my New Testament classes. (Note, I did not write "overwhelming." The response was not exactly "overwhelming," but it was pleasantly surprising and expressed, I believe, a solid interest if not a need.)

The second is something that presses upon me from the pages of the vision itself. I would translate my feeling as a sense of urgency, of a need to move, to prepare, to be ready. John's invocation upon all those who receive the revelation is rendered by the King James translators: "Blessed is he that readeth, and they that hear the words of this prophecy, and keep those things which are written therein: for the time is at hand" (Rev. 1:3).

The last phrase, "for the time is at hand," is what urges me. The Greek (*ho gar kairos eggus*) can be translated as the King James Version does it, but I fear that with that rendering we are likely to misunderstand John's thrust. The sense is that time is limited, or that time presses. This captures the idea of how the inner tempo, the spiritual vigor of the age, will escalate as mankind enters the apocalyptic era. As the earth prepares for the coming of her Lord, time becomes laden with force, charged with an irresistible destiny. The Greek does not employ the ordinary word for time (*chronos*) but speaks of the *kairos:* time that has matured, that has found fulfillment.

Closely connected with the thought is a phrase repeated three times near the end of the book: "Behold, I come quickly" (Rev. 22: 7, 12, cf. 20). The Lord is not telling the early Christians to expect him at any moment. Rather, the phrase characterizes a dynamic quality of time. The Lord is saying that he comes in the pressing, the urgent time—the time bearing within it a measureless spiritual hastening that moves to crescendo upon a humanity unmoved, unrepentant, and unprepared. One scholar said, "That Christ comes quickly can very well mean that He comes 'too quickly' for an unprepared and sleeping humanity. That the time is 'near' may mean that it is 'short'; that it is actually too short considering the slowness and laziness of human souls."[3]

In order to fulfill the need for a clear analysis of Revelation, I have done four things: translated the document paying close attention to variations found in the different preserved manuscripts, including the Joseph Smith Translation; studied the most important Jewish and Christian apocalypses, drawing out what I could from them; consulted the studies of scholars both within and without the Church; and most importantly, pulled together those insights gained from the Standard Works and the teachings of the modern prophets.

Further, I have not ignored the historical setting in which the work was composed. To do so would have impoverished the study as it would that of any literature. Though a person may enjoy Shakespeare without a knowledge of Elizabethan England, understanding and appreciation are greatly increased when he has at least some of that knowledge. The same holds true for Revelation, and for that matter, the New Testament as a whole.

Even so, not all the questions concerning John's vision are answered in this book, nor are they answerable. For this reason some may find this study disappointing. The plain fact is that there are portions of Revelation that cannot be fully understood at present. It will take either time or further revelation to make them clear. I have not ignored these difficult areas. Various theories have been presented so that the reader can be aware of the arguments and problems. Often no solution is proposed.

The reader needs to be aware of three additional points. First, this book brings together only the material from the scriptures and the prophetic teachings, both ancient and modern, that clarify John's message. Therefore, this book is neither a compendium of statements about nor a study of the last days. Further, it is not a complete commentary carefully examining each verse of John's vision. It is an analysis of the message of the book of Revelation, overall and chapter by chapter. Second, many biblical quotes will differ from those in the King James Version (hereafter noted as KJV). In most cases I am using my own translation (hereafter noted as AT), and less frequently, the Joseph Smith Translation (hereafter noted as JST) in order to make a passage clearer. Note, however, that the text of the KJV is quoted for reference in its entirety at the beginning of each sectional study. Third, there are a number of references to classical sources and ancient Jewish and Christian apocryphal and pseudepigraphical texts and documents. The citations for these follow the abbreviation and note style found in the *Oxford Classical Dictionary* and the *Interpreter's Dictionary of the Bible*.[4]

I am indebted to a host of people for their assistance and suggestions on this endeavor. I would like to give special thanks to Vic Werlhof, whose enthusiasm for the project was a great source of encouragement and whose generous financial contributions made this work possible; to my colleagues Larry E. Dahl, Robert L. Millet, and Paul H. Peterson, who read portions of the text and offered valuable suggestions; to my daughter Jessica E. Draper, who turned a rough draft into a product that I was not ashamed to show others; to my research assistants Amy B. C. Rossiter, Lara K. Harris, and Robert B. Bennett for their painstaking work on checking sources, notes, style, and grammar. I extend special thanks to Richard L. Anderson, who read the entire manuscript and whose insights and recommendations have made this work more sound. Finally, I extend appreciation to my wife, Barbara, not only for her continued support in this product, but also for everything that makes life meaningful.

Though I have sought to be in harmony with Church doctrine, to faithfully interpret the scriptures, and to accurately represent the power of the message of Revelation, all conclusions and assertions in this book represent my own understanding.

CHAPTER 1

"AS A FLAMING FIRE AND A MINISTERING ANGEL"

(D&C 7:6)

POWER OVER DEATH

To his disciples Jesus said, "Verily I say unto you, There be some standing here, which shall not taste of death, till they see the Son of man coming in his kingdom" (Matt. 16:28, KJV). One wonders if the Lord's gaze fell upon John. Not many months later, the Savior said to him, "John, my beloved, what desirest thou? For if you shall ask what you will, it shall be granted unto you" (D&C 7:1). Standing before the Lord of life, John asked what would otherwise have been the inconceivable: "Lord, give unto me power over death, that I may live and bring souls unto thee" (v. 2). His desire was granted. "Because thou desirest this," affirmed the Lord, "thou shalt tarry until I come in my glory, and shalt prophesy before nations, kindreds, tongues and people" (v. 3).

John's aspiration set on course the fulfillment of a prophecy made nearly six hundred years earlier. The American prophet Nephi, caught away in vision, saw the entire history of the world. Like others, he was forbidden to write but not without explanation:

The angel spake unto me, saying: Look! And I looked and

1

beheld a man, and he was dressed in a white robe. And the angel said unto me: Behold one of the twelve apostles of the Lamb. Behold, he shall see and write the remainder of these things; yea, and also many things which have been. And he shall also write concerning the end of the world.

Wherefore, the things which he shall write are just and true; and behold they are written in the book which thou beheld proceeding out of the mouth of the Jew; and at the time they proceeded out of the mouth of the Jew, or, at the time the book proceeded out of the mouth of the Jew, the things which were written were plain and pure, and most precious and easy to the understanding of all men.

And behold, the things which this apostle of the Lamb shall write are many things which thou hast seen; and behold, the remainder shalt thou see. But the things which thou shalt see hereafter thou shalt not write; for the Lord God hath ordained the apostle of the Lamb of God that he should write them.

And also others who have been, to them hath he shown all things, and they have written them; and they are sealed up to come forth in their purity, according to the truth which is in the Lamb, in the own due time of the Lord, unto the house of Israel.

And I, Nephi, heard and bear record, that the name of the apostle of the Lamb was John, according to the word of the angel (1 Ne. 14:18–27).

Thus, it fell to John to give the vision to the world. But as he did so, he also chronicled the history through which he himself would live. He knew in broad terms the entire history of the last two millennia. It is unlikely, however, that he knew of the spiritual manifestation that awaited him after a Roman ruler, perhaps Domitian himself, banished him for some time to a little Greek island in the Aegean Sea.

THE SETTING OF THE REVELATION

Patmos is a small, roughly butterfly-shaped volcanic island southwest of the Turkish city of Ephesus. It measures about ten by five miles. The earliest references to it are found in Thucydides and later in Strabo.[1] The writings of Pliny note that under Rome a number of islands were used as penal settlements. In addition to Patmos, there were Pontia, off the coast of Latium, and Gyara and Seriphus in the Aegean Sea.[2] At that time Patmos was fertile though it relied heavily upon rain for its water supply. The prisoners were thus able to take care of themselves. Today, though no longer fertile, the island boasts a population of about 2,400 fishing families.[3]

The revelation came while John was serving time in that penal colony. He notes that his crime was declaring "the word of God, and for the testimony of Jesus Christ" (Rev. 1:9, KJV).[4] The exact nature of his punishment is unknown, but it consisted at least in part of banishment. Among the Romans there were two types of exile: *deportatio* and *relegatio*. *Deportatio* was permanent and consisted of the loss of rights and property. Only the emperor could impose it. *Relegatio* ran in length from one-half to ten years and involved no loss of rights or property. The Roman senate, a city prefect, or other officials could inflict it. John seems to have suffered the milder *relegatio*, probably imposed by a governor of the Roman province of Asia if not by the emperor himself.[5] At any rate, he was later freed and able to continue his work.

Establishing a firm date for John's imprisonment is impossible.[6] According to his testimony, it was at a time when the Christians were being persecuted on a fairly large scale. Since some forms of harassment were going on from the mid-40s and continued off and on throughout the first and later centuries after the birth of the Lord, no period is totally exempt. Two times vie for the most support among scholars as the period of greatest persecution: the late-60s and the 90s. During the former, Nero launched his persecution against the Christians at Rome. During the latter, Domitian pushed his empire-wide pogrom of all Christians.

Those who favor the Neronian era use evidence from Revelation itself. For example, they point to the head of the beast that was wounded and came alive (see Rev. 13:3) as a reference to Nero. Because this fits certain legends that sprung up shortly after the death of the emperor, they insist that John had him in mind. Those who favor Domitian's time base their evidence on the early sources, which are quite unanimous on the subject. The decade of the 90s also best fits the evidence.

During this decade the triangular struggle between pagans, Jews, and Christians escalated in Asia Minor. This was an area that had a tradition for religious strife often sparked by the frequent natural disasters. About A.D. 92 there was an anti-Christian outbreak due in part to a serious famine blamed on the Saints because they refused to pay homage to pagan gods. Boycotts and trade sanctions were directed against the churches. Arrests, imprisonments, banishments, and even executions followed. The famine first affected Pisidian Antioch and later Prusa in the north of the province. Apparently, even areas outside this province were hit.[7]

In addition, the emperor Domitian launched a wide pogrom specifically against the Christians. He had a profound hostility toward any form of religious unorthodoxy, that is, any religion he felt was antithetical to Roman belief. Prominent citizens who lapsed too blatantly into an "external religion" such as Christianity or Judaism came under his censure even to the point of banishment and death. Further, he became megalomaniacal late in his career, eventually persuading himself he was lord and god. He demanded that his court address him as such. He ordered libations to be made and incense to be offered before his statues. Those who refused, many Christians included, were punished.[8]

Under these or similar circumstances John received a sentence of banishment to the island. There he remained probably for years.[9] At what point he received the apocalypse is unknown, but one may rest assured that this was not the only time John enjoyed comfort from the Spirit during his long vigil "for the testimony of Jesus." Finally the day came for his release. According to one tradition, he retired to western Asia Minor (present-day Turkey) and there continued the work of the ministry.[10]

JOHN'S PURPOSE IN WRITING REVELATION

John wrote the book of Revelation with a definite objective in mind. His intent grew out of the visionary experience. It was to fulfill the commandment given him directly by Jesus Christ himself (see Rev. 1:11). However, there were other factors at play. Many of the Saints were discouraged, even frightened. They were in the midst of the greatest crisis yet faced by the early Church. The ordeal through which they were passing had terrifying prospects. Rome, the seemingly omnipotent master of their world, had determined that holding to the Christian faith constituted a crime worthy of death. The churches in Asia already knew the effect of that brutal decision. Many undoubtedly wondered how a few powerless Christians could survive against the Latin colossus.

But more than external danger threatened the life of the fledgling Church. Indeed, a far greater threat overshadowed them than the injustice of the cold Roman master. This was the period in which apostasy was visibly gaining the upper hand after a half century of struggle. The Savior's apostles and prophets knew it was coming. It was one of the themes on which the Lord had dwelt during his forty-day ministry after his resurrection (see Acts 1:3).[11]

From the days of that ministry, the shadow of the Antichrist haunted the peace of the Saints. Paul warned the Thessalonians, the Melitians, and others that a "falling away" would occur because men would not endure sound doctrine (see 2 Thes. 2:1–5; 2 Tim. 4:3–4; Acts 20:29–31). "Also of your own selves," he told them, "shall men arise, speaking perverse things, to draw away disciples after them" (Acts 20:30, KJV). As a result of this falling away the "man of sin," a son of perdition, would be revealed "who opposeth and exalteth himself above all that is called God, or that is worshipped; so that he as God sitteth in the temple [i.e., the church] of God, [showing] himself that he is God" (2 Thes. 2:3–4, KJV).

The Greek word Paul used that is translated as "falling away" is *apostasia*. It meant literally to stand apart in immovable opposition, and in a civil sense, "rebellion" or, better, "revolution" or "mutiny." It carried the idea of an internal takeover by parties hostile to established authority, leadership, and constitution.[12] Paul warned the Church for over three years that there would be such a rebellion. Once the rebellion succeeded, those leaders whom the Savior chose would be replaced by others of a perverse nature (wolves in sheep's clothing) who would change the doctrine (constitution) of Christ to fit their own base desires. Paul's warning shows that the Church was not in danger of totally disappearing. Rather, those antichrists, who would replace Christ's gospel with the doctrines of men, would assume control.

John fought against these stubbornly disobedient and defiant individuals. We know the names of some of them: Diotrephes, Alexander the coppersmith, Hymenaeus, and Philetus (see 3 Jn. 1:9–10; 1 Tim. 1:20; 2 Tim. 2:17; 4:14). These and others perverted the doctrine by setting themselves up as leaders and replacing the teachings of Christ with their own. It appears that in many areas local officers also struggled to supplant the authority and leadership of the prophets and apostles. Presbyters and bishops vied for power and claimed authority that was not theirs.[13]

The situation was critical. A false prophetic circle arose that competed with the true prophets for ecclesiastical authority and theological acceptance. False apostles infiltrated the church at Ephesus (see Rev. 2:2); at Pergamos a faction upheld what John called the "doctrine of Balaam" (Rev. 2:14, KJV), which was probably a move to incorporate into Church practice certain elements of the pagan religion of the Romans; while at Thyatira a false prophetess with quite a number of followers seduced many with her teachings (see v. 20). Heresy was spreading everywhere.

We see in the first of John's epistles the thrust that the apostasy was taking. There he admonishes his readers to "believe not every spirit, but try the spirits whether they are of God: because many false prophets are gone out into the world" (1 Jn. 4:1, KJV). Apostolic authority with its basis in true prophecy must be followed, he admonished, because "we are of God: he that knoweth God heareth us; he that is not of God heareth not us. Hereby know we the spirit of truth, and the spirit of error" (v. 6, KJV).

A better grasp of these passages is gained when one understands the nature of the prophetic office in the early Church. The Apostles were the ranking authorities (see 1 Cor. 12:28); indeed, the very foundation of the Church consisted of apostles and prophets (see Eph. 2:20). However, this led to a problem: certain persons arose claiming the prophetic gift and, on that basis, Church authority. This happened as early as the mid-fifth decade.

Paul pointed out the necessity of discerning between the alternate voices claiming to speak by the Spirit (see 1 Tim. 6:20–21) and laid down some basic rules for distinguishing the true from the false (see 1 Cor. 12:3). The need seems to have become even more acute a few decades later when John told his followers to "test the spirits" (1 Jn. 4:1, AT).[14] And this problem was still being felt a half century after that. The writer of the *Didachē* warned his readers that a man was not a prophet who sponged off the community of believers and demanded meals or money while in purported prophetic ecstasy.[15]

At the time John wrote Revelation, a power struggle raged within the Christian community. John wrote his work for those who yet clung to the truth. He warned against false prophets and their source of inspiration, and emphasized that God would not allow them to continue without consequence. If the churches chose to reject God's officers, he would come out in judgment by abandoning the churches and allowing the false leaders to take over. However, this condition would only last for a time. Eventually, the apostate church would be consumed under a blaze of truth and light.

But what of the nation that was the political seat of persecution and whose authority even the least of the Christians felt? The Revelator had an answer. God would move against Rome and the other recreant nations that would follow. His authority would prevail over even these seemingly omnipotent masters. And the powers of hell, which undergirded and supported the corrupt governments and from which they drew both their strength and inspiration, would also incur the terrible wrath of God. Driven into a war lust, they would fight against themselves until the time God would intervene and stop all fighting, rendering them eternally impotent.

Thus, the focus of Revelation — the core around which everything revolves — centers on the issue of authority. Who really overmasters the world? Is it the political institutions? the powers of evil? or God? To the faithful few, struggling against external pressure and deadly persecutions and being buffeted by alternate voices, the message of Revelation with its omnipotent, wrath-filled yet caring God, must have brought comfort and hope with the promise of final victory.

But all was not bliss. There was no promise of relief from suffering outside of death. The picture John portrayed gave no illusion of peace but of an extended period of warfare. The future, until the end of time, was to be ruled by Satan who, though mortally wounded, would fight desperately using his minions both incorporeal and mortal.[16]

Some have viewed John's intent as nothing more than keeping the Saints in line by holding out the promise of eternal reward.[17] But John's aim seems far more noble. It is true that the course of history he presents stressed the ultimate, rather than the immediate triumph of goodness over evil, and yet the call was for the Saints to work out their salvation in the present and to place their trust in God who was not yet ready to expose his mastery over history. Triumph was not immediately at hand. The Saints had to exercise faith through a hope that made no demands upon the present. They could not escape history. The work of God would continue for a long period within its confines. Even today, an aspect of faith is a willingness to allow God to operate in his own way in the present, to take what comes, and to continue strong. God, through his Saints, will achieve ultimate victory. John's readers had to accept the agony of the present as travail necessary to bring into being a glorious future.[18]

CONCLUSION

Of John, the Savior said, "I will make him as flaming fire and a ministering angel; he shall minister for those who shall be heirs of salvation who dwell on the earth" (D&C 7:6). Surely in writing Revelation John partially fulfilled the Lord's intent. He wrote a message of testimony and hope to those "heirs of salvation" who lingered in his own day. But he also wrote for the Lord's people living in the latter days. For those who understand, the flaming fire of his testimony still lights the way to the Lord and Savior of the world.

CHAPTER 2

THE REVELATION OF ST. JOHN THE DIVINE

REVELATION – A BOOK TO BE UNDERSTOOD

As a trumpet calls soldiers to battle, a voice deep as eternity summoned John away from his Sabbath meditations. Turning toward the sound, he saw a radiant being surrounded with indescribable light. The heavenly being announced that John was about to have a revelation that he was to record and then send to the churches of God. The title given to this work in the KJV is most appropriate: "The Revelation of St. John the Divine." The term *divine*, as used here, is not an adjective describing one who is godly, but rather a noun denoting one who foresees. The breadth of the Seer's vision encompassed all earthly time and reached even into eternity.

This revelation has come forth as a testament of the fore-knowledge of God, giving many hope and assurance through nearly two millennia. Its message, for those who are willing to pay the price to understand it, continues to proclaim comfort. This is especially true for the Saints living during the last days. It does this primarily by assisting them in preparing for the Second Coming of the Son of the Most High. Indeed, there is no other people for whom it is more germane.

A scholar described Revelation as a book that finds a man

mad or leaves him that way.[1] Many who have labored through its maze would agree. But God gave the vision and preserved it for a purpose. He meant his Saints to understand it. It is not, however, a book for the spiritual novice. The Revelator received it by the power of prophecy, and one can best understand it by that same power. It was in this vein that Joseph Smith declared that the book "is one of the plainest books God ever caused to be written."[2] To those who live in the day when prophets of God again walk the earth, who have access through the prophets to eternal truths and thus to the gift of prophecy, the central message of the book is clear.

In response to the question, "Are we expected to understand the book of Revelation?" Elder Bruce R. McConkie stated:

> Certainly. Why else did the Lord reveal it? The common notion that it deals with beasts and plagues and mysterious symbolisms that cannot be understood is just not true. It is so far overstated that it gives an entirely erroneous feeling about this portion of revealed truth. Most of the book—and it is no problem to count the verses so included—is clear and plain and should be understood by the Lord's people. Certain parts are not clear and are not understood by us—which, however, does not mean that we could not understand them if we would grow in faith as we should. The Lord expects us to seek wisdom, to ponder his revealed truths, and to gain a knowledge of them by the power of his Spirit.[3]

His point is that Latter-day Saints are in an excellent position to understand the Apocalypse. To us the Lord has stated, "Unto you it shall be given to know the signs of the times, and the signs of the coming of the Son of Man" (D&C 68:11). And again:

> For thus saith the Lord—I, the Lord, am merciful and gracious unto those who fear me, and delight to honor those who serve me in righteousness and in truth unto the end. Great shall be their reward and eternal shall be their glory. And to them will I reveal all mysteries, yea, all the hidden mysteries of my kingdom from days of old, and for ages to come, will I make known unto them the good pleasure of my will concerning all things pertaining to my kingdom. Yea, even the wonders of eternity shall they know, and things to come will I show them, even the things of many generations (D&C 76:5–8).

He admonishes further, "The coming of the Lord draweth nigh, and it overtaketh the world as a thief in the night — therefore, gird up your loins, that you may be the children of light, and that day shall not overtake you as a thief" (D&C 106:4–5). These scriptures show that the Lord has no intention of hiding the future from his Saints. The book of Revelation proves this fact. As further evidence that God is willing to share this knowledge, we can look to Joseph Smith's latter-day example. He saw the entire history of the earth. Of the experience, he stated: "After I got through translating the Book of Mormon, I took up the Bible to read with the Urim and Thummim. I read the first chapter of Genesis and I saw the things as they were done. I turned over the next and the next, and the whole passed before me like a grand panorama; and so on chapter after chapter until I read the whole of it. *I saw it all!*"[4]

JOHN'S VISION AND THE SEALED PORTION
OF THE BOOK OF MORMON

Numerous prophets have been privileged to see panoramic visions that sweep through time, but to John was given the privilege of recording the comprehensive vision of the beginning to the end. The Book of Mormon prophet known as the brother of Jared saw, like John, the entire history of the world (see Ether 3:25–27). Though there have been few prophets who could rival the seeric power of Jared's brother, the sacred knowledge given to him was not to be shared with a faithless world. The Lord gave him explicit instructions:

> Behold, thou shalt not suffer these things which ye have seen and heard to go forth unto the world, until the time cometh that I shall glorify my name in the flesh; wherefore, ye shall treasure up the things which ye have seen and heard, and show it to no man. And behold, when ye shall come unto me, ye shall write them and shall seal them up. . . .
> When the Lord had said these words, he showed unto the brother of Jared all the inhabitants of the earth which had been, and also all that would be; and he withheld them not from his sight, even unto the ends of the earth. . . . And the Lord said unto him: Write these things and seal them up; and

I will show them in mine own due time unto the children of men (Ether 3:21-22, 25, 27).

The Jaredite prophet Ether preserved and eventually bequeathed, through the people of Lamoni, the record to the Nephites. After the Savior's appearance to his American disciples, the record was translated and became a part of their scriptures. Because of ensuing disbelief, the vision was lost to them. Moroni, however, preserved it as a part of his record. His translation constituted at least part of the sealed portion of the Book of Mormon plates, which Joseph Smith was expressly forbidden to translate with these words: "Touch them not in order that ye may translate; for that thing is forbidden you, except by and by it shall be wisdom in God" (Ether 5:1). That vision has remained sealed ever since. However, another saw and recorded the same vision. The sealed portion of the Book of Mormon "contains the same revelation which was given to John upon the isle of Patmos," albeit Jared's brother apparently wrote with a great deal more detail.[5]

The unique feature about John's revelation is that the prophet was commanded not to seal it up. Indeed, John seems to be the only prophet commissioned to publish the vision up to this time. Daniel and Nephi also saw and wrote these things, but, like Jared's brother, they were commanded to seal them up that they might later come forth in their purity (see Dan. 12:4, 9; 1 Ne. 14:25-26). Nephi was expressly forbidden to write what he saw (1 Ne. 14:28).[6]

Someday, the Lord has promised, the revelation recorded by the brother of Jared will be revealed. This will be in conjunction with the restoration of the gospel. As the Lord said to the house of Israel:

> When ye shall rend that veil of unbelief which doth cause you to remain in your awful state of wickedness, and hardness of heart, and blindness of mind, then shall the great and marvelous things which have been hid up from the foundation of the world from you — yea, when ye shall call upon the Father in my name, with a broken heart and a contrite spirit, then shall ye know that the Father hath remembered the covenant

which he made unto your fathers, O house of Israel (Ether 4:15).

Until then John's record will have to fill the gap. Fortunately, this is far from being a burden. Unto Moroni the Lord stated, "And then [when Israel comes to accept the Savior] shall my revelations which I have caused to be written by my servant John be unfolded in the eyes of all the people. Remember, when ye see these things, ye shall know that the time is at hand that they shall be made manifest in very deed" (Ether 4:16). Reading and understanding Revelation can result in a sensitivity to the latter-day events as they unfold.

THE VISION GIVEN IN CODE

John wrote far less than he knew. Joseph Smith on one occasion stated that the Seer "saw the same things concerning the last days, which Enoch saw."[7] The statement may allude to the vision of Enoch recorded in Moses 7:41–67, which says in part, "The Lord showed Enoch all things, even unto the end of the world; and he saw the day of the righteous, the hour of their redemption, and received a fulness of joy" (v. 67).

There was, however, a problem with recording that information. Both John and Nephi seemed to have been aware of it, but Nephi articulated it, stating that the Bible would go through the hands of the "great and abominable church, which is most abominable above all other churches; for behold, they have taken away from the gospel of the Lamb many parts which are plain and most precious; and also many covenants of the Lord have they taken away" (1 Ne. 13:26). This was done in a deliberate attempt to pervert the gospel and lead men astray (see 1 Ne. 13:14–28). The problem was to get the message through the editors of the great and abominable church.

John did not choose the form of the vision; God did. The form is now called *apocalyptic*. It provided John with the means of being able to write in a kind of divine code. And it seems to have worked well for him. Though there are more variant manuscript readings of the text of Revelation than those of any other

New Testament book, these are not sufficient to cause uncertainty on the meaning of a single paragraph taken as a whole. In the four hundred verses of Revelation, there are about 1,650 variant readings (these do not include different spellings of the same word) in the five available uncials. For comparison the general epistles contain 432 verses and contain about 1,100 variants with considerably more manuscript sources and, therefore, the potential for an even greater number of discrepancies.[8]

APOCALYPTIC LITERATURE

John's vision is often called "The Apocalypse." This title is derived from the ancient Greek word *apokaluptō,* which means to make bare, disclose, or uncover.[9] In a religious sense it carries the idea of disclosing divine secrets and making known holy mysteries.[10] Ancient Greek-speaking Jews and early Christians used the word to signify a vision with its interpretation, as opposed to a revelation or prophecy (see Rom. 16:25; 2 Cor. 12:1; Gal. 1:12). Thus, "The Apocalypse" is an appropriate title for John's revelation.

So far as is known, his is the earliest work in which the word *apokalupsis* was actually used in the title.[11] It is not the only example of this type of literature, however;[12] the Old Testament provides such examples as Isaiah 6, Ezekiel 1, 40–48, and Daniel 7–12; the Book of Mormon contributes 1 Nephi 8, 11–14. This mode of expression was popular among some Jewish writers from the second century before Christ into the first century after him. It held some appeal for Christian writers until the second century of our era.

Broadly speaking, this genre includes actual and purported visions of the heavenly world and deals chiefly with the coming millennium. The forms, symbols, methods of composition, and certain characteristic conceptions make apocalyptic a distinct class of religious literature. While John's writing is superior to and different from all other apocalyptic writers in important particulars, he does share basic ideas, imagery, language, and style. Indeed, his debt to those writers, especially those of the

Old Testament, can be observed in nearly every chapter. This makes a knowledge of their writings most helpful in a study of the Revelation of John.[13]

THE BASIC THEOLOGICAL FOUNDATION OF APOCALYPTIC LITERATURE

A basic theological foundation forms the ground that gives apocalyptic literature a unique religious perspective.[14] This is composed of three elements. First, it is nearly always eschatological. That is, it focuses on a period of time yet future when God will disrupt the flow of history to bring about the end of wickedness and institute a new order of righteousness and peace. It is God's breaking into the flow of history and altering it that distinguishes the apocalyptic panorama from its counterpart, prophecy. Prophecy, like apocalyptic, is predictive but concentrates on a future that arises out of the present such that historical flow is not interrupted. Apocalyptic looks to the end time when God will discontinue the course of history, turn it to his own purposes, and bring about a new beginning. Therefore, apocalyptic ignores, and in this way denies, man's capacity to create a peaceful future by overcoming wickedness. The united witness of apocalyptic literature is that the consummation will come from outside the flow of history, thereby disrupting it to bring about God's own ends.[15]

Second, apocalyptic literature is dualistic. That is, apocalyptic reality consists of two irreducible elements or opposing principles: good and evil. This dualism is not metaphysical but works on the historical and the temporal plane. The present age is subject to the powers of evil. Satan and his hosts reign. But his world will collapse into a new timeless age of perfect righteousness under the authority of ultimate goodness, the Lord Jesus Christ.

Third, a rigid determinism marks the whole. Revelation testifies that all things move in concert toward a divinely predetermined end. Everything is inevitable; nothing is left to chance. The problem of human agency or free will within the context of God's omniscience never surfaces. But there is a tacit insistence that God's ultimate victory is worked out within the framework of human freedom. Yet apocalyptic writers in general, and John in particular, are very pessimistic about mankind's being able to combat evil and rise out of the present wicked world. Though individuals can and will repent, as John insists throughout his revelation, the world as a whole will not. Thus, God alone has the power to overcome the power of Satan and the wickedness that exist in it. Therefore, central to the apocalyptic framework is faith in God and in his power to control the future and turn all things to the blessing of the righteous.[16]

Though John's Revelation shares these elements, it is unique. No other piece has the sweep, power, organization, and grandeur of this masterwork, to say nothing of authentic inspiration. In its light, the nonbiblical apocalypses found in the apocrypha and pseudepigrapha[17] appear crude, confused, and strange. They seem the product of unbridled fancy, written to titillate and mystify rather than edify. In contrast, Revelation stands orderly, dignified, serious, and purposeful. Further, it bears an apostolic stamp. Unlike other apocalypses that use pseudonyms (the unknown author claiming his work to be that of some great person in the past, like Enoch or Moses), Revelation identifies its writer from the first and keeps him ever before the eye of the reader.[18]

UNDERSTANDING THE BOOK OF REVELATION

A few basic keys are very helpful in grasping the message of the book. Elder McConkie gives seven basic guidelines in his article "Understanding the Book of Revelation." These are 1) "know that the book of Revelation deals with things that are to occur after New Testament times, particularly in the last days"; 2) "have an overall knowledge of the plan of salvation and of the nature of God's dealing with men on earth"; 3) "use various latter-day revelations which expand upon the same subjects in similar language"; 4) "study the sermons of Joseph Smith relative to the book of Revelation"; 5) "use the Inspired Version of the Bible"; 6) "reserve judgment on those things for which no interpretation is given"; and 7) "seek the Spirit." Others have identified different keys to understanding the book.[19]

The keys explored here are understanding: the importance of having the Spirit as a guide, the time period covered in Revelation, John's Hebrew perspective, the structure of the book, and the apocalyptic style and methods John used. This portion of the chapter is quite technical, but the reader will be well repaid for the time spent reading it.

A most important key to understanding John's work is the spirit of revelation and prophecy. This is centered in the living apostles and prophets and is found in modern scripture. As the Saints hearken to both the living prophet and the Standard Works, the Lord will reveal his will line upon line and precept upon precept. The result will be a sensitivity among the Saints to the signs of the times and the signs of the coming of the Son of Man (see D&C 98:12; 45:39; 68:11). A response to this sensitivity will prepare the Saints for the great day of the Lord. Without it—well, the parable of the ten virgins may yet prove fully prophetic: half of their number, having done much but not all, were caught unprepared (see Matt. 25:1–13).

In addition to assistance through the scriptures and the spirit of revelation, recognition that most of the book deals with events yet future is most helpful. Over the centuries a strong difference of opinion has marked the discussions on the time period covered by Revelation. Questions such as "Did John write only of things near his own day, or of things far into the future?" have been asked and answered again and again.[20] The debate is settled for the Latter-day Saint. Joseph Smith stated, "The things which John saw had no allusion to the scenes of the days of Adam, Enoch, Abraham or Jesus, only so far as is plainly represented by John, and clearly set forth by him. John saw that only which was lying in futurity and which was shortly to come to pass." On another occasion he stated, "John had the curtains of heaven withdrawn, and by vision looked through the dark vista of future ages, and contemplated events that should transpire throughout every subsequent period of time, until the final winding up scene."[21]

John's Hebrew perspective greatly assisted him in comprehending what he saw. Like many other books in the New Testament, but more thoroughly, Revelation is recursive; that is, it represents the present and future by alluding to earlier biblical prophecies, especially those found in Genesis, Exodus, Ezekiel, Daniel, and Zechariah.[22] In this way John incorporated and confirmed the biblically defined design of the course and cause of history. Breaking with Greek and Roman models based on the theory of cyclism (the idea of eternal recurrence), biblical prophecy reveals a single and sharply defined plot: a beginning with creation under God's direct power; a catastrophe in the Fall; a solution in the incarnation, atonement, and resurrection of Christ; a climactic battle between the forces of good and evil; and a resolution in the Second Coming of the Lord of glory. All this transforms the tragedy of human history into a divine triumph.[23]

The overall design of Revelation is that of a great arc moving resolutely back to its beginning—from paradise to paradise. This, however, is not the arc of a circle, but that of a spiral. The intent is not to return back to Eden from which man fell but to move to a higher Eden that exceeds the peace, joy, and glory found in the original. This is seen in the recurrence of the edenic motif in John's vision of the new heaven and the new earth. The new Eden has the tree of life and more; the waters of life flow from there as well (see Rev. 22:1–2). The Fall, then, becomes one of man's greatest fortunes. Through it man not only finds Christ but also merits—not merely inherits as at the first—the ultimate paradise through grace and works, the perfect unity between God and man.[24]

John's perspective is revealed in the structure of the revelation itself. Not just because it is at the end of the New Testament, but because of its perspective, Revelation puts a finishing touch on the apostolic witness. Its companion writings focus on the Christian communities themselves; they never take notice of the broader world. The Apocalypse focuses on the Church in its relationship to the world and to the future.[25] It does this in part through its structure.[26]

Three major divisions make up the work: Chapters one through three contain the introduction and the message to the seven Asian churches; four through eleven contain a brief survey of earth history and then focus on the time just before the Second Coming of the Lord; and twelve through twenty-two begin at John's day and again move toward and through the Second Coming, then on through the Millennium to the end time, but from a different perspective.[27] The latter two divisions are full of instructive interludes, flashbacks, and flash-forwards. Appendix A in this book contains a detailed outline of the contents of Revelation. A careful study of that material may prove very helpful in understanding the structure and flow of John's material.

Not only is an understanding of the structure of Revelation helpful in getting at its message, but also an understanding of the apocalyptic style and methods John used is profitable. Appendix B gives a detailed list and examination of these elements. However, a few items need to be noted here. Most of the New Testament was written primarily for those who have ears to hear; this is not so with Revelation. It was written more for those who have eyes to see. John received the revelation through impressions and symbols. To these he added some explanations to assist his readers.

The Book of Mormon allows the process to be examined. Lehi received a vision that he related to his children (see 1 Ne. 8). Symbols formed the basis of what he saw and experienced. These he transmitted without interpretation, apparently feeling quite comfortable with what it all meant. Nephi, however, was perplexed. After prayer, a vision opened to him. An angelic messenger interpreted the symbols, thus allowing Nephi to understand the realities behind the images.

John's experience matched that of Lehi. There is little doubt that he understood perfectly what the visions meant. But acting as a deliberate composer, somewhat like Nephi, he added explanatory material by way of elaboration and example. These expanded the symbols and served to allow the reader to better understand them.

The question naturally arises whether or not John actually saw the things he describes. Apparently this is indeed the case. Joseph Smith declared:

> There is a grand distinction between the actual meaning of the prophets and the present translation [of the Bible]. The prophets do not declare that they saw a beast or beasts, but that they saw the *image* or *figure* of a beast. Daniel did not see an actual bear or a lion, but the images or figures of those beasts. The translation should have been rendered "image" instead of "beast," in every instance where beasts are mentioned by the prophets. But John saw the actual beast in heaven, showing to John that beasts did actually exist there, and not to represent figures of things on the earth. When the prophets speak of seeing beasts in their visions, they mean that they saw the images, they being types to represent certain things. At the same time they received the interpretation as to what those images or types were designed to represent.[28]

Note that John, in this instance, saw actual beasts. However, this is not the case throughout the book. The beasts to which the Prophet Joseph Smith referred are those mentioned in chapter four, not those in chapters twelve and thirteen. The JST specifically states that the beasts in the latter were only images representing earthly beings or conditions. Nonetheless, John actually saw the image he describes, but, as noted above, he also "received the interpretation as to what those images or types were designed to represent."

Again, using Lehi's vision as a model is instructive. The best and perhaps only study of the nature of apocalyptic visions is found in 1 Nephi 8 and 11. Lehi was taken into a dream world where apparently he actually saw a tree, an iron rod, a building without foundation, and so on. These things did not exist in reality but were types or images of historical events and peoples. In his report of the vision, Lehi felt no need to interpret, possibly because to him the interpretation was perfectly clear, having been conveyed during the presentation of the vision. However, his sons, including Nephi, found only perplexity at not being able to come to understanding on their own. Only after Nephi inquired of the Lord was he granted an interpretation that confirmed that his father both saw the images he reported and also understood their meaning.

Likewise, the Spirit left it up to John to translate what he comprehended into human language, but the vision did not come to him that way. The physical senses were superseded by those of the Spirit. Indeed, Spirit communicated directly with spirit through forms, images, and impressions. In this way nothing was lost in the interchange. Unfortunately John did not have that privilege when he wrote. He had to use the language of his readers to make plain his testimony. To make up the difference, John used earthly symbolisms through which a weak, yet somewhat effective, understanding of what he grasped might be conveyed.

A dozen times in the course of the revelation John was commanded to write. As he did so, full of the Spirit, he became a deliberate composer—a prophet, an artist, a poet—attempting to communicate the sweep of the grand vision presented to him. It was beyond the possibilities of adequate portrayal through the normal use of words. His understanding had compassed marvelous scenes surpassing the natural man's ability to grasp. Forces, both natural and supernatural, had collided before his eyes. All heaven and hell had been set in motion, not on some ethereal plane but on this very planet.

John chose to write in the very form of the vision. Therefore, the key ingredient for understanding was to remain the Spirit. In this way God accomplished two ends: comprehension of the marvelous insights could be gained by those spiritually in tune, and at the same time the vision was protected from those who would pervert it. In the process he revealed history to the end time and built into a unified picture the profound theme of God's full knowledge of history.[29]

One cannot fully appreciate the message of the book until he can see past the symbols to the vast realities for which they stand. Fortunately, John is very helpful in the task. Though the Seer interpreted his symbols only in a few instances,[30] he did not design them to contradict or confuse. Therefore, use of major symbols is uniform throughout Revelation. The trumpets, seals, bowls, beasts, and so forth all have a fixed and consistent meaning.[31] The context allows most of the meanings to be ascertained. Further, modern revelation helpfully elucidates and provides the key to understanding others. But, it needs to be understood that some images remain obscure, and their full interpretation must wait for further light; these, however, constitute but a small portion of the book.[32]

John uses his symbols as a means of presentation rather than as an attempt to analyze or prove a point.[33] One of the values of symbolic representation is the multiplicity of meaning that can be generated. John's intention seems to have been to have the reader fix his attention not upon the image but upon the ideas that the image generated. Such is the nature of Near Eastern symbolic usage. God did not design the images for pictorial representation. They come through the eyes of a poet, not the brush of a painter.[34] Further, John consistently records the full complement of his images to produce understanding about the prophetic matrix upon which he is focusing.

CONCLUSION

The strength of the Apocalypse lies in its ability to communicate its prophetic message by inviting the reader to imaginative participation. God designed the symbols to communicate ideas in a vivid and arresting manner while John developed the narrative flow of Revelation to produce emotions, reactions, and understanding that would have been much more difficult, if not impossible, through conventional language.[35]

Before leaving this chapter, a word must be said about numbers as they appear in Revelation. Near Eastern literature, not just Hebrew, reveals a fondness for using numbers to communicate ideas. Why certain numbers became laden with symbolic meaning is unknown; in most cases this arose in prehistoric times and is now lost to us. Interestingly there is a general consistency across cultures to the meaning of certain numbers. That is not to say that numbers are never used as numbers. Certainly they mostly signify only literal quantity. However, in certain contexts they express ideas. This is the case in Revelation. One should interpret numbers just as the other symbolic representations. Fortunately, they are used consistently. For example, the numbers 4, 7, 12, and 1,000 denote aspects of wholeness, or completeness: the first to the world, the second to totality or perfection, the third to priesthood, and the last to superlative greatness.[36]

One last note seems necessary. Not every detail described by John has deep significance. Some of the vision's particulars reflect what John saw and round out the image, giving vividness and power to his presentation. Flaming eyes, feet burning as brass, or various colored stones are all means by which John catches and holds the mind's eye. There, individual meaning must never be taken out of the context of which the images are a part.

The real difficulty in understanding the message of Revelation is twofold: the structure of the text, and its use of symbols. This book has been designed to assist the reader in overcoming both. A word of warning, however. For those whose mental stomachs are unaccustomed to a feast of wild imagery and rapid movement, such as Revelation sets, the banquet can quickly satiate. Often taking each course a little at a time, savoring, tasting, and digesting it are best. Prayer, study, and meditation are indispensable.

CHAPTER 3

THINGS WHICH MUST SHORTLY COME TO PASS

(AN ANALYSIS OF REVELATION 1–3)

THE OPENING OF THE VISION (1:1–2)

1 The Revelation of Jesus Christ, which God gave unto him, to shew unto his servants things which must shortly come to pass; and he sent and signified it by his angel unto his servant John:

2 Who bare record of the word of God, and of the testimony of Jesus Christ, and of all things that he saw.

The first chapter of Revelation, indeed the first sentence, introduces the theme of the entire vision. It is *the* revelation of Jesus Christ. But the genitive form of the Greek verb can be taken two ways: either as the revelation the Lord gives, or as the revelation that unveils him. The first interpretation emphasizes the purpose of the vision (to disclose the order of future events), the second emphasizes the importance, the work, and the role of the Savior. Both views are valid and are not mutually exclusive. But the direction of the vision as a whole emphasizes the preeminence of the second. That is, the revelation proclaims the mission, ministry, and importance of the Lord and Savior.

The source of the revelation was God, who revealed Jesus Christ. This is in keeping with the role of the Father who has never appeared to fallen man, except to bear record of the Son.[1] Therefore the central focus of the vision, and that to which the

Father testifies through it, is the important work of the Son.
The recipient was John, as the JST makes clear (see Rev 1:1),
whose duty was to act as witness of the things that were given
to him. We see from verse one that God intended the vision to
circulate. He wanted it read and listened to. He wanted it understood. He did not give it to be a mystery, a puzzle, or an enigma
that his people could not solve. He ordered John to disclose
truth that otherwise would have remained hidden. God's purpose was to enlighten and lift the spirits of those who were
faithful to him. John's responsibility was to record and to circulate the revelation.[2]

So important was the vision that an angel "signified it" (v.
1, KJV). The term *signify* is a translation of the Greek *sēmainō*
and means not only to foretell, but also to give a sign or identifying token.[3] The English term comes from the Latin *signum*,
which carries much of the same idea, that is, representing, in-
dicating, or validating something by a sign, mark, or token.[4]
Apparently the angel gave John a sign or a token that authen-
ticated the vision.[5] John then witnessed this confirmation for
his readers.

Such stress on the validation of the vision emphasizes its
importance in the sight of both God and of John. Therefore, it
had to be communicated precisely. John's responsibility was to
write neither less nor more than he received. He stressed that
he bore "record of the word of God, and of the testimony of
Jesus Christ, and of all things that he saw" (v. 2, KJV). In this
way he reassured his readers that he kept the vision pure.

BLESSED ARE THEY WHO UNDERSTAND (v. 3)

3 Blessed is he that readeth, and they that hear the words of this prophecy, and keep those things which are written therein: for the time is at hand.

Verse three invokes the first of seven beatitudes found in the
revelation. (The others are found at 14:13; 16:15; 19:9; 20:6; 22:7,
14.) The blessing was pronounced both upon "he who reads"
and "they who hear" (AT), provided that they respond to the

admonition written therein. The singular "he who reads" and the plural "they who hear" reflect a practice of worship in the early Church. Patterned after the service of the synagogue, one person read a scripture or message while the congregation listened.[6] John declared a blessing upon those who were obedient to his writings whether they read his words or heard others read them.

The JST adds an insight to verse three. It states, "Blessed are they who read, and they who hear and understand the words of this prophecy, and keep those things which are written therein." Joseph Smith's modifications point to conditions in which many would be able to read and hear the words of the prophecy. He seems to have the present in mind. Upon any one who receives it, regardless of the time frame, rests the responsibility not only to read, but also to understand and to do. One must pay the price to realize the blessing.

THE ALMIGHTY (vv. 4–8)

4 John to the seven churches which are in Asia: Grace be unto you, and peace, from him which is, and which was, and which is to come; and from the seven Spirits which are before his throne;

5 And from Jesus Christ, who is the faithful witness, and the first begotten of the dead, and the prince of the kings of the earth. Unto him that loved us, and washed us from our sins in his own blood,

6 And hath made us kings and priests unto God and his Father; to him be glory and dominion for ever and ever. Amen.

7 Behold, he cometh with clouds; and every eye shall see him, and they also which pierced him: and all kindreds of the earth shall wail because of him. Even so, Amen.

8 I am Alpha and Omega, the beginning and the ending, saith the Lord, which is, and which was, and which is to come, the Almighty.

In verse four, John identifies those who were to receive his letter. They are seven of the churches in the Roman province of Asia. Elder James E. Talmage has suggested that these seven were the last bastions of faith, the great apostasy having eaten up all the other areas. John was writing a letter of comfort and warning to the surviving remnant of the true Church.[7]

However, implications from John's symbolic use of numbers

should not be overlooked. John possibly uses seven to denote that the message is universal for all branches of the church, even those outside of Asia, and those beyond John's day. After all, equally important were the churches at Troas (see Acts 20:5ff), Colosse (see Col. 1:2), and Hierapolis (see Col. 4:13).[8] If this is the case, then the seven churches become symbolic of the church of God anytime, anywhere, and the message applicable wherever similar conditions are faced.

With the words, "Now this is the testimony of John to the seven servants who are over the seven churches in Asia" (v. 4), the JST makes it clear that the letter contains the testimony of John, the last testimony, to be directed to the local leaders. But that testimony was not for the leaders alone. John directed that it be shared with the congregations as well, and he invokes a blessing of grace and peace upon these faithful servants from a three-fold source.

The first "from he who is and who was and who is to come" (v. 4, AT) is a partial quote of the name of God given to Moses in Exodus 3:14–15 as translated in the Septuagint (cf. Jer. 1:6; 14:13; 32:17, where the names of God would also translate "He who is"). The Greek phrase begins with *apo*, "from," which takes the genitive case but here is followed by three nominative phrases joined by the connective *kai*, "and." By keeping the form in the nominative, John underscores the idea that God is always the subject: he holds the initiative; things happen because he orders all thing according to his will. Men do not force his hand but work, even in their rebellion, to his purposes (see Rom. 9:15–18; John 10:18; Ezek. 38:4, 14–22). John seems to have intended the phrase to be as one word, an undeclinable noun, a paraphrase of the tetragrammaton, Y-H-W-H, "He who is."[9] This rephrase of the divine name reminds John's reader that God is eternally existent, without beginning of days or end of years.

Through the use of the title, John brings Jehovah into the arena of history. Jehovah stands as the Lord of the past, the present, and the future. The temporal order holds significance because the present is when he works out his purposes. Yet his eternal present embraces the past and the future.[10] Such a rendering would be especially appropriate at this moment when the Church approached its final hours. The Saints could find hope in the face of a disheartening future on the grounds that God, by virtue of his eternal existence, exercises power and fulfills his purposes through the course of history.[11]

The second source of blessing to the churches is the seven spirits who stand before the throne of God. We run into these spirits again in chapters 4 and 5, still standing before the throne of God. In Revelation 4:5, these spirits are identified as fiery lamps, and 5:6 calls them the eyes of the Lamb "sent forth to all the world" (AT).[12] JST 1:4 makes it clear that these spirits are symbolic of the leaders of the various branches and that an angel was sent to testify to them of the things of God. The image of the seven servants could be a foreshadowing of both their future destiny as well as their present responsibility.[13] As they labor, they act as the eyes of God overseeing the affairs of the Church. In doing so, their calling and election are made sure, and thus they gain eternal life. It is little wonder, then, that these devout servants were a source of blessing to the struggling branches.

The final source of blessing is again from the Lord, but this blessing grows not out of what he is (the God of all time), but out of what he did. John identifies the Savior as "the prince of the kings of the earth," "the faithful witness," and "the first born from the dead" (v. 5, AT). The latter term also appears in Colossians 1:18, when Paul uses the title to declare Christ sovereign over the Church by virtue of his resurrection from the dead. The ideas conveyed by these titles are those of priority and sovereignty, with the latter dominating. John's reference echoes Psalm 89:27, KJV, which states, "I will make him my firstborn, higher than the kings of the earth."

The term *witness* comes from the Greek *martus*. It came to mean in Christian circles one who bore testimony through the giving up of his life. The Savior was the epitome of the faithful witness, or martyr, in this sense. However, death could not hold him, and so he is also the first born from the dead. Because he now exercises sovereign control, he can bestow the powers both of life and of kingship on those who follow him. These will reign with him a thousand years (see Rev. 20:4–6).[14] He can do this because, through his love, he shed his blood so that all can be cleansed from sin.

The JST states, "I, John, the faithful witness, bear record of the things which were delivered me of the angel, and from Jesus Christ" (1:5). This passage emphasizes three points. First, the revelation had dual attestation (the angel and the Lord), and thus fulfilled the law of witnesses (see Deut. 17:6; Matt. 18:16). Second, angelic and divine administration were coupled in such a way that the Savior himself was somehow involved in the process of the revelation. It was not merely about him but through him. And third, John was true to the charge given him to declare the message accurately.

Verse six focuses on the end result of the resurrection and supremacy of the Lord: he is able to make his followers kings and priests unto God.[15] The seven servants mentioned twice in Revelation 1:4, JST, apparently were to achieve this rank and blessing through their faithfulness. The idea of becoming priests and kings unto God was earlier expressed in Exodus 29:6 and Isaiah 61:5–6. It is repeated in 1 Peter 2:9. The Greek of the Septuagint and of 1 Peter would translate "a kingdom of priests," the idea being that the Savior has set up his kingdom composed of those who hold his priesthood. This kingdom was meant to endure forever, and those who are members are eternal heirs of glory. The kingship John speaks of is an everlasting possession based on the power and authority anchored in the priesthood. According to Bruce R. McConkie, the kings and priests were

> holders of the Melchizedek Priesthood [who] have power to press forward in righteousness, living by every word that proceedeth forth from the mouth of God, magnifying their callings, going from grace to grace, until through the fulness of the ordinances of the temple they receive the fulness of the priesthood and are ordained kings and priests. Those so attaining shall have exaltation and be kings, priests, rulers, and lords in their respective spheres in the eternal kingdoms of the great King who is God our Father.[16]

That the same program is still going on is evident from the Lord's admonition in Doctrine and Covenants 78:15: "That you may come up unto the crown prepared for you, and be made rulers over many kingdoms, saith the Lord God, the Holy One of Zion, who hath established the foundations of Adam-ondi-Ahman."

Knowing that the Lord possesses such power, we should not be surprised that John closed this portion of his epistle with the doxology, "to him be glory and dominion for ever and ever. Amen" (v. 6, KJV). The JST adds John's exclamation, "he cometh in the clouds with ten thousands of his saints in the kingdom" (v. 7). The cloud (Greek *nephelē*) was a sign of the presence of God (see Matt. 17:5; Mark 9:7; Luke 9:34–35) and the vehicle of the Second Coming (see Dan. 7:13; Matt. 24:30; 26:64; Mark 13:26; D&C 133:3, 20).[17] Many will inherit his kingdom and return to reign with him in glory. When he does return, all will see him together and know, some to their shame, not only who he is, but what he did for those who believed.[18] Nothing can stop him from bestowing his favor upon the faithful. As he says, "I am . . . the beginning and the ending, . . . the Almighty" (v. 8, KJV).

The Lord himself proclaimed these titles, reminding the reader that even though the world may appear godforsaken, the Lord is in control of all things. The last title, "the Almighty," is most significant. The Greek *pantokratōr*, "almighty," does not designate one who can do anything, but rather one who holds together and regulates all things.[19] Therefore, this title alone epitomizes the central message of Revelation. That message is further underscored in modern scripture, which declares that the Savior "ascended up on high, as also he descended below all things, in that he comprehended all things, that he might be in all and through all things, the light of truth" (D&C 88:6). It is this "light which is in all things, which giveth life to all things, which is the law by which all things are governed" (v. 13). Thus, the Lord overmasters the sun, the moon, and even the stars with all the world systems that surround them. He is indeed God, the Almighty.

THE VISION OF THE SON OF MAN (vv. 9–18)

9 I John, who also am your brother, and companion in tribulation, and in the kingdom and patience of Jesus Christ, was in the isle that is called Patmos, for the word of God, and for the testimony of Jesus Christ.

10 I was in the Spirit on the Lord's day, and heard behind me a great voice, as of a trumpet,

11 Saying, I am Alpha and Omega, the first and the last: and, What thou seest, write in a book, and send it unto the seven churches which are in Asia; unto Ephesus, and unto Smyrna, and unto Pergamos, and unto Thyatira, and unto Sardis, and unto Philadelphia, and unto Laodicea.

12 And I turned to see the voice that spake with me. And being turned, I saw seven golden candlesticks;

13 And in the midst of the seven candlesticks one like unto the Son of man, clothed with a garment down to the foot, and girt about the paps with a golden girdle.

14 His head and his hairs were white like wool, as white as snow; and his eyes were as a flame of fire;

15 And his feet like unto fine brass, as if they burned in a furnace; and his voice as the sound of many waters.

16 And he had in his right hand seven stars: and out of his mouth went a sharp twoedged sword: and his countenance was as the sun shineth in his strength.

17 And when I saw him, I fell at his feet as dead. And he laid his right hand upon me, saying unto me, Fear not; I am the first and the last:

18 I am he that liveth, and was dead; and, behold, I am alive for evermore, Amen; and have the keys of hell and of death.

This section of the revelation contains John's explanation of how the revelation came. It was Sunday, the Lord's day, and John was "in the Spirit" (v. 10, KJV). He heard a voice that he describes as a trumpet. One must not picture a musical instrument, but an instrument used to give orders in battle, or to announce a message from a king. Thus, the voice was that of a herald summoning John, as it were, to battle, or preparing him for a notice from the King. The voice commanded him to write upon a scroll (translated "book") what he was about to see and hear, and to send it to the seven churches. This prophecy, composed of several separate visions, constitutes the book of Revelation.

Three scrolls are identified in the course of the vision: the one John was to produce (chapter one), the one opened by the Lamb of God (chapter five), and the one delivered to John by an angel (chapter ten). John's consistent use of the scroll image specifies its meaning: each contains the divine secrets of God so far as a portion of the earth's destiny is concerned. Therefore, the scroll symbolizes the whole of the divine plan.[20] John's writings contain the guidance of God to his churches in preparing for the coming of the Son of Man.

As John turned, he saw a figure resplendent in glory standing in the midst of seven lamp stands. The latter image recalls the menorah, the seven-branched lamp stand of the temple (see Ex. 25:31–37; Zech. 4:2). Here, however, each lamp has its own base. Even so, the figure of the temple cannot be far off, for Solomon placed ten separate lamp stands in the Holy of Holies during the temple dedication (see 1 Kgs. 7:49). Tying the vision even closer to the temple was the figure's dress. The words John used to describe the robe are the same as those in the Septuagint for the costume of the high priest (see Ex. 28:4; 29:5; Dan. 10:5). This is combined with the symbol of royal office: the golden girdle or clasp worn just under the armpits.[21] Thus, John seems to present the Savior as both high priest and king, offices associated with the temple and the fullness of priesthood (see D&C 124:28).

John describes the glorious figure as "like unto a Son of man" (v. 13, KJV). The phrase "son of man" is found in all the Standard Works usually referring to the Savior, though the Old Testament (see Num. 23:19; Ps. 8:4; Isa. 51:12) uses it primarily to distinguish mortals from Gods, especially when the context is one of judgment. The term emphasizes the anthropomorphic nature of deity. But Moses 6:57 suggests that John may have had in mind a higher meaning. There the name is capitalized "Son of Man," showing that it is a proper name or title. According that passage, "in the language of Adam, Man of Holiness" is the name of God, "and the name of his Only Begotten is the Son of Man, even Jesus Christ, a righteous Judge." Therefore, the name designates he who is the Son of the Man of Holiness.[22]

The phrase in Revelation implies that John did not actually see the Son of Man but rather one like him. This is not the case. There are a number of instances in the scriptures where the phrase "like unto the Son of man" has definite reference to the Lord himself, in Abraham 3:27, for example, where there is no doubt that the Lord is being referred to, and in Revelation 14:14. That the divine being is not an angel is further borne out by the fact that he allows John to worship him whereas the angel in Revelation 22:8 rebukes John's attempt to worship him even though the angel is speaking through the divine investiture of authority. Therefore, the personage John saw was the Lord himself in glory. Later in the vision angels are the ones who actually speak to John. Therefore, the context must be used to determine whether the Lord is administering directly or through one of his divine servants.

The resplendent figure stood with the lamp stands—which symbolized the churches—surrounding him (see v. 20). The image is appropriate. Lamp stands do not create the light but make it available to others. The Church is to carry the light of Christ to the world. The Savior stated, "I am the law, and the light. Look unto me, and endure to the end, and ye shall live" (3 Ne. 15:9). He further admonished, "Hold up your light that it may shine unto the world. Behold I am the light which ye shall hold up" (3 Ne. 18:24; cf. Matt. 5:14–16).[23]

However, the Church is to do more than merely reflect the light. The Lord stated unequivocally, "I give unto you to be the light of this people. . . . Therefore let your light so shine before this people, that they may see your good works and glorify your Father who is in heaven" (3 Ne. 12:14, 16). Further, the Lord is ever with his Church; he stands among his Saints as their king and high priest, knowing every facet of their lives and struggles, giving counsel through their leaders and comfort to all. The leaders are, as it were, in his right hand where he can sustain, uphold, and direct them. Thus, the Church can find security in following them.

Through symbolic representation, John describes the power, glory, and purity of the Lord: "His head and his hairs were white like wool, as white as snow; and his eyes were as flaming fire" (v. 14, AT). The description rings with power. But the image becomes somewhat hard to picture when the text states,

"And out of his mouth went a sharp twoedged sword" (v. 16, KJV). Two Greek words are translated "sword" in the KJV. These are *machaira* and *rhomphaia*. Though both terms were used for swords in general, the term *machaira* could also describe a knife such as a butcher or surgeon uses. The *rhomphaia*, the term John chose to use, designated particularly a Thracian broadsword, but the word also denotes a lance or spear with a broad double-edged head.[24]

The symbolism goes back to Isaiah 11:4 — "he shall smite the earth with the rod of his mouth" (the Septuagint replaces "rod" with "word") — and 49:2 — "he hath made my mouth like a sharp sword." Either sword is an excellent symbol for the executive and judicial powers of God: that which severs, cuts, opens, and reveals. But what John seems to portray in particular is the word of God which is "quick and powerful, sharper than a two-edged sword, to the dividing asunder of the joints and marrow, soul and spirit; and is a discerner of the thoughts and intents of the heart" (D&C 33:1).

Before giving his final commission to John, the Lord stated, "[I] have the keys of hell and of death" (v. 18, KJV). This statement surprises many. They believe wrongly, that Lucifer holds those keys. Keys give access or control; they symbolize authority. In New Testament times, Hell (Greek *hadēs*) was the world of spirits where the wicked await the day of judgment in torment.[25] God rules both paradise and spirit prison. His justice places the wicked in torment that they might be purged in the fire and prepared for glory.

Through his atonement the Savior gained power over hell and death. In exercising the keys of the resurrection, the Lord demonstrated his complete authority. John here echoes Peter, who stated that Christ taught the spirits in prison. Thus, neither death nor hell can resist the power of the risen Lord. The Savior does more than rescue the faithful from death and hell. He entered death's domain as a conquering hero and preached his gospel, bringing life to those who heeded.[26] Some day, at the Lord's command, hell will empty itself so that all may stand to be judged.

JOHN'S FINAL COMMISSION (vv. 19–20)

19 Write the things which thou hast seen, and the things which are, and the things which shall be hereafter;

20 The mystery of the seven stars which thou sawest in my right hand, and the seven golden candlesticks. The seven stars are the angels of the seven churches: and the seven candlesticks which thou sawest are the seven churches.

Chapter one closes with a reiteration of the commandment for John to write and identifies the immediate audience for what he was to write. However, here it expands to give the outline of the remainder of the book. He must write "the things which thou hast seen, and the things which are, and the things which shall be hereafter" (v. 19, KJV). What he has seen is the vision of the Son of Man that he recorded in the preceding verses. The "things which are" constitutes his message to the seven churches (chapters 2–3). What "will come hereafter" comprises most of the rest of the book.

THE MESSAGES TO THE SEVEN CHURCHES
(chaps. 2–3)

Rather than move through specific section-by-section analyses of these two chapters, I will here treat the chapters through a more general analysis, identifying the themes and messages common to all sections. The last verse of the previous chapter identified the audience, symbolized by golden candlesticks, as the seven churches in Asia, that is, Ephesus, Smyrna, Pergamos, Thyatira, Sardis, Philadelphia, and Laodicea (see 1:11). The Lord then gives John a particular but at the same time universal message to each church.

Scholars have speculated that the reason the Lord chose these seven churches as recipients of his letter was because they were postal centers all linked by a common road that formed a sort of inner circle around the province, binding together the most populous, wealthy, and influential areas. Once delivered to these churches, the Revelation could easily spread to all the other branches.[27] As attractive as this hypothesis is, it doesn't work. There were other postal cities (Troas, Adramyttium, and

Colossae for examples) that lay on this same route. But the Lord selected only seven, probably, as noted in the preceding chapter, because of the symbolic meaning of the number. The whole church seems to be meant, but the specific churches mentioned exemplified the problems faced by all. The instruction to each church was universal for it tells "what the Spirit is saying to the churches" (AT)—all the churches. Note that the phrase is repeated in Revelation 2:7, 11, 17, 29; 3:6, 13, 22.[28]

The purpose of the letter was to sound a warning to the Church as a whole. Apostasy was running full steam, fired by false prophets and apostles. Entire branches were ignorantly or willfully falling into it. The message to the churches sounded a clear warning that God would abandon the churches unless they returned to him. Each congregation was responsible to stop the spread of heresy, to hold on to the truth, and to thereby gain salvation.

John, the Seer, followed a general format in his admonition to each church. There is a complimentary opening introduced by the phrase "I know thy works," followed by a rebuke beginning with "I have something against thee," and ending with a promise "to him that overcometh" (KJV). The exceptions to this format are Smyrna (2:8–11) and Philadelphia (3:7–13), which receive no condemnation, and Sardis (3:1–6) and Laodicea (3:14–22), which receive no compliments.

From the content of the letters, the Church's spiritual life foundered in six areas. Two were external: a willingness to compromise with paganism and a denial of Christianity due to Jewish harassment. Four were internal: the acceptance of unauthorized leaders, approval of false doctrine promulgated by pseudo-prophets, halfheartedness and indifference, and a loss of love for the Church and her master. Succumbing to any one of these would have sounded the death knell for the Church. And in fact, in some areas the white flag of surrender to the world's ways already flew.

Of the problems listed, the one of greatest concern in the book of Revelation was authority, that is, the question of who had the right to preside and to define the doctrine of the Church.

The problem was not new. Peter cautioned the Church that "there were false prophets also among the [Old Testament] people, even as there shall be false teachers among you, who will secretly bring in opinions of destruction, even denying the Master that bought them, and bring upon themselves swift destruction. And many shall follow their licentiousness; by reason of whom the way of truth shall be blasphemed" (2 Pet. 2:1–2, AT). Paul warned the Saints, "Of your own selves shall men arise, speaking perverse things, to draw away disciples after them. Therefore watch, and remember, that by the space of three years I ceased not to warn every one night and day with tears" (Acts 20:30–31, KJV).

By the time John wrote his epistles, these prophecies were reality. In sorrow because the time had come, he wrote, "Little children, it is the last time: and as ye have heard that antichrist shall come, even now are there many antichrists; whereby we know that it is the last time. They went out from us, but they were not of us" (1 Jn. 2:18–19, KJV). Note the root of the problem: men and women deliberately perverting the way of God, willing to deny Christ even though they knew differently. These were not ignorant deceivers, but deliberate workers of darkness.

Peter says that they "walk after the flesh in the lust of uncleanness, and despise constituted authority. Self-satisfied darers, they fear not to blaspheme dignities" (2 Pet. 2:10, AT). Well did Paul brand at least some among them as "that man of sin . . . the son of perdition" (2 Thes. 2:3, KJV), men and women "who were once enlightened, and have tasted of the heavenly gift, and were made partakers of the Holy Ghost," who "tasted the good word of God, and the powers of the world to come." These apostates could not be renewed "again unto repentance; seeing they crucify to themselves the Son of God afresh, and put him to an open shame" (Heb. 6:4–6, KJV). Spurning authority, despising truth, loving error and the glory of men, these hell-inspired antichrists, like spiders, carefully spun their web of half truths, counterfeit ordinances, and false doctrines. Luring and trapping a people no longer willing to follow living prophets and becoming ever more devoid of the Spirit, these spinners of heresy were able to suck out the juice of their spiritual lives.

Revelation gives names to some of the doctrines these false prophets and apostles of darkness taught. There was the doctrine of Balaam and the associated doctrines of the Nicolaitans (see Rev. 2:6, 14). These were coupled with those of a woman the Seer branded as Jezebel, who led some into "the depths of Satan" (2:24, KJV). The exact aspect of these doctrines is unknown, but we can make some general observations. For instance, we know something of Balaam. This Old Testament prophet-turned-apostate introduced into Israel the worship of Baal with its orgiastic perversions (see Num. 22:1–25:9; 31:16). The use of his name suggests that false prophecy was an issue.

The Nicolaitans may have been a pseudoprophetic group since Nicolas is mentioned with the seven presbyters of whom at least four were considered prophets (see Acts 6:5).[29] Doctrine and Covenants 117:11 warns Newel K. Whitney to "be ashamed of the Nicolaitane band and of all their secret abominations." The language is strong, suggesting that whatever the heresy was, the Lord considered it abhorrent.

Jezebel's activities earned her the sarcastic epithet "woman . . . who calls herself a prophetess" (2:20, AT). We know that Christian women held prophetic power (see Acts 21:8–9). But at Thyatira the gift had been turned to fight against the truth. Based on the conditions of the day, a gentile area would not have had any problem accepting and promoting a prophetess. At that time "sibyls," women easily excited into an ecstasy, became mediums and spoke as oracles. A number of these found their way into the Church. Out of their responses came a collection of maxims known in apocryphal literature as the Sibylline Books.[30]

Based on Numbers 25:1–2 and 31:16, where the doctrine that Balaam preached is theologically defined, apparently the Nicolaitans and the self-styled prophetess were preaching a form of idolatry that included spiritual fornication. The phrase "to eat meat offered to idols" (v. 20, AT), associated with both the Nicolaitans and Jezebel, referred not only to food consecrated to an idol, but also to participation in pagan feasts with its rites. Therefore, it would seem that Jezebel and the Nicolaitans were part of the same heretical group working within the cloisters of the Church to pull people to their salacious ways. Their doctrine probably appealed to spiritual prostitution rather than physical, but the imagery depicting extreme sensuality gives an accurate feel for their allure. The false apostles who appeared at Ephesus may have been migrant missionaries perhaps belonging to the same group.[31]

From their teachings then, it would appear that the Nicolaitans were spiritual libertines working within the Church in Asia Minor. They set up a prophetic tradition standing opposite that of John and those associated with him. They refused to recognize his authority, or that of authorized representatives of the Lord. They presented a real threat to the true church. Many of its members were persuaded by the new seduction, not only leaving the truth, but also fostering the evil. Therefore, the Lord warned them through John, "Repent, and do the first works; or else I will come unto thee quickly, and will remove thy candlestick out of his place" (2:5, KJV).

John gives no hint that the churches could or would survive this crisis. Though he offers promises of salvation, they are not to the body of the Church but to individuals. Indeed, for the most faithful among the branches, the church at Smyrna, the Lord holds no promise of continuance: "Fear none of those things which thou shalt suffer: behold, the devil shall cast some of you into prison, that ye may be tried; . . . be thou faithful unto death, and I will give thee a crown of life" (2:10, KJV).

The promises to the faithful individual symbolize exaltation and come loaded with allusions to the temple. The promise is that they shall eat of the tree of life in paradise and of the hidden manna (see 2:7, 17), both considered to be the food of angels, but the former with particular significance. In it was the seed of "eternal lives" (D&C 132:24) and immunity to death (see D&C 132:19–22; Gen. 3:12–24). Each will receive "a white stone, and in the stone a new name written, which no man knoweth saving he that receiveth it" (Rev. 2:17, KJV). According to Doctrine and

Covenants 130:10–11, this stone acts as "a Urim and Thummim to each individual who receives one, whereby things pertaining to a higher order of kingdoms will be made known; and a white stone is given to each of those who come into the celestial kingdom, whereon is a new name written. . . . The new name is the key word." Further, the Savior promises, "He that overcometh, the same shall be clothed in white raiment," and him "will I make a pillar in the temple of my God, and he shall go no more out: and I will write upon him the name of my God, and the name of the city of my God, which is the new Jerusalem, which cometh down out of heaven from my God: and I will write upon him my new name" (Rev. 3:5, 12, KJV).

CONCLUSION

John's commission was to publish the vision of God to the churches when apostasy and persecution were about to destroy what remained of the Church established by the Master. While John languished on Patmos, counterfeit authorities made their way through the ranks of the Church.

The pattern seems to follow that portrayed in the Book of Mormon when "the people did harden their hearts, for they were led by many priests and false prophets to build up many churches, and to do all manner of iniquity" (4 Ne. 1:34). Further, "they did not dwindle in unbelief, but they did wilfully rebel against the gospel of Christ" (v. 38), and "they did continue to build up churches unto themselves, and adorn them with all manner of precious things" (v. 41). Soon "there were many churches in the land; yea, there were many churches which professed to know the Christ, and yet they did deny the more parts of his gospel, insomuch that they did receive all manner of wickedness, and did administer that which was sacred unto him to whom it had been forbidden because of unworthiness. And this church did multiply exceedingly because of iniquity, and because of the power of Satan who did get hold upon their hearts" (vv. 27–28).

With all this, a power struggle developed between the false

leaders and those leaders, known as the three Nephites, whom the Lord appointed. Death could not touch them and, therefore, the false churches had to move against them in other ways (vv. 30–33). Eventually, though the wicked could neither destroy the three nor weaken their testimony, the apostate leaders were finally able to silence them, probably through banishment. The picture in Revelation is about the same. False leaders continuously gaining authority and strength were finally able to silence John's influence among the Church members. But they did not silence his testimony. His revelation endured in spite of their machinations.

To the Saints living in the Roman province of Asia, John bequeathed, through the book of Revelation, a strong testimony that God lived and that Jesus was the Messiah. His message was a light that pierced the darkness of the gathering apostasy and told of the eventual triumph of God. It reassured the Saints that the present distress was not the end of the war but of a single battle. Though God seemed vanquished, he was not, and would turn seeming defeat into glorious victory. The Revelation showed how. Thus, it became a beacon of hope to the faithful until, one by one, they passed away. With their passing the light of truth dimmed and then went out.

CHAPTER 4

THE THRONE IN HEAVEN

(AN ANALYSIS OF REVELATION 4)

THE VISION OF HEAVEN

Chapter four presents a change of scene and subject. Up to this point only the earth has been in view; now John's vision expands to encompass heaven. In an instant, John leaves behind him the troubles, the apostasies, the dissensions, and the apprehensions of the earthly church and passes into an atmosphere of perfect tranquility and assurance. Here not even an echo of earthly turmoil disharmonizes the songs of adoration and trust of the heavenly hosts. Everywhere there prevails an infinite harmony of righteousness and power. The might of God thunders, and flashes, and radiates, permeating all heaven with his glory while angelic choirs proclaim the holiness of him whose sovereignty the earth will follow even in its rebellion.[1]

THINGS WHICH MUST COME HEREAFTER (v. 1)

1 After this I looked, and, behold, a door was opened in heaven: and the first voice which I heard was as it were of a trumpet talking with me; which said, Come up hither, and I will shew thee things which must be hereafter.

The phrase "And after these things I looked and behold" (AT) is used throughout the revelation to introduce a new vision.[2] A voice, carrying the commanding sound of a battle trump, summons John to leave the scene of earthly unrest and worry and to approach a portal of heaven that now stood open. The door is not small. The Greek word *thura* (door), as used here, suggests a double or folding door such as the entry to a Roman manor or Jewish great house.[3] It is the entrance to the dominion of God where his power remains ever unveiled.

John's experience perhaps would have been similar to that of Joseph Smith, who reported, "The heavens were opened upon us, and I beheld the celestial kingdom of God, and the glory thereof, whether in the body or out I cannot tell. I saw the transcendent beauty of the gate through which the heirs of that kingdom will enter, which was like unto circling flames of fire" (D&C 137:1–2). The purpose for John's elevation was for perspective. From this post he could better see "things which must be hereafter."

THE THRONE IN HEAVEN (vv. 2–3)

2 And immediately I was in the spirit: and, behold, a throne was set in heaven, and one sat on the throne.
3 And he that sat was to look upon like a jasper and a sardine stone: and there was a rainbow round about the throne, in sight like unto an emerald.

At this point the vision enters into its second stage and appears to elevate the Seer to an even higher state of ecstasy from that he was already in. John was, of course, already in the Spirit (see Rev. 1:10). What he does now is emphasize the idea. Here the time frame is that of heaven. In this eternal moment, past, present, and future become one. From this perspective John is given to understand the relationship of the parts to the whole and how God overmasters all. Omnipresence takes on a new meaning. Not only is God everywhere present, he is also everywhen present. The context of John's vision seems to rest on the same ground as the statement of Joseph Smith that "the past, the present, and the future were and are, with Him, one eternal 'now.' "[4]

John sees the great Lord of time sitting on his throne, symbol of his absolute omnipotence, in resplendent glory. The description echoes Ezekiel 1:26–28 where the throne appears as a sapphire surrounded by a rainbow.[5] The Greek *thronos,* the term John uses, was reserved for kings and gods—those who were absolute rulers. The heavenly throne is frequently referred to in the Old Testament (see 1 Kgs. 22:19; Isa. 6:1; Ezek. 1:26; Ps. 47:8; Dan. 7:9) and in apocalyptic literature to denote the dominion, sovereignty, and monarchial majesty of God.[6]

John's description, however, keeps the person of God ever hidden. He makes no attempt to portray God's features or form. The Seer focuses on God's splendor and tries to describe and impress this upon his reader: light sparkling, radiating, and scintillating in hues of deep green and blood red—"he that sat was to look upon like a jasper and a sardine stone: and there was a rainbow round about the throne, in sight like unto an emerald" (v. 3, KJV). The sardine stone (more popularly known as sard) is blood red. The name jasper was given to a number of stones mostly green in color, though there was a red and yellow variety.[7] John combines the colors symbolizing life and death and has them radiating from the one who is the God of both. By this means the mind's eye beholds the unmistakable testimony of divine power—God covered "with light as with a garment" (Ps. 104:2, KJV), dwelling "in unapproachable light, whom no [natural] man has ever seen or can see" (1 Tim. 6:16, AT; cf. John 6:46).

With each new symbolic representation, the Seer deepens our understanding of the majesty and power of God. A rainbow radiates out from and encircles the royal seat, sign of the covenant between God and Noah, suggesting that his judgment does not eclipse his mercy (see Gen. 9:8–17). But John does not give us a prismatic bow; it shimmers of but one hue, green, suggesting that life overarches all God is and all He does (cf. Moses 1:39). The presence of the rainbow is most important. According to Caird, it suggests that "there is to be no triumph for God's sovereignty at the expense of his mercy, and it warns us not to interpret the visions of disaster that follow as though God had forgotten his promise to Noah."[8]

THE TWENTY-FOUR ELDERS
AND THE SEA OF GLASS (vv. 4–6)

4 And round about the throne were four and twenty seats: and upon the seats I saw four and twenty elders sitting, clothed in white raiment; and they had on their heads crowns of gold.

5 And out of the throne proceeded lightnings and thunderings and voices: and there were seven lamps of fire burning before the throne, which are the seven Spirits of God.

6 And before the throne there was a sea of glass like unto crystal: and in the midst of the throne, and round about the throne, were four beasts full of eyes before and behind.

In these verses John rounds out his vision. Surrounding the central point of light stands another circle, not vertical like the rainbow, but horizontal. It is composed of twenty-four seats, or more accurately, thrones. Upon these sit, in majesty of their own, Elders.[9] The title John gives them (Greek *presbuteros*, used to designate prominent political and religious leaders) suggests that while mortal they had been men of importance, probably leaders within the congregations.[10] They "had been faithful in the work of the ministry and were dead; [they] belonged to the seven churches, and were then in the paradise of God" (D&C 77:5). Actually the men may have yet been alive as John wrote for what John saw was their future state.[11] These men won the promise God holds out for all: "He will take you up in a cloud, and appoint every man his portion. And he that is a faithful and wise steward shall inherit all things" (D&C 78:21–22).

The number and dress of the Elders suggests that John used them to represent the final reward of all the faithful.[12] The number *twelve* represents priesthood. Here its multiple is used to suggest fullness. There were twenty-four priestly courses and Levitical orders among the Jews, whose heads were also called Elders (see 1 Chr. 24:7–18; 25:9–31).[13] According to Hailey, "the number twenty-four suggests a combination of the twelve patriarchs of the twelve tribes of Israel and the twelve apostles, thus representing the redeemed of both covenants now united through Christ."[14]

The Patriarchs and Apostles are later linked in the description of the New Jerusalem (see Rev. 21:12, 14), where the names of the apostles are placed on the foundation stones and the names of the patriarchs are inscribed over the gates. Further, there is a certain homogeneity depicted between the Old and the New Covenant for the redeemed sing the song of Moses and the Lamb (see Rev. 15:3). In John's vision the Elders hold the two patriarchal offices of priest and king. Their white garments represent priestly holiness and their golden crowns and thrones royalty.[15] That they represent all the faithful seems apparent from Revelation 20:6, where those who come forth in the first resurrection are kings and priests.[16]

Out of the throne around which the the Elders sat "proceeded lightnings and thunderings and voices" (v. 5, KJV). In his attempt to capture the power of the rays and currents that flowed from the throne, John adopted the imagery of a great storm.[17] The word translated "voices" (Greek *phōnē*) in the KJV could well be translated as sounds, tones, or noises. These mighty phenomena symbolize divine power, majesty, and glory that almost overwhelm the beholder. Lightning, thunder, and noises also combine to give another aspect of the authority of God. To Sinai, Jehovah had come in the midst of thunders and lightnings and with the voice of the trump (see Ex. 19:16–19). Thus, they manifest the presence of God. But on later occasions when he manifested himself in this manner, it was in judgment against his enemies (see Rev. 8:5; 11:19; 16:18; Ps. 18:13–14; 144:6). Though God is a God of mercy, he is also a God of judgment. Only when justice is satisfied can mercy claim her own (see Alma 42:22–25).

Associated with these powers, John sees "seven lamps of fire burning before the throne, which are the seven servants of God" (JST, v. 5), imagery and wording that echo Ezekiel 1:13 and Zechariah 4:2. Here again we meet, symbolically, the seven men who presided over the churches. John depicts them as lamps burning before the throne of God, acting, it would appear, as God's witnesses in judgment upon the unfaithful portion of the churches.

But the burning lamp stands are not the only things near the throne. John saw before it a sea of glass like crystal, perhaps similar to the "molten sea" or brass basin in Solomon's temple (cf. v. 6 and 1 Kgs. 7:23–26). The adjective glass-like (Greek *hualinos*) suggests the idea of clear, calm, shimmering. Crystal had a long association with glory and fire (see Ex. 24:9–10, 17; Ezek. 1:22, 27). The two symbols are allied but not quite the same. Glass is a manufactured product while crystal grows in nature. Thus the "glass" of the sea suggests a produced state of purity, and the "crystal," what is native in God's holy nature.[18] The word *sea* (Hebrew *ya'm*) referred to both the fresh-water ocean, the source of all life and fertility according to tradition, and to a basin of holy water in the temple. Thus the sea of glass becomes a perfect symbol for this earth "in its sanctified, immortal, and eternal state" (D&C 77:1). In that state it will be one of the celestial orbs, a source of the power of life for worlds and a retainer of holiness.

THE FOUR LIVING CREATURES (vv. 6–8)

6 And before the throne there was a sea of glass like unto crystal: and in the midst of the throne, and round about the throne, were four beasts full of eyes before and behind.

7 And the first beast was like a lion, and the second beast like a calf, and the third beast had a face as a man, and the fourth beast was like a flying eagle.

8 And the four beasts had each of them six wings about him; and they were full of eyes within: and they rest not day and night, saying, Holy, holy, holy, Lord God Almighty, which was, and is, and is to come.

Also associated with the throne are beasts, whose description in verse six echoes those of the living creatures of Ezekiel 1:5–10; 10:14; Isaiah 6:2–3; and Daniel 7:3–7. They form the first of the concentric circles, the Elders the second. John portrays these beasts as honoring and reverencing God.[19] As John saw real Elders, he saw actual beasts, or better, living creatures. The word chosen by John is *zōon*, meaning living being. This stands in contrast to *thērion* (wild beast), which he later uses to describe the associates of Satan.

Joseph Smith taught that these beasts probably "had lived on another planet, and not ours."[20] Expanding this idea, the prophet stated "that John's vision was very different from Daniel's prophecy—one referring to things actually existing in heaven; the other being a figure of things which are on earth."[21] Joseph Smith's information was based on revealed fact. He had asked the Lord, "Are the four beasts limited to individual beasts, or do they represent classes or orders?" The Lord had responded, "They are limited to four individual beasts, which were shown to John, to represent the glory of the classes of beings in their destined order or sphere of creation, in the enjoyment of their eternal felicity" (D&C 77:3). Thus, like the Elders they are real but also stand as symbols: "They are figurative [i.e., symbolic] expressions, used by the Revelator, John, in describing heaven, the paradise of God, the happiness of man, and of beasts, and of creeping things" (D&C 77:2).

The descriptions of the animals with their various faces like a man, an ox, a lion, and an eagle are highly symbolic. John seems to epitomize the orders of beings—mankind, domestic animals, wild animals, and fowl and other living things—through the representation of the creatures' faces. Their wings and eyes are also symbolic: "Their eyes are a representation of light and knowledge, that is, they are full of knowledge; and their wings are a representation of power, to move, to act, etc." (D&C 77:4).[22]

Besides praising God, these living creatures may have another important function. In other apocalyptic literature such creatures, called cherubim, act as guardians of the throne of God and at times as guides.[23] Cherubs are always associated with God but more especially in two capacities: as his steeds or chariots, as in Ezekiel 1, and as guardian figures keeping safe the way of God, as here in Revelation. They seem to work with the Seer particularly in the capacity of guides. At specific points they open up portions of the vision for him to view.

THE SCENE OF PRAISE (vv. 9–11)

9 And when those beasts give glory and honour and thanks to him that sat on the throne, who liveth for ever and ever,

10 The four and twenty elders fall down before him that sat on the throne, and worship him that liveth for ever and ever, and cast

their crowns before the throne, saying,
11 Thou art worthy, O Lord, to receive glory and honour and power: for thou hast created all things, and for thy pleasure they are and were created.

Chapter four concludes in a tremendous symphony of worship and praise to God. The Seer declares that the living creatures never cease to extol God (v. 8) and then states that, "whenever the living creatures give glory, honor, and thanks to him who sits on the throne, . . . the twenty-four elders fall down before him who sits on the throne and worship him" (vv. 9–10, AT). The idea is that all beings in heaven worship God constantly. The Elders reverence their Creator by casting their crowns before him. In this way they acknowledge that their authority is delegated from God. The act of casting the crowns before the throne of God symbolizes the full devotion of the Elders to the law of consecration and stewardship. They act as stewards over their domain but consecrate all back to him.[24]

The act of praise focuses on the life-giving principle in God. The Revelator's frequent reference to the color green has underscored this idea. Because God is the creator of life, mortal and eternal, he is worthy of all honor and glory. But there is another dimension. Not only did God give life—"you created all things"—but "by your will, . . . they have their being" (v. 11, AT). He, at every moment, sustains all life. John saw streaming from the throne light—green light. It is this "which giveth life to all things, which is the law by which all things are governed, even the power of God who sitteth upon his throne, who is in the bosom of eternity, who is in the midst of all things" (D&C 88:13). Thus, he generates all life everywhere, even in the heavens.

CONCLUSION

Encouragement and hope flow out of chapter four. It centers on the powers of God, his glory, majesty, and might. In symbolic terms the Seer conveys to the mind of the reader a vision and understanding of God's greatness. He stands at the center of heaven surrounded by all creatures he has saved as well as the faithful to whom he has given power and authority. Light and life proceed from him. He is the essence of being and the principle of all existence — even eternal existence. The exalted ones recognize this and return to him praise and glory forever. This vision marks a transition from John's present to "things which shall come hereafter." Thus, the vision appropriately looks to the future celestial kingdom when God will have fully wrought his designs for this world that will be fully restored into his presence. The vision also serves as the introduction to the rest of the revelation through which the Seer comes to understand how God executes his will.

CHAPTER 5

THE LAMB SLAIN FROM THE FOUNDATION OF THE WORLD

(AN ANALYSIS OF REVELATION 5)

THE SCROLL OF DESTINY (vv. 1–5)

1 And I saw in the right hand of him that sat on the throne a book written within and on the backside, sealed with seven seals.

2 And I saw a strong angel proclaiming with a loud voice, Who is worthy to open the book, and to loose the seals thereof?

3 And no man in heaven, nor in earth, neither under the earth, was able to open the book, neither to look thereon.

4 And I wept much, because no man was found worthy to open and to read the book, neither to look thereon.

5 And one of the elders saith unto me, Weep not: behold, the Lion of the tribe of Juda, the Root of David, hath prevailed to open the book, and to loose the seven seals thereof.

As the revelation of the eternal throne room continues, John sees on the right hand of God a scroll of unparalleled significance, "written within and on the backside, sealed with seven seals" (v. 1, KJV).[1] Through modern revelation we understand that it contains "the revealed will, mysteries, and the works of God; the hidden things of his economy concerning this earth during the seven thousand years of its continuance, or its temporal existence" (D&C 77:6; cf. 88:108–10). John notes that the scroll was full, both on the front and the back, which parallels Ezekiel 2:10. Nothing had been left out, and no more could be added. It was the scroll of destiny.[2] John's imagery bears a mind-set frequently found in apocalytpic literature that from the beginning God determined the end of history.

We need to clarify here the difference between the view point of Revelation that God has ordained future events and the false idea that individual salvation is predetermined and that therefore there is no individual agency. One of the powers ascribed to God is expressed by the Greek words *prognōsis*, and *proginōskō*. These words are respectively translated "foreknowledge" and "predestine" and catch the idea not only of knowing something beforehand, but of choosing someone beforehand. Paul understood that God, because of his foreknowledge, had marked or set the course of history through the use of individuals who would bring about his will (see Rom. 8–9). That is, God ordered things through the means of sending down spirits when and where he chose. These spirits, without any other manipulation on the part of God, act in ways he knows. Thus, by selection of these souls, God can order the course of history while still maintaining agency.

A major thesis of Revelation is that God set the path of all things and nothing will stray from his design. This idea is symbolized in the scroll where the sovereign will of God has been recorded, where all history has been foretold. Though the idea that God has determined the course of world events may grate on some, it was a source of comfort and hope for those to whom John wrote.

The document is sealed with seven seals. The use of seals was common during ancient times to prevent adulteration of important papers and, more importantly, to prove their authenticity. The verb *sphragizō*, to provide with a seal, carried the idea of assured content and authenticity. But the idea of ownership was important because the owner protected the document. In John's day, seals carried the mark of the owner who guaranteed the contents and was responsible for carrying out the agreements, if any, contained therein. Out of this grew the association of the seal with the idea of protection and safety. This forms the symbolic base of the use of the term by the early

Christians. To be sealed by the Holy Spirit (see Eph. 1:13) meant more than being provided with a means of identification. It assured that an individual could endure to an eternal reward because, belonging to God, protective power would be given from above.

Archaeologists found in Israel a document such as John describes, dating from about the time the apocalypse was written. It was an important legal contract.[3] Its discovery confirmed the belief that the Seer was making symbolic reference to a binding agreement or covenant. One such type of covenant was the Roman will, which also bore seven seals. Such testaments could not be administered until all the seals were broken.[4] Only a person of authority could break the seals and execute the will.

Working from this imagery, John describes the heavenly search for the a person with power to open the scroll and execute the demands contained therein. In this case the scroll is the primary symbol for the fullness of time, containing as it does the aggregate of God's will concerning this earth. Unless someone is found who can minister the will of God, the purposes of this earth will fail.

A "strong angel" conducted the search. Just what John meant by the adjective is not known. The Greek term is *ischuros* and can be translated as strong, mighty, or powerful. The expression often applies to gods and angels. John's use of it suggests that there exists rank among the ministers of heaven.[5] Possibly the angel John had in mind was Gabriel, Hebrew for "God is my strength," but Michael, the commander of the forces of the Lord of Hosts and the angel of top rank, also fits the description. The Seer may have had him in mind.[6] Whatever the case, this mighty being cried forth the fateful question: "Who is worthy to open the scroll and to loosen the seals of it?" (v. 2, AT).

He could find no one in the entire cosmos to open the scroll, or even "to look thereon" (v. 3, KJV). To look meant more than just to view. John could clearly see the scroll from where he was. To open and look meant to comprehend, disclose, and execute the contents of the document. No one responded because no one "was able." The Greek (*dunamai*) suggests that no one had the power or ability in or of himself to do the task, not even the mighty angel asking the question.[7]

This failure brought an instant and sorrowful response from John: "and I mourned deeply."[8] However, his pathos did not last long. One of the Elders reassured him that "the Lion of the tribe of Juda, the Root of David, hath prevailed" and could therefore open the scroll (v. 5, KJV). Both of these titles come directly out of Jewish messianism. The first echoes Genesis 49:9–10 in which Judah is called a "lion's whelp" and promised that scepter would not depart from him "until Shiloh [i.e., the Messiah] come" (KJV).[9] The second title suggests Isaiah 11:1, which refers to the root of Jesse, the future ideal king of David's line, who was to usher in the period of peace.

THE LAMB SLAIN (vv. 6–7)

6 And I beheld, and, lo, in the midst of the throne and of the four beasts, and in the midst of the elders, stood a Lamb as it had been slain, having seven horns and seven eyes, which are the seven Spirits of God sent forth into all the earth.

7 And he came and took the book out of the right hand of him that sat upon the throne.

As John looks he does not see a lion, symbol of power and majesty. Instead he sees a lamb "in the midst of the throne" (v. 6, KJV). The phrase suggests that the lamb was at the position nearest to the throne, sharing, as it were, the central place. In this way the Seer symbolizes the principal reality. The Lamb is the center of all things, having preeminence over all God's creations.

The Lamb, though living, bore the marks of a violent death. The Greek verb used, *sphazō* (slaughter), refers to the act of sacrificing. John could have had the paschal lamb in mind. If so, he was tying the image to Israel's Egyptian exodus, which he considered the prototype of ultimate and final victory through the Messiah.[10] Indeed, Jewish apocalyptic looked to a conquering lamb that was to appear in the days of the final judgment to destroy all evil.[11] Through this powerful symbol, Revelation underscores a central theme of the New Testament: victory through sacrifice.[12] The Lamb prevails (see John 16:33) not by sovereign might but by sacrifice grounded in love.[13] He is worthy because he purchases God's people with his own blood. The Seer's metaphor emphasizes both the high value of those he purchased, costing him his blood and life, and the universality of the Lord's action in redeeming all the faithful from death and hell.[14]

John described the Lamb as having seven eyes and seven horns. Again, the image created suggests symbolic interpretation rather than visual reconstruction. The eyes depict knowledge, the horns represent power. The possession of seven eyes echoes Zechariah 4:10, where they are symbols of God's omniscience. The horn is the Old Testament symbol for power (see Num. 23:22; Deut. 33:17; 1 Sam. 2:1; 1 Kgs. 22:11; Ps. 75:4; 89:17). Thus, it was the mark of kingly dignity (see Ps. 112:9; 148:14; Zech. 1:18; Dan. 7:7, 20; 8:3).[15]

Christ possesses a fullness of the omnipotence and omniscience of God; he is "the power of God, and the wisdom of God" (1 Cor. 1:24, KJV). To these the Seer adds, through the symbolism of the "seven Spirits of God" (Rev. 5:6, KJV), the fullness of administrative authority. All this connects to earthly government, which the Lamb is about to assume in his redemptive character "as . . . slain" (v. 6, KJV). Through "the seven spirits sent forth in all the earth" (v. 6, AT), the Lamb is omnipresent. With this imagery, John does more than invest the Savior with the attributes of deity; he redefines omnipotence. Often felt to describe God's power of unlimited coercion, the Seer reveals its true nature as the power of infinite persuasion, the invincible strength of self-sacrificing love.[16]

The JST adds insight and clarity. It describes the Lamb as having twelve horns and twelve eyes, "which are the twelve servants of God, sent forth into all the earth" (v. 6). Here the prophet defines the nature of the power of the Lamb. Twelve, as has been noted previously, is the priesthood number, and all priesthood centers in the Lamb. Thus, he is called the "great high priest" Heb. 4:14, KJV).[17] According to Doctrine and Covenants 107:1–6,

There are, in the church, two priesthoods, namely, the Melchizedek and Aaronic, including the Levitical Priesthood. Why the first is called the Melchizedek Priesthood is because Melchizedek was such a great high priest. Before his day it was called *the Holy Priesthood, after the Order of the Son of God.* But out of respect or reverence to the name of the Supreme Being, to avoid the too frequent repetition of his name, they, the church, in ancient days, called that priesthood after Melchizedek, or the Melchizedek Priesthood. All other authorities or offices in the church are appendages to this priesthood. But there are two divisions or grand heads — one is the Melchizedek Priesthood, and the other is the Aaronic or Levitical Priesthood.

Further, "The Melchizedek Priesthood holds the right of presidency, and has power and authority over all the offices in the church in all ages of the world, to administer in spiritual things" (D&C 107:8). All this power centers in the Lamb and flows from him to his leaders. By its authority, the Savior acted to bring about the Atonement, and he continues to minister its saving power in the world. This is the central deed in the scroll of destiny, for all history pivots on this one act. It alone allowed for the complete fulfillment of the Father's will.

The JST notes that the eyes and horns symbolized the servants of God, those sent forth as ministers. The Greek word *apostellō* is translated "sent forth," and from this the noun *apostolos*, or "apostle," is derived. In its Judeo-Christian context, however, the word *apostle* took on a different nuance than it normally had. For the Greeks, the one sent was the one empowered or commissioned to act for the one doing the sending. For the Jews and Christians, the term designated anyone commissioned and empowered by God: one who had authority to speak his word and administer his ordinances. The Greek term was used to translate the Hebrew *shaleha,* one commissioned to act for God. The Rabbis recognized two groups. The first was the priesthood body as a whole, the second, a small number of outstanding prophets, especially Moses, Elijah, Elisha, and Ezekiel.[18] The Savior used this term for his chosen leaders. Therefore, the JST shows us that John looked to the foundation of the Church, the apostles and prophets, as the means through whom the Lamb exercises his authority upon the earth. These authorized ministers hold the keys of life and salvation under the Lord for all the world.

THE NEW SONG (vv. 8–14)

8 And when he had taken the book, the four beasts and four and twenty elders fell down before the Lamb, having every one of them harps, and golden vials full of odours, which are the prayers of saints.

9 And they sung a new song, saying, Thou art worthy to take the book, and to open the seals thereof: for thou wast slain, and hast redeemed us to God by thy blood out of every kindred, and tongue, and people, and nation;

10 And hast made us unto our God kings and priests: and we shall reign on the earth.

11 And I beheld, and I heard the voice of many angels round about the throne and the beasts and the elders: and the number of them was ten thousand times ten thousand, and thousands of thousands;

12 Saying with a loud voice, Worthy is the Lamb that was slain to receive power, and riches, and wisdom, and strength, and honour, and glory, and blessing.

13 And every creature which is in heaven, and on the earth, and under the earth, and such as are in the sea, and all that are in them, heard I saying, Blessing, and honour, and glory, and power, be unto him that sitteth upon the throne, and unto the Lamb for ever and ever.

14 And the four beasts said, Amen. And the four and twenty elders fell down and worshipped him that liveth for ever and ever.

Exultation erupts as the Lamb takes the scroll. The moment to open it has arrived. The elders take up their harps to sing praises to God and the Lamb (see vv. 8–9). A new song is necessary because the death of the Lamb established a new covenant. This covenant is not new merely in point of time, but more important, it is new and distinctive in its superiority to the old one.[19]

The Greek words translated "a new song" (ōdēn kainēn) suggest those songs expressive of gratitude for mercies granted to those in need (see, e.g., Ps. 33:3; 40:3; 96:1; Isa. 42:10). In Isaiah 42:9–10 the Lord states, "Behold, the former things are come to pass, and new things do I declare: before they spring forth I tell you of them. Sing unto the Lord a new song, and his praise from the end of the earth, ye that go down to the sea, and all that is therein; the isles, and the inhabitants thereof" (KJV).

These verses express the full context of the phrase that corresponds to a deeper sense of "new things."

Appropriately, the new song comes just at that point when one cycle of events has been fulfilled and another is about to begin. However great the things of the old earth were, they are about to be dimmed by the coming of the new paradise.[20] Such gratitude does not belong to the elders alone. Along with their harps they carry incense burners from which flows sweet smoke representing the outpouring of gratitude from the Saints. This refreshing savor perfumes the divine halls of heaven.

Verses 9–14 bring chapters four and five to a climax as the assembly sings three glorious hymns of praise. Already, John has heard a hymn sung to the majestic power seated upon the throne (see 4:10–11). It focused on God with his holiness, almightiness, and everlastingness as manifested in life and creation. The first song in chapter five is the song of the Elders, dwelling on the redemptive power that is in the Lamb. He is worthy because he has purchased creation with his blood. The testimony of the Elders supports the witness of much of the New Testament (see, e.g., Acts. 20:28; 1 Cor. 6:20; 7:23; 1 Pet. 1:18–20; 2 Pet. 2:1). Because of what the Lamb did, the redeemed are now kings and priests who will reign forever (see v. 10).

A larger chorus made up of millions of exalted beings now joins with the Elders in singing the second anthem. It too proclaims the Lamb's worthiness.[21] No sooner do its strains die than the climax begins, uniting in one grand closing hymn all creation, the very cosmos. Nature itself praises God and the Lamb, "saying, Blessing, and honour, and glory, and power, be unto him that sitteth upon the throne, and unto the Lamb for ever and ever" (v. 13, KJV).

CONCLUSION

The point of the chapter is that the Lamb was able to do what no one else could: to execute the will of the Father. The vision specifies why the Lamb was able to open the book and look thereon: he was slain. He, God, gave himself as sacrifice to appease the demands of justice and allow the twin powers of mercy and grace to flow. Victory grew out of death, redemption out of blood. This allowed the will of the Father to operate.

The hymns express the adoration of heaven, earth, and all creation in recognition of that sacrifice. Worthiness is the focus, but other honors are mentioned: blessing, glory, power, and wisdom. The hymns are not requests that the Lord receive these honors but a celebration of adoration because he possesses them. Thus, the cosmos rejoices in a grand recognition of the dual powers of the Father and the Son, the law- and life-givers of the universe.

CHAPTER 6

THE SIX SEALS

(AN ANALYSIS OF REVELATION 6)

THE SEVEN SEALS AND THE FOUR HORSEMEN

As the songs of adoration cease, the Lamb begins the task only he can do. One by one he breaks the seven seals. As he does so, John beholds in vision the dramatic events associated with them. Each seal attached to the scroll of destiny symbolizes a set portion of earth's history: "The first seal contains the things of the first thousand years, and the second also of the second thousand years, and so on until the seventh" (D&C 77:7).[1] According to the Doctrine and Covenants, the seals will be opened in connection with the Second Coming:

> Then shall the first angel again sound his trump in the ears of all living, and reveal the secret acts of men, and the mighty works of God in the first thousand years. And then shall the second angel sound his trump, and reveal the secret acts of men, and the thoughts and intents of their hearts, and the mighty works of God in the second thousand years—and so on, until the seventh angel shall sound his trump; and he shall stand forth upon the land and upon the sea, and swear in the name of him who sitteth upon the throne, that there shall be time no longer; and Satan shall be bound (88:108–110).

The breaking of the seals does not open any portion of the document. The scroll will not open until the seventh seal breaks. All must wait until then for the will of God to be fully executed.

Before that day, evil will rule. But judgment, fully fueled by the indignation and wrath of God, will be executed when the seventh seal is broken.

John uses horses and their riders to symbolize the events of the first four thousand years. The symbolism is found in the Old Testament. In Revelation it is modified for a purpose, but it definitely echoes the two visions of Zechariah, one of four horsemen, the other of four chariots (see 1:8–11; 6:1–8). However, in Zechariah's vision both sets were but patrol squads whose purpose was to report on the peaceful condition upon the earth. Like John's, the horses Zechariah saw were of different colors, but they corresponded to the different winds or points of the compass.[2] In Revelation the four colors indicate a significant aspect of each millennium: conquest (white), bloodshed and war (red), plague and famine (black), and death (pale or livid).[3]

THE FIRST SEAL (vv. 1–2)

1 And I saw when the Lamb opened one of the seals, and I heard, as it were the noise of thunder, one of the four beasts saying, Come and see.

2 And I saw, and behold a white horse: and he that sat on him had a bow; and a crown was given unto him: and he went forth conquering, and to conquer.

As the Lamb breaks the first seal, one of the living creatures summons John to "come and see" (v. 1, KJV).[4] With that command, the first vision opens and the first rider appears on a white horse. The color suggests two things: purity and victory. It was the Near Eastern custom for conquerors to ride white horses in their triumphs.[5] The color reflects the nature of the horseman. He is one of God's own, a prophet of power and light. He carries the bow, a symbol of war, suggesting a period in which righteousness was on the offensive. The rider receives "a crown," not the sign of political rule (Greek *diadēma*) but of victory (Greek *stephanos*, the laurel crown won through athletic achievement).[6] Thus, victory goes to the one sitting on the white horse who conquers and receives commission to continue his conquests.

The use of the passive voice, "a crown was given unto him" (v. 2, KJV), is instructive. John uses this voice continuously throughout Revelation. By doing so, he indicates that an unseen power operates behind history, shaping it, molding it, making it conform to a specific will. That power is God, as John has already indicated, working through the Lamb.

The first thousand years of earth's history saw the beginning of wickedness, apostasy, and war but saw also what could be considered the greatest triumph for good yet achieved. During this period Enoch and his people laid the foundations of Zion, and righteousness truly was on the offensive. Note "that what John saw was not the establishment of Zion and its removal to heavenly spheres, but the unparalleled wars in which Enoch, as general over the armies of the saints, 'went forth conquering and to conquer.' "[7]

They waged battles in ways never seen before or after. The primary weapons of the righteous were faith and the word of God: "So great was the faith of Enoch that he led the people of God, and their enemies came to battle against them; and he spake the word of the Lord, and the earth trembled, and the mountains fled, even according to his command; and the rivers of water were turned out of their course" (Moses 7:13). Having subdued earthly enemies, the people of Zion subdued earthly appetites, passions, sickness and pain, and eventually even death. Truly, righteous conquest was the highlight of the era.

THE SECOND SEAL (vv. 3–4)

3 And when he had opened the second seal, I heard the second beast say, Come and see.

4 And there went out another horse that was red: and power was given to him that sat thereon to take peace from the earth, and that they should kill one another: and there was given unto him a great sword.

But righteousness did not prevail into the next millennium. Zion fled, and corruption gained the day. As John sees the second seal broken and hears the command "Come and see" (v. 3), a horse with its rider charges into view. The Seer describes the horse as *purros* in color. The word means literally red as fire (the dragon in chapter twelve has the same color). The color suggests death by violent means, usually by bloodshed. But it also represents sin, especially the sin that moves against humanity.[8] Of those living early in the second millennium, the Lord said,

> For these many generations, ever since the day that I created them, have they gone astray, and have denied me, and have sought their own counsels in the dark; and in their own abominations have they devised murder, and have not kept the commandments, which I gave unto their father, Adam. Wherefore, they have foresworn themselves, and, by their oaths, they have brought upon themselves death; and a hell I have prepared for them, if they repent not (Moses 6:28–29).

Enoch saw the result. To him the Lord said, "Look, and I will show unto thee the world for the space of many generations" (Moses 7:4). Enoch describes what happened:

> I beheld in the valley of Shum, and lo, a great people which dwelt in tents, which were the people of Shum. And again the Lord said unto me: Look; and I looked towards the north, and I beheld the people of Canaan, which dwelt in tents. And the Lord said unto me: Prophesy; and I prophesied, saying: Behold the people of Canaan, which are numerous, shall go forth in battle array against the people of Shum, and shall slay them that they shall utterly be destroyed (Moses 7:5–7).

The second millennium saw the advent of organized warfare with the objective of genocide. Clearly, the red horse galloped supreme.

The horse's rider received the curved bladed saber (Greek, *machaira*), the favorite weapon of the cavalry.[9] Like the color red, it symbolized violent death coupled with all the fury of war (cf. Rom. 8:35; Gen. 31:26). But it also carried the idea of authority to punish evildoing (see Rom. 13:4). Therefore, there is a sense of judgment about it. As Mormon said, "The judgments of God will overtake the wicked; and it is by the wicked that the wicked are punished; for it is the wicked that stir up the hearts of the children of men unto bloodshed" (Morm. 4:5). John states that the horseman was given power "to take peace from the earth, and that they should kill one another" (6:4, KJV). The phrase "kill one another" (Greek, *allēlous sphaxousin*) indicates both international and civil strife.[10]

The rider could easily be the devil, reigning supreme during this period of gross wickedness. So great were the abominations that Noah was pained and God judged the nations with the Flood.[11] But Satan's rule was more apparent than real. Note how John again uses the passive voice. The rider possessed neither the sword nor the power. They were given to him. War, strife, bloodshed must come, but God overrules even here, setting bounds on who carries the sword, how hard it is swung, and how long.

THE THIRD SEAL (vv. 5–6)

5 And when he had opened the third seal, I heard the third beast say, Come and see. And I beheld, and lo a black horse; and he that sat on him had a pair of balances in his hand.

6 And I heard a voice in the midst of the four beasts say, A measure of wheat for a penny, and three measures of barley for a penny; and see thou hurt not the oil and the wine.

At the command of the living creature, "Come and see" (v. 5), the third horse thunders forth, its blackness symbolic of death, especially by plague, famine, pestilence. The engine of want drove the third millennium. Even the Lord's people knew the gnawing of hunger. Abraham's brother, Haran, died of starvation, and the famine forced the prophet himself to move into Canaan and eventually into Egypt to survive (see Abr. 1:29–30; 2:2–15). The same held true for Jacob and his sons (see Gen. 41–44).[12] Vast movement marked the whole era from 2,000 to 1,200 B.C. It is called the *Volkswanderungenzeit,* the time of the people's wandering—an era of mass migrations when peoples collided against peoples. Strife and war resulted, and tumult ruled the day.

The rider holds a scale on which to make weight, and a voice hocks his wares: "A measure of wheat flour for a denarius, and three measures of barley meal for a denarius" (v. 6, AT). A measure, Greek *choinix,* was equal to about a U.S. quart. The silver denarius, or "penny" in the KJV, was the daily wage for a common laborer (see Matt. 20:2). Ordinarily, a denarius would buy between ten and sixteen quarts of wheat flour or twice that of barley meal. Here, under famine conditions, a day's work supplied only enough flour to keep a person alive for one day, or enough meal for three.[13]

The warning against hurting the oil and the wine follows John's principle of showing that God is in charge. Limits are set on how far the famine could go.[14] It is unlikely that only wine and oil are meant. The terms were used as a standing formula designating the nutritive products of the earth in both times of plenty and want (see, e.g., Deut. 7:13; 11:14; 28:51; 2 Chr. 32:28; Neh. 5:11; Hosea 2:8; Joel 2:19).[15] The point is that God controlled the breadth of the famine. Though much could be taken, the world would not succumb to the dearth. Further, the Lord had prepared a way of escape for his faithful people.

There is an aspect of this that is interesting. In the Temple Scroll (one of the Qumran scrolls), two previously unknown Jewish feasts are mentioned: the Feast of Oil and the Feast of New Wine. Both products were closely associated with the burnt offering of the temple in which they acted as sacrificial elements along with the animal. They were stored in a special place and handled only by the priests. Josephus described the horror coming out of sacrilege as the temple was plundered by one John and his troops who drew every drop of sacred wine and oil and anointed themselves and drank freely. He concluded this alone warranted the destruction of Jerusalem.[16] The Seer may have been suggesting that God's house would survive the famine.[17]

THE FOURTH SEAL (vv. 7–8)

7 And when he had opened the fourth seal, I heard the voice of the fourth beast say, Come and see.

8 And I looked, and behold a pale horse: and his name that sat on him was Death, and Hell fol-lowed with him. And power was given unto them over the fourth part of the earth, to kill with sword, and with hunger, and with death, and with the beasts of the earth.

With the command "Come and see" (v. 7), the last of the horses lunges into view. Its color is a sickly pale green (Greek, *chlōros*). Not inappropriately, the rider is death himself riding roughshod between 1,000 B.C. and the period of the Lord's birth. And he rides not alone — Hell follows with him. Surely no period before this saw more vicious generals and armies. It was the time when some of the world's greatest empires rose and fell: Babylon, Assyria, Persia, and Macedonia among them. As armies marched, men died in droves, and Hell gaped open wide its jaws to receive them.

Caught up in all this strife were the people of Jehovah. Palestine was often a hotly contested area. Pulled by the forces of the day, its political leaders tried to play power politics to their shame and destruction. The great prophets, Hosea, Amos, Isaiah, and later Jeremiah and Lehi, tried to warn them of their folly. They would not heed. Too caught up in idolatry to repent, too licentious to reform, too hard-hearted to feel, they warred among themselves and weakened their nation. As a consequence, they left Jehovah and life eternal. Hell was truly their reward.

The power of Death and Hell, symbolized in the great barbarian broadsword (*rhomphia*), exacted its due. The sphere of operation of these two horsemen was a fourth part of the earth. John's use of the fraction suggests a limited sphere. Not all the earth was under their domain. Their means of destruction was fourfold: war, famine, pestilence, and the wild beasts of the earth. The fourfold means of destruction corresponds to the four sore judgments found in Ezekiel 5:16–17; 14:21.[18] The latter suggests the general conditions of the era. So many were destroyed that whole areas became depopulated to the point where wild beasts ran free. Few were left to protect the weak or ill.

With these horsemen John continues his underlying theme. Note that Death and Hell possess no power of their own. It is given to them. Their area of operation was limited. Only a fourth part of the earth, a determined amount, was subject to them. Most of the earth lay outside their domain. The rest came under the protection of another — the one John keeps hidden. And even that portion over which they held sway was not given up totally to them: their fearsome weapon being given to them by he who directs all things.

Note how both death and destruction have been escalating through the course of the revelation. After Righteousness, War rode affecting the nations, primarily the soldiers and men of war. Famine followed bringing distress upon whole populations. Next came Death and Hell, which affected a fourth part of the earth. This pattern of ever-greater circles of destruction continues through the rest of the vision: trumpets bring destruction upon one-third of the earth (see 8:7–8, 10, 12), and the vials bring total annihilation to all wickedness (16:1–17).

THE FIFTH SEAL (vv. 9–11)

9 And when he had opened the fifth seal, I saw under the altar the souls of them that were slain for the word of God, and for the testimony which they held:

10 And they cried with a loud voice, saying, How long, O Lord, holy and true, dost thou not judge and avenge our blood on them that dwell on the earth?

11 And white robes were given unto every one of them; and it was said unto them, that they should rest yet for a little season, until their fellowservants also and their brethren, that should be killed as they were, should be fulfilled.

At the breaking of the fifth seal, no horse thunders forth. Instead the Revelator sees the fulfillment of a prophecy given for his own day. The fifth seal represents John's era, the era in which the Son of God was born, ministered, and atoned for all mankind. It was the era during which the new covenant was established and the keys of resurrection were first manifested. Interestingly, John depicts none of these things. The event on which the vision focuses is the deliberate destruction of those who stood as witnesses of the Word of life. As mentioned earlier, John already knew the way his dispensation would end. The Lord had made this abundantly clear. He told his disciples that after he departed, "then shall they deliver you up to be afflicted, and shall kill you: and ye shall be hated of all nations for my name's sake. And then shall many be offended, and shall betray one another, and shall hate one another" (Matt. 24:9–10, KJV). John viewed the terrible fulfillment of that dire prophecy. Those men and women he saw in vision who had died for the Word's sake were in reality yet giving up their lives.

John saw the souls of the righteous under the altar of heaven. The image of the altar suggests sacrifice. The direct association of these saints with the altar implies that their lives had been given in sacrifice because of their loyalty to God. Their position under the altar suggests that they were martyrs, their souls resting there only because their lives had been offered, as it were, upon it. During sacrificial rites the blood of the victim, symbolic of its life, was poured out at the altar's base, seeping beneath it (see Lev. 4:7; 17:11). John's view of the life, or soul, of the martyr as under the altar probably echoes this practice.[19] What made their lives a sacrifice for righteousness was not in dying for the faith but in living for it. As Paul admonished, "I beseech you therefore, brethren, by the mercies of God, that ye present your bodies a living sacrifice, holy, acceptable unto God which is your reasonable service" (Rom. 12:1, KJV).

The idea that the souls of the righteous awaited their reward from under the altar of heaven was popular a little later in Judaism. The Rabbis taught that those buried in Israel were just as if they had been buried under the altar, and those buried under the altar were as if they were buried under the throne of glory.[20] The whole idea suggested that martyrs were in a state of holiness and peace within the kingdom of God. These men and women had given their lives on the strength of their testimony. They had received their witness directly from the Savior himself, and this witness is what they bore, as John makes clear when he states that they "were slain on account of the word of God, even the testimony borne by Jesus" (v. 9, AT). Most manuscripts include the words "of the Lamb" (*tou arniou*), suggesting that the testimony of the martyrs was the same as that of the Lord.

That testimony emphasized his divinity. He was the Messiah, the Son of God (see, e.g., Matt. 16:16–20; John 4:42; Acts 18:5). It was because they held to this that they were killed. Other passages in which we find this expression (see Rev. 1:2, 9; 20:4) leave no doubt that the witness is that borne by the

Savior himself and which the disciples share by revelation.[21] As Elder McConkie has said,

> Martyrs of religion are found in every age in which there have been both righteous and wicked people on earth. Christ himself was a martyr who voluntarily laid down his life, according to the Father's plan, that immortality and eternal life might become available for his brethren (John 10:10–18). 'Greater love hath no man than this, that a man lay down his life for his friends' (John 15:13). . . . True martyrs of religion receive eternal life. 'Whoso layeth down his life in my cause, for my name's sake, shall find it again, even life eternal' (D&C 98:13; Mark 8:35; John 12:25; Rev. 2:10). But the mere laying down of one's life standing alone is not gospel martyrdom. Both the righteous and the wicked have and do sacrifice their lives for friends or country without gaining thereby any hope or assurance of exaltation. Those on the other hand who have the truth and who could escape death by denying it are the martyrs who shall receive a martyr's reward—eternal life. When they seal their testimony with their blood, they are honored and their murderers are condemned (D&C 136:39).[22]

John hears the cry of the martyrs to God, asking how long "dost thou not judge the nations and avenge our blood" (v. 10, AT). Their appeal is for judgment through which vindication of their testimonies would come. The world must stand trial for the witness it has received and violently rejected. However, the Seer learned that the time for judgment was not to be during the fifth millennium; during that period the martyred Saints would be comforted and would enter into the rest of the Lord, but they would not yet be vindicated. White robes, symbolic of the purity of their lives and of their ultimate victory, were given to them, and patience was enjoined.

The rest into which they entered was not their final reward. The Greek word (*anapauō*) carried the idea of rest from toil, weariness, distress, and pain. These martyrs were "received into a state of happiness, which is called paradise, a state of rest, a state of peace, where they shall rest from all their troubles and from all care, and sorrow" (Alma 40:12). Their rest was grounded on the assurance that their word would be avenged. For the time being, they were to be patient; the register of martyrs was not yet full.[23] Others must die as well. These, how-

ever, would not be from the fifth seal, but from the sixth and
the seventh.

THE SIXTH SEAL (vv. 12–17)

12 And I beheld when he had opened the sixth seal, and, lo, there was a great earthquake; and the sun became black as sackcloth of hair, and the moon became as blood;

13 And the stars of heaven fell unto the earth, even as a fig tree casteth her untimely figs, when she is shaken of a mighty wind.

14 And the heaven departed as a scroll when it is rolled together; and every mountain and island were moved out of their places.

15 And the kings of the earth, and the great men, and the rich men, and the chief captains, and the mighty men, and every bondman, and every free man, hid themselves in the dens and in the rocks of the mountains;

16 And said to the mountains and rocks, Fall on us, and hide us from the face of him that sitteth on the throne, and from the wrath of the Lamb:

17 For the great day of his wrath is come; and who shall be able to stand?

With the sixth seal, we enter into the modern era. As the Lamb
broke it, a terrible scene of cosmic proportions met the eyes of
the Seer. A tremendous earthquake rocked the planet, affecting
every mountain and island. The sun ceased to shine, the moon
hung blood red, and the stars seemed to fall from heaven. In
ancient Jewish thought, cosmic order depended upon man's
obedience to God. They felt that when man became so wicked
that he attempted to set up his own system against God, the
constellations would abandon their harmony and the universe
would begin to disintegrate (see, e.g., Ps. 19).[24] The Revelator's
point seems to be that man cannot sin without influencing
heaven and earth (cf. Moses 7:28, 37, 48). The cosmos will echo
back his unholy deeds.

John could have well understood the idea of the cosmos in
turmoil from popular apocalyptic belief that had its roots in
earlier prophetic portrayals of the end of time. Not every detail
is to be taken literally.[25] For example, the moon will not become
blood though it may take on a sanguine hue. (John prophesied
that the moon would become red, the color of the second horse,
and the sun black, the color of the third.) But behind the symbol

stands reality. The cosmos really does react to events on earth, and the earth itself reacts through great convulsions.

Biblical literature regularly associated the earthquake with divine visitation. When God revealed his presence on Mount Sinai, "the whole mount quaked greatly" (Ex. 19:18, KJV). Isaiah stated that men would hide in caves from the terror of the Lord "when he ariseth to shake terribly the earth" (Isa. 2:19, KJV). "For thus saith the Lord of hosts; Yet once, it is a little while, and I will shake the heavens, and the earth, and the sea, and the dry land; and I will shake all nations" (Hag. 2:6–7, KJV).[26] Thus by use of the earthquake, the Lord shows his incredible power as he begins to warn the nations. Such power will be sufficiently terrifying to drive men to wish for death rather than face vengeance. John's forceful symbols dramatically convey the great natural disasters that bring the sixth millennium to a close and act as forerunners to the final catastrophes.[27]

The portrayal in Revelation could be quite literal in these verses. The Lord revealed to Joseph Smith those events destined to occur as the sixth seal closed: "Not many days hence and the earth shall tremble and reel to and fro as a drunken man; and the sun shall hide his face, and shall refuse to give light; and the moon shall be bathed in blood; and the stars shall become exceedingly angry, and shall cast themselves down as a fig that falleth from off a fig-tree" (D&C 88:87; see also Isa. 34:4). On another occasion the Lord said, "Before that great day shall come, the sun shall be darkened, and the moon be turned into blood; and the stars shall refuse their shining, and some shall fall, and great destructions await the wicked" (D&C 34:9).

Elder McConkie states that "some heavenly meteors or other objects, appearing as stars, will fall 'unto the earth.' Indeed, the events of that day shall be so unprecedented and so beyond human experience, that the prophets are and have been at an almost total loss for words to describe those realities pressed in upon them by the spirit of revelation."[28] The threat of the awesome desolation of the world will bring all to their knees.

Another event will transpire of such consequence that only symbolic language can describe it: "The heaven departed as a scroll when it is rolled together" (v. 14, KJV). John gives the sky the attributes of a flexible material expanse that can be withdrawn by being rolled up like an ancient scroll. Just what is meant here is unknown. The Greek word *apochorizein* does not mean to split or rend, but rather to remove to another place. The present heaven, from the standpoint of those on earth, will be removed (see Mark 13:31; 2 Pet. 3:10). Doctrine and Covenants 88:95 suggests that after the folding up of the heavens, there shall be an unfolding in which "the face of the Lord shall be unveiled."

The Seer notes seven consequences to the wickedness of mankind: (1) the earthquake, (2) the darkened sun, (3) the reddening of the moon, (4) the stars falling, (5) the heavens rolling up, (6) the mountains and islands moving out of their places, and (7) the universal consternation of mankind. Further, he notes seven classes of men who will be affected: (1) kings, (2) great men, (3) rich men, (4) chief captains, (5) mighty men, (6) bondmen, and (7) free men. Such numbering seems deliberate on his part. It emphasizes the idea of completeness: no enemy of God, no matter how high or low born, will escape the wrath of the Lamb.[29] He will move in his fury when patience ceases to be a virtue: "It shall come to pass, because of the wickedness of the world, that I will take vengeance upon the wicked, for they will not repent; for the cup of mine indignation is full; for behold, my blood shall not cleanse them if they hear me not" (D&C 29:17).

CONCLUSION

John associates a major event with the breaking of each seal. He catches the major characteristic of each millennium through the fifth. When he arrives at the sixth, his pace slows, and he gives more detail. He notes not just one event, but seven. It seems fitting that his rapid narrative should slow at this point. This is the moment just before the final millennium begins — the preparation period for it. It is the time when the Lord will reach out in terrible majesty and shake the very foundations of the earth in an attempt to break the hard-heartedness of the race. The Lord explained his purpose in these words:

> Hearken, O ye nations of the earth, and hear the words of that God who made you. O, ye nations of the earth, how often would I have gathered you together as a hen gathereth her chickens under her wings, but ye would not! How oft have I called upon you by the mouth of my servants, and by the ministering of angels, and by mine own voice, and by the voice of thunderings, and by the voice of lightnings, and by the voice of tempests, and by the voice of earthquakes, and great hailstorms, and by the voice of famines and pestilences of every kind, and by the great sound of a trump, and by the voice of judgment, and by the voice of mercy all the day long, and by the voice of glory and honor and the riches of eternal life, and would have saved you with an everlasting salvation, but ye would not! Behold, the day has come, when the cup of the wrath of mine indignation is full (D&C 43:23–26).

This scripture suggests that the Lord will try everything from promises to punishments to bring people to him. But once all is tried, the retribution will follow: he "would have saved" them, but now they are left to his anger. Little wonder that the wicked will cry "to the mountains and rocks, Fall on us, and hide us from the face of him that sitteth on the throne, and from the wrath of the Lamb" (Rev. 6:16, KJV).

What transpires in the sixth seal is a severe warning, but it is not the end. It is God's attempt to get men to repent and come to him. Looking at this same time period, an angel prophesied to Nephi saying,

> Wo be unto the Gentiles if it so be that they harden their hearts against the Lamb of God. For the time cometh, saith the Lamb of God, that I will work a great and a marvelous work among the children of men; a work which shall be everlasting, either on the one hand or on the other—either to the convincing of them unto peace and life eternal, or unto the deliverance of them to the hardness of their hearts and the blindness of their minds unto their being brought down into captivity, and also into destruction, both temporally and spiritually, according to the captivity of the devil, of which I have spoken (1 Ne. 14:6–7).

Therefore, the Lord will use the sixth seal to call people to repentance in ways that will shake the very foundations of the earth. Given every opportunity, unrepentant men and women will feel the wrath of the Lamb. The fullness of that wrath is revealed in chapters eight and nine. But what of the righteous? What happens to them as the world is gripped by the mailed fist of justice? That is the subject of chapter seven.

CHAPTER 7

THE SEAL OF THE LIVING GOD

(AN ANALYSIS OF REVELATION 7)

THE FOUR ANGELS (v. 1)

1 And after these things I saw four angels standing on the four corners of the earth, holding the four winds of the earth, that the wind should not blow on the earth, nor on the sea, nor on any tree.

John has prepared his reader for the crashing of God's judgment upon the world as the Lamb breaks the last seal. The Seer concluded chapter six with "the kings of the earth, and the great men, and the rich men, and the chief captains, and the mighty men, and every bondman, and every free man, [hiding] themselves in the dens and in the rocks of the mountains," crying in terror against the face of God and the Lamb, "for the great day of his wrath is come; and who shall be able to stand?" (Rev. 6:15, 17, KJV). But that wrath does not explode from chapter seven. Just at the moment of greatest crisis, an interruption occurs; the vision changes, and an interlude begins, bringing a moment of quiet and explanation to the reader.

Such a break in flow characterizes the Seer's pattern. At each turning point, as events are about to get ugly, he pauses to give encouragement and hope through explanation. Chapters four and five do this for the six seals, chapter ten for the third woe, chapter fourteen for the seven vials, and chapter 20:1–6 for the battle of Gog and Magog. This is exactly the case here.[1] Chapter seven answers the question posed in 6:17: "Who shall be able to stand?" (KJV).

As the new vision opens, John sees four angels standing on the four corners of the earth. The repetition of the number four suggests geographical fullness — all the world will be involved in the events of chapter seven. These angels hold in check the wind so that it "should not blow on the earth" (v. 1, KJV). The Greek word *anemos*, translated "wind," indicates a storm wind, sometimes almost hurricane-like.[2] Such winds brought drought, heat, insect plagues, and desolation. The mention of sun and withering heat in verse sixteen suggests that John had in mind the sirocco, a scorching wind that burnt up vegetation and left the land dust dry.[3] Biblical people viewed such winds as displays of divine wrath (cf. Hosea 3:15; Rev. 16:9, "great heat" being from a scorching wind). In this light, the angels play the role of divine executioners with power to destroy the whole earth.

Modern revelation confirms this view and adds depth. God commissioned these four angels and gave them "power over the four parts of the earth, to save life and to destroy; these are they who have the everlasting gospel to commit to every nation, kindred, tongue, and people; having power to shut up the heavens, to seal up unto life, or to cast down to the regions of darkness" (D&C 77:8). These angels have, as it were, two faces. They are not only destroying angels, but saving angels as well. What makes the difference is how men respond to the message they dispense.

The angels have long since left their home in heaven and are now on the earth. President Wilford Woodruff stated that these angels have been loosed and are at work here. However, their job is not just to destroy but to commit the gospel as well.[4] Their main period of operation is the sixth seal, or the period just preceding the Millennium. Thus, angelic administration is combining with mortal efforts to assure the world-wide preaching of the gospel during that time (see D&C 77:10).[5] Only after they fulfill that commission will they unleash the winds of destruction.[6]

The signs associated with the sixth seal—the earthquake, the plagues on the sun and moon, the stars falling—play a major role in the objectives of the sixth seal. Their function is not primarily destruction. They represent additional effort on the part of God to bring all men to him. The four angels symbolize the spiritual forces that oversee and assist in fulfilling this objective. But one must keep in mind that the same power that can save the nations also can destroy them. That power is Jesus Christ. During the sixth seal, the fullness of his gospel will be restored to the earth and both natural and supernatural forces will combine to see that it spreads to all lands and cultures. Those who respond with fullness of heart will enter into the rest of the Lord and find peace and safety. Those who reject it will find vexation and misery.

The world has already rejected the gospel many times, but during the sixth seal it will be in a position where one more rejection will assure its doom. This is because the gospel, preached with tremendous power, will not be easily ignored. Those who reject it will not do so out of ignorance. Therefore, the sixth seal will heighten the ideological conflict between the forces of good and evil. The conflict will not be resolved during the sixth seal, but the battle lines will be clearly drawn.

The Book of Mormon provides insight on how this will be done. In a vision Nephi saw the beginning of a conflict and its advance not long before the second coming of the Lord. He states:

> I looked and beheld many nations and kingdoms. And the angel said unto me: What beholdest thou? And I said: I behold many nations and kingdoms. And he said unto me: These are the nations and kingdoms of the Gentiles.
> And it came to pass that I saw among the nations of the Gentiles the formation of a great church. And the angel said unto me: Behold the formation of a church which is most abominable above all other churches, which slayeth the saints of God, yea, and tortureth them and bindeth them down, and yoketh them with a yoke of iron, and bringeth them down into captivity. And it came to pass that I beheld this great and abominable church; and I saw the devil that he was the founder of it.

> And I also saw gold, and silver, and silks, and scarlets, and fine-twined linen, and all manner of precious clothing; and I saw many harlots. And the angel spake unto me, saying: Behold the gold, and the silver, and the silks, and the scarlets, and the fine-twined linen, and the precious clothing, and the harlots, are the desires of this great and abominable church. And also for the praise of the world do they destroy the saints of God, and bring them down into captivity (1 Ne. 13:1–9).

These verses define the antagonist to righteousness along with its objective and battle plan. The great and abominable church craves the material, lusts after the sensual, and fuels itself on the praises of the world. Because it stands opposite God's kingdom, it grows only as it shuts out the light of the gospel and the refining power of the Holy Spirit. Therefore, for self-preservation, it must destroy the Saints of God.

In cosmic terms, the battle lines will fall between the church of the devil and the church of God. The mortal perspective may not perceive and report it that way, but from a spiritual standpoint the issue is clear. Returning to Nephi's vision, an angel said to him:

> Look, and behold that great and abominable church, which is the mother of abominations, whose founder is the devil. And he said unto me: Behold there are save two churches only; the one is the church of the Lamb of God, and the other is the church of the devil; wherefore, whoso belongeth not to the church of the Lamb of God belongeth to that great church, which is the mother of abominations; and she is the whore of all the earth. And it came to pass that I looked and beheld the whore of all the earth, and she sat upon many waters; and she had dominion over all the earth, among all nations, kindreds, tongues, and people.
>
> And it came to pass that I beheld the church of the Lamb of God, and its numbers were few, because of the wickedness and abominations of the whore who sat upon many waters; nevertheless, I beheld that the church of the Lamb, who were the saints of God, were also upon all the face of the earth; and their dominions upon the face of the earth were small, because of the wickedness of the great whore whom I saw.
>
> And it came to pass that I beheld that the great mother of abominations did gather together multitudes upon the face of all the earth, among all the nations of the Gentiles, to fight against the Lamb of God. And it came to pass that I, Nephi,

beheld the power of the Lamb of God, that it descended upon
the saints of the church of the Lamb, and upon the covenant
people of the Lord, who were scattered upon all the face of
the earth; and they were armed with righteousness and with
the power of God in great glory (1 Ne. 14:9–14).

The armor of the Saints—righteousness and tremendous
power from God—will protect them from the world-embracing
colossus while the destroying angels prepare to move against
it. As noted above, the primary preparation will be the preaching
of the gospel. Pure testimony will flow through the nations
during the sixth seal. Many will respond. Those who do not,
who willfully rebel against the light and who seek to destroy
God's work, will face the wrath of the seventh seal.

THE ANGEL OF THE EAST (vv. 2–3)

2 And I saw another angel ascending from the east, having the seal of the living God: and he cried with a loud voice to the four angels, to whom it was given to hurt the earth and the sea,

3 Saying, Hurt not the earth, neither the sea, nor the trees, till we have sealed the servants of our God in their foreheads.

In concert with the four angels, John sees another angel ascending from the east. The imagery used in these verses reminds one of the rising sun, which recalls the glory of God, spreading light and life. The idea is reminiscent of Ezekiel 43:4, where the glory of Jehovah comes out of the east. This angel "is he to whom is given the seal of the living God over the twelve tribes of Israel; . . . and, if you will receive it, this is Elias which was to come to gather together the tribes of Israel and restore all things" (D&C 77:9). Speaking of this Elias, Elder Bruce R. McConkie has said,

> Correcting the Bible by the spirit of revelation, the Prophet
> restored a statement of John the Baptist which says that Christ
> is the Elias who was to restore all things. (Inspired Version,
> John 1:21–28.) By revelation we are also informed that the Elias
> who was to restore all things is the angel Gabriel who was
> known in mortality as Noah. (D. & C. 27:6–7; Luke 1:5–25;
> *Teachings*, p. 157.) From the same authentic source we also
> learn that the promised Elias is John the Revelator. (D. & C.
> 77:9, 14.) Thus there are three different revelations which name

Elias as being three different persons. What are we to con-
clude?

By finding answer to the question, by whom has the restoration been effected, we shall find who Elias is and find there
is no problem in harmonizing these apparently contradictory
revelations. Who has restored all things? Was it one man?
Certainly not. Many angelic ministrants have been sent from
the courts of glory to confer keys and powers, to commit their
dispensations and glories again to men on earth. At least the
following have come: Moroni, John the Baptist, Peter, James
and John, Moses, Elijah, Elias, Gabriel, Raphael, and Michael.
(D. & C. 13; 110; 128:19–21.) Since it is apparent that no one
messenger has carried the whole burden of the restoration,
but rather that each has come with a specific endowment from
on high, it becomes clear that Elias is a composite personage.
The expression must be understood to be a name and a title
for those whose mission it was to commit keys and powers
to men in this final dispensation.[7]

The angel that John saw, symbolic of all these Eliases, carries
the seal of the living God. He has to place this upon the servants
of God before the end of the sixth seal, before the time when
the destroying angels vent their fury. The seal, as mentioned
in chapter five, is both a guard against defilement and pollution
and a means of security. Both ideas apply here: the seal identifies
the Saints as God's own, and, as its major purpose, it insures
their protection against the coming judgments. The imagery
parallels that in Ezekiel 9:4 where a mark on the forehead protects the righteous from the destruction about to fall on Jerusalem.[8]

Joseph Smith taught that the four angels assisted in "sealing
the blessing upon their [the Saints'] heads, meaning the everlasting covenant, thereby making their calling and election
sure."[9] Peter expounded the doctrine of calling and election (see
1 Pet. 1:3–5; 2 Pet. 1:1–19), and Paul referred to it on a number
of occasions (see Eph. 1:11–14; 4:30; 2 Cor. 1:21–22). The basic
idea is that through faith, repentance, and baptism, a person
can receive the gift of the Holy Ghost. As he responds to its
teachings, he becomes purer and develops the attributes of god-
liness, culminating in Christ-like love. Certain benefits flow out
of this. As Nephi said, "Ye must press forward with a stead-

fastness in Christ, having a perfect brightness of hope, and a love of God and of all men. Wherefore, if ye shall press forward, feasting upon the word of Christ, and endure to the end, behold, thus saith the Father: Ye shall have eternal life" (2 Ne. 31:20).

A person has made his calling and election sure when the promised blessings are sealed to him. Peter admonished the Saints of his day to "give diligence to make your calling and election sure: for if ye do these things, ye shall never fall" (2 Pet. 1:10). The "these things" he referred to include growing in virtue, testimony, patience, brotherly love, and the pure love of Christ. Those who do these things are assured that they shall have eternal life from which they will never fall. Revelation suggests that this power will function widely before the end of the sixth seal.

There is another step one can achieve in mortality, but Peter does not focus on this. He does allude to it when he states, "We have also a more sure word of prophecy; whereunto ye do well that ye take heed, as unto a light that shineth in a dark place, until the day dawn, and the day star arise in your hearts" (2 Pet. 1:19). The Doctrine and Covenants states that the term "the more sure word of prophecy means a man's knowing that he is sealed up unto eternal life, by revelation and the spirit of prophecy, through the power of the Holy Priesthood" (131:5). Thus, a person can receive a revelation that he has attained unto eternal life while in mortality.[10] The symbol of the seal as used by John does not necessarily include the more sure word of prophecy. It does include having the Holy Ghost ratify the covenants that one has entered into and the person maintaining a state of justification through faithfulness.

THE 144,000 (vv. 4–8)

4 And I heard the number of them which were sealed: and there were sealed an hundred and forty and four thousand of all the tribes of the children of Israel.

5 Of the tribe of Juda were sealed twelve thousand. Of the tribe of Reuben were sealed twelve thousand. Of the tribe of Gad were sealed twelve thousand.

6 Of the tribe of Aser were sealed twelve thousand. Of the tribe of Nepthalim were sealed

twelve thousand. Of the tribe of Manasses were sealed twelve thousand.

7 Of the tribe of Simeon were sealed twelve thousand. Of the tribe of Levi were sealed twelve thousand. Of the tribe of Issachar were sealed twelve thousand.

8 Of the tribe of Zabulon were sealed twelve thousand. Of the tribe of Joseph were sealed twelve thousand. Of the tribe of Benjamin were sealed twelve thousand.

The number of those sealed, states the Seer, is 144,000. The number need not be taken literally. The Doctrine and Covenants states "that those who are sealed are high priests, ordained unto the holy order of God, to administer the everlasting gospel; for they are they who are ordained out of every nation, kindred, tongue, and people, by the angels to whom is given power over the nations of the earth, to bring as many as will come to the church of the Firstborn" (77:11). Note that this scripture does not specify a number. Instead it notes that the group is composed of high priests who have a special calling "to administer the everlasting gospel" and "to bring as many as will come to the church of the Firstborn."

Joseph Smith associated them with the temple.[11] The symbolic meaning of the number supports this association. Twelve represents the priesthood. Biblical people squared a number to amplify its symbolic meaning. Thus, 144 suggests a fullness of priesthood authority. But John is not satisfied with that. He gives the image a superlative quality by multiplying 1,000, representing completeness. In this way he shows the strength and breadth of the priesthood in the latter days, in this dispensation that is, indeed, the dispensation of the fullness of times. During this period that complete priesthood authority will operate. It is little wonder that as the world spurns this authority, it will be condemned.

The attachment to the temple fits perfectly since only there can one receive the fullness of the priesthood (D&C 124:25–30). Elder McConkie states that the 144,000 are kings and priests "converted, baptized, endowed, married for eternity, and finally sealed up unto eternal life."[12] Their mission is not merely to bring people into The Church of Jesus Christ of Latter-day Saints. It goes beyond that. Their special assignment centers in getting people sealed into the church of the Firstborn through the administration of the fullness of the endowment (on the church of the Firstborn, see D&C 76:50–70; 93:21–23).

John indicates that the 144,000 will be those sealed from all the tribes of Israel. Curiously, he leaves out Dan, adds Levi, and has Joseph taking the place of Ephraim to get twelve tribes. The Seer gives no hint why he left out Dan. Some early Christians believed that John dropped the tribal name because of a tradition that the Antichrist would arise from there.[13] The disfavor into which Dan fell goes all the way back to 1 Chronicles 7, which also omits Dan from the list of tribes.[14] It may be that Dan's association with idolatry marked the tribe for omission since Jeroboam set up his idols in that tribal territory (see Judg. 18:30; 1 Kgs. 12:29). Since John was writing in part against the influences of idolatry invading the church, he may have omitted Dan as a warning.[15]

THE COUNTLESS MULTITUDE
OF THE SAVED (vv. 9–17)

9 After this I beheld, and, lo, a great multitude, which no man could number, of all nations, and kindreds, and people, and tongues, stood before the throne, and before the Lamb, clothed with white robes, and palms in their hands;

10 And cried with a loud voice, saying, Salvation to our God which sitteth upon the throne, and unto the Lamb.

11 And all the angels stood round about the throne, and about the elders and the four beasts, and fell before the throne on their faces, and worshipped God,

12 Saying, Amen: Blessing, and glory, and wisdom, and thanksgiving, and honour, and power, and might, be unto our God for ever and ever. Amen.

13 And one of the elders answered, saying unto me, What are these which are arrayed in white robes? and whence came they?

14 And I said unto him, Sir, thou knowest. And he said to me, These are they which came out of great tribulation, and have washed their robes, and made them white in the blood of the Lamb.

15 Therefore are they before the throne of God, and serve him day and night in his temple: and he that sitteth on the throne shall dwell among them.

16 They shall hunger no more, neither thirst any more; neither shall the sun light on them, nor any heat.

17 For the Lamb which is in the midst of the throne shall feed

them, and shall lead them unto   God shall wipe away all tears from
living fountains of waters: and   their eyes.

John's vision expanded beyond the 144,000 to include a vast congregation "which no man could number," composed of those saved from all nations and peoples (v. 9, KJV). The enormous throng represents conquerors with their white robes and the palm fronds, the double symbol of victory. The former also signifies their purity, for they have washed their robes in the blood of the Lamb (see v. 14). In joy, they make homage to their God: "Salvation to our God which sitteth upon the throne, and unto the Lamb" (v. 10, KJV).

The word translated "salvation" (*sōtēria*) expresses the idea of a great deliverance by the hand of God through which his people find total victory. But in this context, they are celebrating neither God's salvation nor their own. The victory of God and the Lamb is what makes all other victories possible. Thus, because the Savior prevailed, the throng prevailed. Without his victory, nothing they could have done would have mattered. But the Lamb, slain before the foundation of the world, satisfied justice so that grace could abound, and through that grace the multitude was redeemed and became priestly members of the divine kingdom (see Rom. 3:24; 5:20; Eph. 2:8; 1 Pet. 1:13; 5:5; 2 Ne. 25:23).[16]

Because of the victory of the Lamb, the efforts of the Saints take on meaning. Their faith and good works now play an important part in their own salvation and that of others, which they could not do before. One of the elders explained the nature of their saving acts to John, saying: "These are they which came out of great tribulation, and have washed their robes, and made them white in the blood of the Lamb" (v. 14, KJV). The definite article (present in the Greek but not in the KJV) is significant: "*The* great tribulation" points to a definite prophetic period, not simply to the common troubles that afflict God's people in all ages.[17] *The* period is the final series of woes the angels are about to loose on the world.[18] Verse 14 changes tense to the future. It appears that at this point John begins speaking from the standpoint of a prophet foretelling the future. He views the final abode of the Saints upon the celestialized earth.

Millions will prevail during this time of trial because they heeded the warnings and prepared themselves, "therefore are they before the throne of God" (v. 15, KJV). John's use of the word "therefore" is deliberate. It means that the multitude stand before God because they have been purified from all sin. In this state they "serve him day and night in his temple" (v. 15, KJV). The word *serve* (Greek *latreuō*) specifically denotes the performance of ceremonies associated with God's sanctuary (cf. Heb. 8:5), which these men can perform because they are kings and priests of the Most High. But in this state, they not only serve, but are served in return. The Lamb feeds them and leads them. God himself wipes away their tears. Hunger, thirst, discomfort are all unknown to them, for the one who "sitteth on the throne shall dwell among them" (v. 15, KJV). Having overcome, they are honored by those whom they honor and loved by those whom they love. Such is the state of eternal life.

CONCLUSION

Chapter six, anticipating the outpouring of the wrath of God, asked the question: "Who shall be able to stand?" John answers that question in chapter seven: those who have been sealed against destruction by washing their robes in the blood of the Lamb. By this means they become pure and are able to dwell with the Lord. However, that dwelling need not be just in heaven. There is an earthly counterpart to paradise: Zion. The Lord has said: "Let Zion rejoice, for this is Zion—THE PURE IN HEART; therefore, let Zion rejoice, while all the wicked shall mourn. For behold, and lo, vengeance cometh speedily upon the ungodly as the whirlwind; and who shall escape it? The Lord's scourge shall pass over by night and by day, and the report thereof shall vex all people; yea, it shall not be stayed until the Lord come; . . . nevertheless, Zion shall escape" (D&C 97:21–23, 25).

As early as the first millennium of earth's history, prophets understood the importance of the latter-day Zion as the means of preserving the Lord's people. To Enoch the Lord declared:

> As I live, even so will I come in the last days, in the days of wickedness and vengeance, to fulfil the oath which I have made unto you concerning the children of Noah; and the day shall come that the earth shall rest, but before that day the heavens shall be darkened, and a veil of darkness shall cover the earth; and the heavens shall shake, and also the earth; and great tribulations shall be among the children of men, but my people will I preserve; and righteousness will I send down out of heaven; and truth will I send forth out of the earth, to bear testimony of mine Only Begotten; his resurrection from the dead; yea, and also the resurrection of all men; and righteousness and truth will I cause to sweep the earth as with a flood, to gather out mine elect from the four quarters of the earth, unto a place which I shall prepare, an Holy City, that my people may gird up their loins, and be looking forth for the time of my coming; for there shall be my tabernacle, and it shall be called Zion, a New Jerusalem (Moses 7:60–62).

It is little wonder that, with righteousness and truth sweeping "the earth as with a flood," the judgment of God pours out against those who reject it. As for those who respond, they shall be gathered to places of safety. As the Lord declared, the righteous shall be gathered "upon the land of Zion, and upon her stakes . . . for a defense, and for a refuge from the storm, and from wrath when it shall be poured out without mixture upon the whole earth" (D&C 115:6). The Lord has specified that "those places which I have appointed for refuge, shall be the places for your baptisms for your dead" (D&C 124:36). In other words the Lord shall gather his people to his temples. This brings us back to the 144,000, those special ministers sealed by the four destroying angels against the day of indignation. Those under their care will find

> a land of peace, a city of refuge, a place of safety for the saints of the Most High God; and the glory of the Lord shall be there, and the terror of the Lord also shall be there, insomuch that the wicked will not come unto it, and it shall be called Zion.
> And it shall come to pass among the wicked, that every man that will not take his sword against his neighbor must needs flee unto Zion for safety.
> And there shall be gathered unto it out of every nation

under heaven; and it shall be the only people that shall not be at war one with another. And it shall be said among the wicked: Let us not go up to battle against Zion, for the inhabitants of Zion are terrible; wherefore we cannot stand. And it shall come to pass that the righteous shall be gathered out from among all nations, and shall come to Zion, singing with songs of everlasting joy (D&C 45:66–71).

In this light, the most important work for the Saints of the sixth seal is the establishment of Zion by faithfulness, diligence, and especially purity. Missionary work must spread, temple work increase, and righteousness flow out of the homes and into the communities of the Saints. In this way God will have a people "prepared to receive the glory that I [God] have for them, even the glory of Zion" (D&C 136:31).

CHAPTER 8

THE OPENING OF THE SEVENTH SEAL

(AN ANALYSIS OF REVELATION 8)

SILENCE IN HEAVEN (vv. 1–4)

1 And when he had opened the seventh seal, there was silence in heaven about the space of half an hour.

2 And I saw the seven angels which stood before God; and to them were given seven trumpets.

3 And another angel came and stood at the altar, having a golden censer; and there was given unto him much incense, that he should offer it with the prayers of all saints upon the golden altar which was before the throne.

4 And the smoke of the incense, which came with the prayers of the saints, ascended up before God out of the angel's hand.

The interlude over, John resumes where chapter six left off. But once again, there is no clash of thunder, no outpouring of wrath. The Lamb breaks the seventh seal; the scroll of destiny lies open, but quiet prevails. God's testament, his will for the nations, stands ready to be executed. The day of judgment has come. The world will now receive its inheritance and just reward. Six thousand years of indifference, of carelessness toward God, of transgression, of deliberate corruption of his ways, of willfull rejection and sometimes slaughter of his prophets, of conscious rebellion and evil—all these will now receive their just compensation.

As the seal is broken, "there is silence in heaven for the

space of about half an hour" (v. 1, AT). A solemn moment intervenes before judgment commences. Nothing breaks the solitude, but tension builds as seven angels, as captains over a host, receive seven trumpets and prepare to give their commands.[1] The image of the trumpets creates a feeling of foreboding, for soon their blast will shatter the world. But an interval is needed: a period of preparation, of devotion and worship, of readying before heaven executes God's will, a moment of mourning for a world sick unto death.

John sees an angel approach the altar in heaven holding a golden censer, "and there was given to him much incense, consisting of the prayers of all saints" (v. 3, AT).[2] Thus, both heaven and earth, angels and Saints, combine to create a holy crescendo of expectant, if painful, silence. Never has heaven been filled with the sweet smell of earthly prayers as now. The moment of anguished calm is about to end. But the silence will not end until the heavenly priest, the mighty angel, performs at the altar a priesthood act—the judgment of the nations.[3]

The theological importance of the half hour of silence is derived from the Old Testament. In Habakkuk 2:20, the prophet commands, "the Lord is in his holy temple: let all the earth keep silence before him" (KJV). Then follows a description of the Lord moving in glory and anger against wickedness. The day of judgment has arrived. Zechariah also commands silence as the Lord arouses from his holy dwelling (2:13). Zephaniah does the same thing, "For the day of the Lord is at hand: for the Lord hath prepared a sacrifice" (1:7, KJV), and will move against the wicked (see 1:7–18). In each of these three instances, the silence heralds a wrathful theophany and may indicate a period of mourning before calamity.[4] The Doctrine and Covenants supports this view. The Lord states:

> But the day soon cometh that ye shall see me, and know that I am; for the veil of darkness shall soon be rent, and he that is not purified shall not abide the day. . . . For all flesh is corrupted before me; and the powers of darkness prevail upon the earth, among the children of men, in the presence of all the hosts of heaven—Which causeth silence to reign, and all eternity is pained, and the angels are waiting the great

command to reap down the earth, to gather the tares that they may be burned (38:8, 11–12).

Doctrine and Covenants 88:95 also speaks of a half hour of silence associated with the last days. In this case, it follows the acts of judgment and immediately precedes the coming of the Lord. Though it is out of position with that of Revelation, it carries the same import: it signals a theophany, but this time of total victory.

The period of silence, the Seer states, lasted "about half an hour" (AT). The idea of approximation is clear in the Greek: The word used, hōs, means "approximately" or "nearly." Thus, getting an exact fix on the amount of time John had in mind is impossible. The half hour, it has been speculated, may actually approach twenty-one years, based on the Lord's time being 1,000 years to the day (see Abr. 3:4; 2 Pet. 3:8). If such is correct, it will be a period when all will seem to be at rest, a return to the normal after the pounding taken during the sixth seal. The earth will cease to shake, the stars to fall, and the cosmos will return to a definite pattern. However, no matter what the duration, wickedness will not cease. Therefore, the half hour represents a short interval during which angels and Saints prepare in sorrow for the sentence of destruction to be executed upon the world.

One idea stands out: this is the period in which the heavenly and earthly churches of God will be linked as never before, a period in which the Saints will make their final preparation for what is to come. The Doctrine and Covenants states, "The servants of God shall go forth, saying with a loud voice: Fear God and give glory to him, for the hour of his judgment is come; and worship him that made heaven, and earth, and the sea, and the fountains of waters – calling upon the name of the Lord day and night, saying: O that thou wouldst rend the heavens, that thou wouldst come down, that the mountains might flow down at thy presence" (133:38–40). The devastations that follow will be, at least in part, a response to this prayer of God's servants. Thus, the righteous will not be caught off guard. They will follow the Lord's admonition: "The coming of the Lord draweth nigh, and it overtaketh the world as a thief in the night—therefore, gird up your loins, that you may be the children of light, and that day shall not overtake you as a thief" (D&C 106:4–5).

THE FIRST FOUR TRUMPET BLASTS (vv. 5–12)

5 And the angel took the censer, and filled it with fire of the altar, and cast it into the earth: and there were voices, and thunderings, and lightnings, and an earthquake.

6 And the seven angels which had the seven trumpets prepared themselves to sound.

7 The first angel sounded, and there followed hail and fire mingled with blood, and they were cast upon the earth: and the third part of trees was burnt up, and all green grass was burnt up.

8 And the second angel sounded, and as it were a great mountain burning with fire was cast into the sea: and the third part of the sea became blood;

9 And the third part of the creatures which were in the sea, and had life, died; and the third part of the ships were destroyed.

10 And the third angel sounded, and there fell a great star from heaven, burning as it were a lamp, and it fell upon the third part of the rivers, and upon the fountains of waters;

11 And the name of the star is called Wormwood: and the third part of the waters became wormwood; and many men died of the waters, because they were made bitter.

12 And the fourth angel sounded, and the third part of the sun was smitten, and the third part of the moon, and the third part of the stars; so as the third part of them was darkened, and the day shone not for a third part of it, and the night likewise.

Finally the judgment commences. The angel, performing his priestly service, moves to the altar. He is not one of the seven, but a minister of authority. This angel may have already intervened twice at critical points. He could be the one called "a strong angel" (5:2, KJV), "another angel" (7:2; 8:3; 14:15, KJV), and "another mighty angel" (10:1, KJV). The term "another angel" seems to suggest someone other than the ones who have gone before. However, in each instance where the term is used, it distinguishes one angel from the others just mentioned. It may be that this is Michael or father Adam, the only angel named by John, who holds the keys over this earth.

This conjecture is based on Adam's role as understood by Joseph Smith. Adam acts under Christ over this earth, holding the key of presidency. Angels are under his direction; he reveals the gospel; and he watches over the ordinances.[5] In the Doctrine and Covenants, he is called the seventh angel, perhaps symbolic of the fact that he represents all the angels or that he directs them. He is the one who, in the end, will lead the forces against Satan (see 88:112–13, 115).[6]

This special minister of authority will make the first thrust against the wicked. He takes the censer, fills it with the fire of the heavenly altar, and casts it upon the earth (cf. Ezek. 10:2–7). Noise, thunder, lightning, and earthquake follow. In an instant the silence is shattered. The seventh seal now picks up the destruction scenario of the sixth and multiplies it.

> For not many days hence and the earth shall tremble and reel to and fro as a drunken man; and the sun shall hide his face, and shall refuse to give light; and the moon shall be bathed in blood; and the stars shall become exceedingly angry, and shall cast themselves down as a fig that falleth from off a fig-tree. And after your testimony cometh wrath and indignation upon the people. For after your testimony cometh the testimony of earthquakes, that shall cause groanings in the midst of her, and men shall fall upon the ground and shall not be able to stand. And also cometh the testimony of the voice of thunderings, and the voice of lightnings, and the voice of tempests, and the voice of the waves of the sea heaving themselves beyond their bounds.
>
> And all things shall be in commotion; and surely, men's hearts shall fail them; for fear shall come upon all people. And angels shall fly through the midst of heaven, crying with a loud voice, sounding the trump of God, saying: Prepare ye, prepare ye, O inhabitants of the earth; for the judgment of our God is come. Behold, and lo, the Bridegroom cometh; go ye out to meet him (D&C 88:87–92).

Mankind's chance for repentance is rapidly coming to a close. God tried every means to reclaim them, but they would not hear. Now comes the response to the cry of the earth itself: "Wo, wo is me, the mother of men; I am pained, I am weary, because of the wickedness of my children. When shall I rest, and be cleansed from the filthiness which is gone forth out of me? When will my Creator sanctify me, that I may rest, and righteousness for a season abide upon my face?" (Moses 7:48). The answer is "now," for judgment has commenced.

Four of the angels follow the mighty angel's devastations with additional plagues. Again, the number four is symbolic of geographical totality. The whole earth will fall under the angel's censer, and thus there is the need for the Saints to be sealed against these destructions. But remember that the prayers of the Saints have played an important role in initiating this judgment. Their petitions, at least in part, have unleashed the wrath. This case seems to parallel that of Noah. According to the book of Moses, Noah's "heart was pained that the Lord had made man." The result was that the Lord decided to act, "for it repenteth Noah that I have created them, and that I have made them: and he hath called upon me" (Moses 8:25–26). The result of Noah's petition was the flood. But just what role the Church plays during the period of the seventh seal is not disclosed. It is not in view in chapter eight; only the world is.

The sounding of the trumpets has important symbolic meaning. The Doctrine and Covenants makes it clear that, "as God made the world in six days, and on the seventh day he finished his work, and sanctified it, . . . the sounding of the trumpets of the seven angels are the preparing and finishing of his work, in the beginning of the seventh thousand years—the preparing of the way before the time of his coming" (77:12).

Much work must be done before the Lord comes in glory. The beginning of the Millennium will see the finishing of that work. The term *millennium* can be defined at least three ways. It means literally a period of a thousand years. According to LDS theology, the earth has passed through five full millennia and is about to pass through a sixth. Using this definition, we think of the Millennium as the last thousand years of the earth's history before the "short season." The term can further be defined as that period during which the earth experiences peace and rest—the period when paradisiacal conditions will prevail. Finally the term can define the period during which the Savior will take charge of affairs and reign personally upon the earth. These definitions are not mutually exclusive, and for the vast majority of the last thousand years all three definitions will be correct.

But Doctrine and Covenants 77 states that the seventh seal and the seventh thousand years coincide. That being the case, the Millennium will have begun before the Second Coming at the time the Savior begins to reign on this earth at the great council at Adam-Ondi-Ahman. According to Elder Joseph Fielding Smith, "At that time there will be a transfer of authority from the usurper and imposter, Lucifer, to the rightful King, Jesus Christ. Judgment will be set and all who have held keys will make their reports and deliver their stewardships, as they shall be required. Adam will direct this judgment, and then he will make his report, as the one holding the keys for this earth, to his Superior Officer, Jesus Christ. Our Lord will then assume the reigns of government; directions will be given to the Priesthood; and He, whose right it is to rule, will be installed officially by the voice of the Priesthood there assembled."[7]

So the second coming of the Savior does not usher in the Millennium; the plagues of the seven angels do. That work must first be completed before the Lord appears in glory. The plagues are, therefore, God's last effort to soften the hardened. The plagues have but one purpose: to begin the cleansing process of the earth. But the method is twofold: first, to reclaim any who will repent under the excruciating pain of the last plagues; and second, to destroy those who will not.

As each angel sounds, echoes from Exodus 7–12 are heard. The scourges that God placed upon Egypt become John's type of the millennial plagues. The point seems to be that God will once again make bare his mighty arm before the nations. As Pharaoh hardened his heart and brought the plagues upon Egypt, so the Lord directs trumpet blasts against a world adamant in its hostility toward the Lamb. As happened with Egypt, as the intensity of the judgments increase, so also does the vehemence with which man refuses to repent (see Rev. 9:20–21; cf. Ex. 7:22–23; 8:15, 19, 32; 9:7, 12, 34–35; 10:20, 27–28).

But the trumpet blasts are not designed to destroy the earth. They affect a significant proportion, but not all. Some twelve times the Seer limits the destruction to one-third, symbolically showing that their bounds have been set. They can go only so far. The fraction one-third is used by a number of the prophets in association with what is called "remnant theology," the remnant being the unaffected part. We see this in Ezekiel 5:1–5. The prophet performs his dramatized prophecy (Hebrew 'ot,) against Jerusalem by shaving his head and beard, burns one-third of the hair with fire, cleaves one-third with the sword, and scatters the remainder to the wind. Only the latter one-third remains alive though scattered. It is the remnant. The fraction is used again in Ezekiel 5:12 and in Zechariah 13:8–9. In the latter, one-third is all that remains alive after the divine judgments while another one-third is burned with fire. So the fraction John gives suggests that the purpose of the destruction in Revelation 8 is not so much retribution as a last attempt to turn man to God.[8]

The plagues do not arise out of natural phenomena such as volcanic action. They represent eschatological judgments of which there is no equivalent in Jewish apocalyptic.[9] The picture John paints graphically shows the tremendous power that will rampage upon the earth. When the first trumpet blasts, hail and fire mixed with blood fall to the earth, burning up plant life. John seems to be alluding to the first Egyptian plague (see Ex. 7:20; Ps. 78:44) where the Nile was turned into blood and many creatures died. The Egyptians also saw fiery hail (see Ex. 9:23–25; Ezek. 38:22). But the combination of destructive elements and the extent of the plague John sees make it unique. With the second trumpet, a blazing mountain falls into the sea,[10] killing many of its creatures and disrupting shipping, while the third summons a blazing star against the fresh water systems. Finally, the forth trumpet, in a modification on the ninth Egyptian plague (see Ex. 10:21–23), strikes at the moon and the sun, blotting out much of their light.

In this way John symbolizes the great destructions he saw unleashed. The separate plagues are not to be taken as happening one after the other. Rather, the whole world will likely be set in commotion simultaneously.[11] The attack is directed primarily against nature. Nonetheless, mankind is seriously affected. When the grass and trees are hurt, the wheat and fruit trees go up in flames.[12] When the fresh waters are affected they become as wormwood, a very bitter herb that makes the water impossible to drink.[13] The catastrophes apparently cause the atmosphere to become so polluted that sunlight and moonlight are significantly dimmed. This may cause a drastic change in the weather patterns of the earth. A greenhouse effect may be set up and temperatures rise unusually, resulting in the conditions noted by John in chapter sixteen.

The day of darkness as a symbol of the day of judgment runs thoughout the Old Testament. Amos notes that the Lord's day will be a day of darkness and not of light (5:18). For Joel it will be a "day of darkness and of gloominess, a day of clouds and of thick darkness" (2:2, KJV). As the Savior noted, in the day of the Lord, "the sun shall be darkened, and the moon shall not give her light" (Mark 13:24, KJV; cf. Isa. 13:10). The fourth trumpet plague fulfills these conditions.

In each of the first three instances, fire is an active ingredient in the judgments. However, it is not associated with the fire of the Lord's coming, during which "the elements should melt with fervent heat, and the earth should be wrapt together as a scroll, and the heavens and the earth should pass away" (3 Ne. 26:3: cf. Morm. 9:2). It precedes it. It has been called "the Great Overburn," an apt description of the final holocaust of Revelation, and has been associated with the last great war before the Second Coming—a war of a special nature.[14] It is not described in the usual term of bloodshed and the work of the sword. It is a war of burning in which "the people shall be as the fuel of the fire" (2 Ne. 19:19).

It would take a miracle for anyone to survive such a general holocaust, but that is exactly the point. The destruction is limited. God supervises the whole thing. Further, the fire acts as his agent. Its purpose is not only to destroy, but also to protect his people:

> For the time soon cometh that the fulness of the wrath of God shall be poured out upon all the children of men; for he will not suffer that the wicked shall destroy the righteous. Wherefore, he will preserve the righteous by his power, even if it so be that the fulness of his wrath must come, and the

righteous be preserved, even unto the destruction of their enemies by fire. Wherefore, the righteous need not fear; for thus saith the prophet, they shall be saved, even if it so be as by fire. Behold, my brethren, I say unto you, that these things must shortly come; yea, even blood, and fire, and vapor of smoke must come; and it must needs be upon the face of this earth; and it cometh unto men according to the flesh if it so be that they will harden their hearts against the Holy One of Israel (1 Ne. 22:16–18).

The Lord is perfectly prepared to allow thousands to die in order to protect his people. Some may have trouble with this idea, but the Seer has a very realistic understanding about death. From John's perspective, all must die. The question is when and how. Ultimate destiny is not determined by the moment or manner of death; it is by the manner of life. Those who are destroyed are not annihilated. They have further existence. But for the present they have not been playing the game by God's rules. They have become mean, and so they are thrown into the penalty box, so to speak, for unnecessary roughness while the game goes on. According to Caird, the idea that mortality is so infallibly precious that

the death which robs us of it must be the ultimate tragedy is precisely the idolatry that John is trying here to combat. We have already seen that John calls the enemies of the church 'the inhabitants of earth', because they have made themselves utterly at home in this transient world order. If all men must die, and if at the end heaven and earth must vanish, along with those whose life is irremediably bounded by worldly horizons, then it is surely in accord with the mercy of God that he should send men from time to time forceful reminders of the insecurity of their tenure.[15]

Besides, as already noted, the purpose of the plagues is to drive those who would not otherwise do so to repentance and, thus, into the protective arms of God. Those who will not repent must be accountable to the fire.

CONCLUSION

The Lord has stated, "Mine indignation is soon to be poured out without measure upon all nations; and this will I do when the cup of their iniquity is full" (D&C 101:11). The world will not take advantage of the half hour of silence to repent. Though warned and recognizing the source of that warning, they will not respond. Thus, sin will be added to sin until the measure is complete; when it is, the moment of grace will pass. Then the angels will sound, and the earth will fall under the power of the four trumpets.

As if this destruction were not enough, John hears the ominous cry of a bird of prey (not an angel as in the KJV) preparing to dive for the kill. Most manuscripts have the Greek word *aetos* here, which translates as either eagle or vulture, as in the Septuagint and the New Testament (e.g. Luke 17:37).[16] The image of the vulture hovering over a dying beast or of the eagle ready to swoop down for the kill best expresses the doom that the other three trumpets are about to bring upon unrepentant man. From the high heaven where all are visible to it and it is visible to all, it screeches its dirge: "Woe, woe, woe to the inhabitants of the earth because of the trumpet blasts that are about to be sounded by the other three angels" (v. 13, AT). Real destruction, of which mankind has had only a little taste up to this point, awaits the fifth trumpet blast. Indeed, verse thirteen serves as a "transition between the four plagues brought by God upon nature to lead man to repentance and the subsequent demonic woes in which man will be directly subjected to the forces of the abyss."[17]

CHAPTER 9

THE LOCUSTS

(AN ANALYSIS OF REVELATION 9)

THE FIFTH TRUMPET BLAST
AND THE FIRST WOE (vv. 1–2)

1 And the fifth angel sounded, and I saw a star fall from heaven unto the earth: and to him was given the key of the bottomless pit.

2 And he opened the bottomless pit; and there arose a smoke out of the pit, as the smoke of a great furnace; and the sun and the air were darkened by reason of the smoke of the pit.

As the fifth trumpet blasts, the first of the eagle's woes strikes the earth. A star, symbolic of a once divine being, a premortal power of such proportion his name was "light bearer," unlocks a terror so great that no nightmare can match it. The tense of the verb *fall* in verse one is perfect: "I saw a star fallen from heaven" (AT). John did not see the star fall but knew that it had fallen. The star had become evil and twisted, partaking too long of a poison so strong it could snuff out all light and turn a "son of the morning" into the devil himself. John will have more to say of the fall of this great and terrible being in chapter twelve. For now, the Seer seems to have had the words of the Lord in mind, "I beheld Satan fallen as lightning from heaven" (Luke 10:18, AT). Isaiah's imagery also holds:

> How art thou fallen from heaven, O Lucifer, son of the morning! how art thou cut down to the ground, which didst

weaken the nations! For thou hast said in thine heart, I will
ascend into heaven, I will exalt my throne above the stars of
God: I will sit also upon the mount of the congregation, in the
sides of the north: I will ascend above the heights of the clouds;
I will be like the most High. Yet thou shalt be brought down
to hell, to the sides of the pit (14:12–15, KJV).

John witnesses Satan turn the key to unleash the very powers
of hell upon an unsuspecting world. The predator's intent is to
destroy the earth. From the onset of this millennial battle, John
shows that Satan leads the hosts forth upon the earth. Before
this, God overmastered the plagues through the destroying angels. From this point on, Satan personally directs the operations
bringing the misery that fuels hell to the surface of the earth.
The Seer reveals the Adversary at his worst—venting anger,
frustration, and rage. The world will feel the full thrust of his
fury.

John sees the evil pour out of the pit in the abyss.[1] Ancient
writings show this place to be the abode of Jehovah's enemy
and a kind of holding tank for fallen angels or even Satan
himself.[2] The key Satan uses to open the pit symbolizes power,
authority, and ownership. But note, Satan does not own the
key. He receives it. Once again, John reveals that someone acts
behind the scenes, controlling and directing even the machinations of the Evil One. Ironically this potent one, for all his
flaunted authority, cannot free the might of hell until God gives
him the key. In this way John shows that Perdition's dominion
starts and ends where the Lord dictates. Satan's limits are firm—
he cannot go beyond them (cf. Job 1:12; 2:6).[3] But in the last
days, because of the wickedness of men, the devil will have
great power, "For I [God] am no respecter of persons, and will
that all men shall know that the day speedily cometh; the hour
is not yet, but is nigh at hand, when peace shall be taken from
the earth, and the devil shall have power over his own dominion" (D&C 1:35).

As the pit is opened, smoke billows forth and obscures the
light of the sun. Darkness reigns. Through this powerful symbol,
John reveals the nature of the first thrust against mankind: a
blow against the light. The darkness of false philosophy and

theology must first hide the truth.[4] The Destroyer must mitigate the positive effects of the sixth seal and the first four trumpets. So he sends forth deceptions and delusions after the pattern he has used before with tremendous success.

At an earlier time, when none could ignore the signs and many began to believe, Satan's smoke billowed forth: "From this time forth there began to be lyings sent forth among the people, by Satan, to harden their hearts, to the intent that they might not believe in those signs and wonders which they had seen" (3 Ne. 1:22). Yes, "Satan did stir them up to do iniquity continually; yea, he did go about spreading rumors and contentions upon all the face of the land, that he might harden the hearts of the people against that which was good and against that which should come" (Hel. 16:22). His plan worked well. Under his influence men began to rationalize against the continuing fulfillment of the words of the prophets, saying: "Some things they may have guessed right, among so many; but behold, we know that all these great and marvelous works cannot come to pass, of which has been spoken" (Hel. 16:16). History is about to repeat itself.

THE LOCUSTS (vv. 3–11)

3 And there came out of the smoke locusts upon the earth: and unto them was given power, as the scorpions of the earth have power.

4 And it was commanded them that they should not hurt the grass of the earth, neither any green thing, neither any tree; but only those men which have not the seal of God in their foreheads.

5 And to them it was given that they should not kill them, but that they should be tormented five months: and their torment was as the torment of a scorpion, when he striketh a man.

6 And in those days shall men seek death, and shall not find it; and shall desire to die, and death shall flee from them.

7 And the shapes of the locusts were like unto horses prepared unto battle; and on their heads were as it were crowns like gold, and their faces were as the faces of men.

8 And they had hair as the hair of women, and their teeth were as the teeth of lions.

9 And they had breastplates, as it were breastplates of iron; and the sound of their wings was as the sound of chariots of many horses running to battle.

10 And they had tails like unto scorpions, and there were stings

in their tails: and their power was to hurt men five months.

11 And they had a king over them, which is the angel of the bottomless pit, whose name in the Hebrew tongue is Abaddon, but in the Greek tongue hath his name Apollyon.

Out of this smoke of the abyss comes an appalling nightmare. The portrait of horror John describes focuses on one monstrosity: the locust. This dreaded engine of destruction ravages vegetation to such an extent that famine invariably follows. Coming out of the desert, locusts invade fertile areas in search of food. Some of their columns reach hundreds of feet in breadth and up to four miles in length. They strip the land bare of all vegetation. In Algiers, for instance, a plague of locusts created a famine that left two hundred thousand people dead.[5] The Bible used locust plagues in a special symbolic sense that John follows: judgment against the rebellious. Pharaoh received this judgment from God because of his rebellion (see Ex. 10:4–20; Ps. 105:34–35). God told his own people that if they turned from him, he would send the locust plague upon them (see Deut. 28:38; 1 Kgs. 8:35, 37; 2 Chr. 7:13–14). Infestations of these swarming beasts were so dreaded that, even on the Sabbath, the *shophar* (the ram's horn trumpet blown only for sacred and very special occasions) would sound the alarm.

These insect demons were often associated with darkness. This was not accidental. The cloud they form is often so compact that it obscures the light of the sun.[6] However, John's monsters do not cause the darkness; they result from it. They are men, blinded by the lack of light due to sin and corruption. According to the Doctrine and Covenants 93:39, "that wicked one cometh and taketh away light and truth, through disobedience, from the children of men." The result is a frenzy of evil not unlike the feeding frenzy of the locusts.

John's symbolism follows that of Joel 1–2, which describes a plague of natural locusts but which shows elements that appear to spring from mythology. They come, like John's, from the north instead of the south or southeast as is usual (see Joel 2:20). Joel and John are probably both picking up the Gog-Magog motif from Ezekiel 37–38 and Amos 7:1, where, in the Septuagint, a locust plague is specifically associated with the armies of Gog, that great leader of the anti-God host who fights against God in the last days.[7]

They are not real locusts, as John makes clear in his statement, "It was said to them, Do not harm the grass of the earth, or any green thing, nor any tree, but only those men who have not the seal of God upon their forehead" (v. 4, AT). Their objective, unlike real locusts', is men. But not all men. Only those who do not wear the seal of the living God upon their foreheads. This verse glances back at chapter seven and the sealing of God's servants. Further, God forbids the locusts to kill, "but only to torture them [i.e. the unsealed men] five months" (v. 5, AT).

Note again that the nature, the length, and the target of the torment are all specific. The locusts must not kill, at least not at first. God permits them initially only to cause spiritual and mental anguish. The Greek word *basanisthēsontai* used by John and translated "torment" is from the noun *basanismos*, which occurs only in Revelation: twice here in 9:5, once of those who worship the beast in 14:11, and three times in 18:7, 10, 15 in association with the anguish of the Great Whore. In each instance it indicates mental and spiritual suffering, not physical.

The time limit given to the monstrous insects is five months, the normal life expectancy of a locust. However, the time reference may be symbolic: the Seer appears to be using it to show that there is a limited period in which the tormentors will be allowed to operate. Their target is confined to those men who do not bear the mark of the living God. The righteous have nothing to fear from these demonic hordes. Once again John does not let the reader forget that a power is moving behind the scenes, setting the limits, determining how far and how long things will go. The plague, though driven by the minions of hell, is under sovereign control.[8]

Just how the locusts are able to torment the wicked is not known. But John insists that the anguish is real, for "in those days men will seek death, but will not find it; they will long to die, but death will elude them" (v. 6, AT). The scene is not pretty, but it is not as though there is no means of relief; righteousness, however, is the price. For these men and women, that price is too high. Death appears much cheaper; to melt into nothingness seems more desirable. Of course, this is an illusion. Nevertheless, they will cling to it as their only hope of escape.

Again, a parallel comes from the Book of Mormon. During the final battles that destroyed the Nephite nation, as blood and carnage swept through the land, "no man could keep that which was his own, for the thieves, and the robbers, and the murderers, and the magic art, and the witchcraft [i.e. sorceries] which was in the land" (Morm. 2:10). Everyone was out for everyone else's wealth. As a result of the butchery and thievery, many were filled with sorrow and mourned, but "their sorrowing was not unto repentance, because of the goodness of God; but it was rather the sorrowing of the damned, because the Lord would not always suffer them to take happiness in sin" (Morm. 2:13). As a result, "they did curse God, and wish to die. Nevertheless they would struggle with the sword for their lives" (v. 14).

Note that in both Revelation and the Book of Mormon, "it is by the wicked that the wicked are punished; for it is the wicked that stir up the hearts of the children of men unto bloodshed" (Morm. 4:5). The locusts breed their sadistic torment and pour it out upon the corrupt. God's judgment comes fully, but God needs to do nothing. In fact, his judgment is to do nothing.

John describes the locusts as wearing gold like crowns. The Greek word here is *stephanos* (the award for athletic prowess, as noted before), not *diadēma,* "royal crown." This is the only place where the word is associated with any other than the Lord and the Saints. However, these are not crowns of permanent victory. John makes it clear that "they wore something like crowns of gold" (v. 7, AT), but not the real thing: his phrase *stephanoi homoioi chrusō* means "laurels like unto gold." Victory of the wicked is at best only an imitation of the genuine; it is never lasting or true. The locusts, though terrifying in their appearance and crushing in their initial onslaught, cannot conquer.[9]

Their human faces, women's hair, and lion's teeth heighten

their demonical appearance. If John had some other purpose in mind by reporting these images it is unknown. Speculation gives three meanings to the long hair of the locusts: seductive power, antennae of real locusts, or the ancient locks worn by Parthian horsemen.[10] Whatever his purpose, he does continue to finish the fearful portrait of the monsters. Breastplates of iron make them nearly impregnable, wings give them great mobility, but the scorpions' tails hold the greatest fear. The Seer uses the threat of the poisonous sting as the symbol of that which causes men to be in torment.

A single king drives the frenzied host. Though not identified specifically as such, he is the fallen star, Satan who is the angel of the abyss. John gives him both a Hebrew and Greek epithet. In the Hebrew he is called *Abaddōn*. The name is derived from *abad,* meaning "to perish," and the noun meaning "he who causes to perish," or "the destroyer." The Greek *Apolluōn* means "destroyer" as well.[11] No matter what the language is, the message is the same. Satan, an unseen general, pushes the horde forward. They are his minions, aping his nature, being led by his demonic inspiration. Their rise and torment constitute the fifth trumpet blast and the first period of woe. There are still two more woes to go.

THE SIXTH TRUMPET BLAST
AND THE SECOND WOE (vv. 12–19)

12 One woe is past; and, behold, there come two woes more hereafter.

13 And the sixth angel sounded, and I heard a voice from the four horns of the golden altar which is before God,

14 Saying to the sixth angel which had the trumpet, Loose the four angels which are bound in the great river Euphrates.

15 And the four angels were loosed, which were prepared for an hour, and a day, and a month, and a year, for to slay the third part of men.

16 And the number of the army of the horsemen were two hundred thousand thousand: and I heard the number of them.

17 And thus I saw the horses in the vision, and them that sat on them, having breastplates of fire, and of jacinth, and brimstone: and the heads of the horses were as the heads of lions; and out of their mouths issued fire and smoke and brimstone.

18 By these three was the third part of men killed, by the fire, and

by the smoke, and by the brim- mouth, and in their tails: for their
stone, which issued out of their tails were like unto serpents, and
mouths. had heads, and with them they do
  19 For their power is in their hurt.

As the sixth trumpet sounds, John hears a voice coming from
the horns of the altar in heaven. The horns are a symbol of
God's power that people obtain through faithful worship, especially through sacrifice. These horns have special significance
in two ways. First, on the Day of Atonement the high priest
sprinkled them with the blood of the offering to bring reconciliation between God and Israel. Second, they serve as an asylum for malefactors (e.g. 1 Kgs. 2:28–35, where Joab caught hold
of the horns of the altar to avoid death at Solomon's hands).
Therefore, one might expect the voice from the horns to offer
reconciliation and asylum to the world. However, this is not the
case. Instead, it commands the sixth angel to "release the four
angels who are bound at the great river Euphrates" (v. 14, AT).[12]
That the voice comes from the horns of the altar suggests that
in some way the second woe is connected with or a result of
the prayers of the Saints, for the voice that commands the inflic-
tion comes from the very place, the altar, on which their prayers
were offered (see 7:3–4).[13]

These angels, kept in check while the Saints of God were
sealed against destruction, now unleased their fury "for to slay
the third part of men" (v. 15, KJV). Though the KJV has them
coming from the Euphrates, the prophetic northernmost part
of the kingdom of Israel, the JST makes it clear that they come
out of the pit of the abyss (see 9:14). Thus, Satan frees them at
the same time he unleashes his demons. With these angels now
fully in charge, the plagues are no longer directed at the earth.
Now men become the sole target. These angels have been prepared specifically for this moment, for "they had been kept
ready" (v. 15, AT). Here the Greek participle *hoi hētoimasmenoi*
(a reflexive perfect passive) is "those having been prepared,"
or "those having been made ready." The use of the perfect tense
heightens the idea of their purpose. At an exact moment, and
not a second before, Satan will release the demonic tetrad. But

the destroying angels do not have complete reign. John once again uses the symbolic number one-third to show that there is a limit to what they can do. God continues to hold sway even at this moment.

Quite abruptly the Seer shifts his gaze to the engines of destruction: an unbelievably large cavalry force no longer depicted as locusts. The terror of a mounted attack by armored riders becomes John's means of symbolic communication. The Seer hears (or as the JST states "sees") their number.[14] The number is twice 10,000 × 10,000 or 200,000,000 mounted troops. As usual, this number should not be taken literally. John has given us a multiplied myriad: an expression of incalculable immensity.[15] The main idea in the passage is that of a vast army exceeding by far any before witnessed. A revised version reads, "the *armies* of the horsemen": not one army, but "armies," not a host, but many. The Greek reads, *ho arithmos tōn strateumatōn tou hippikou dismuriades muriadōn,* literally, "The number of the bodies of soldiers of the cavalry [was] two myriads of myriads." John seems to use the plural rather than the singular to show that more than one invasion into the territory will be attempted and will succeed.[16]

Another terrifying aspect of the vision is the horses with their mouths filled with lion's teeth, the embodiment of cruelty and destruction, out of which issue fire, smoke, and brimstone, symbolic of the torment of hell and underscoring the diabolical nature of the horde. John's horses echo the monster Leviathan of Job 41:19–20, who breathes out fire and smoke. By this imagery, John shows that it is grounded in the very heart of Satan's domain.

The fire-breathing monsters succeed in their mission of destruction, killing a staggering number of people. Fire, smoke, and brimstone execute the judgment and inflict the judicial power of Satan. They do not represent the quick and clean death of the sword but the agonizing misery upon which hell feeds. John sees more than mere human slaughter by modern scientific methods. Combined with these, and driving them, are the destructive forces of the pit let loose upon a "third part of men," to kill. The slaughter appears to be selective, for there is a remnant that remains.[17] Perhaps only the more wicked part succumb to the three agents of death.

THE REST OF THE MEN REPENTED NOT (vv. 20–21)

20 And the rest of the men which were not killed by these plagues yet repented not of the works of their hands, that they should not worship devils, and idols of gold, and silver, and brass, and stone, and of wood: which neither can see, nor hear, nor walk:

21 Neither repented they of their murders, nor of their sorceries, nor of their fornication, nor of their thefts.

As amazing as it seems, those that are not killed continue to worship the very forces that worked for their destruction.[18] They refuse to give up their materialistic idolatry. Their hearts continue to crave gold, silver, brass, and other material objects that, as John points out, "neither can see, nor hear, nor walk" (v. 20, KJV). Though their world is collapsing because of it, these wicked souls sell themselves as the lackeys of the Never-living and the Destroyer-doomed-to-destruction. Thievery, murder, and fornication, specifically prohibited in the ten commandments, all continue apace.

To the list John adds sorcery (see v. 21). The Greek word he uses is *pharmakeia,* from which the word *pharmacy* is derived. *Pharmakeia* indicates the use of drugs, elixirs, and contraceptive potions associated with the occult. When freely accepted, these narcotics addict, desensitize, and deceive the nations, resulting in blindness and the inability to change. The use of drugs, simple and potent, is the same means by which the Mother of Abominations is able to deceive the nations (see Rev. 18, particularly v. 23).

CONCLUSION

John's two images, combining to reveal the nature of the latter-day nightmare, give the reader a feel for the horror that Satan will free against the wicked. The vision creates a picture composed of the most horrible images that can be imagined; not so much to detail what actually will be but to give the reader, through the use of powerful metaphors, a feeling for the reality behind what will be. But the real horror is neither the horses nor the horsemen. It is those men and women who will live through the evil day and not be humbled, who will continue to cling to their idols of gold, silver, brass, stone, and wood. Inanimate objects, which neither see, nor hear, nor feel, will become masters and bind to themselves these demented souls. Thus, these people practice the most blatant form of idolatry—placing material things before God—even in the face of the reality that their idols do them no good.

And all this will "be accomplished after the opening of the seventh seal, before the coming of Christ" (D&C 77:13). The Second Coming does not usher in the millennial era. The woes pronounced by the trumpets do. Let me emphasize, Christ will not appear in glory as the millennial day dawns. Instead, Satan's inferno-creating horses and sadistic hoards "having fiery breast-plates, dusky red, and sulfurous" will (v. 18, AT).

The Millennium, for the purpose of this study, begins at the time the Savior commences his reign on the earth. But to begin his rule, he does not have to have appeared to the world. His reign begins as he collects the keys he has given to the prophets through the ages and directs affairs personally. Daniel gives a hint when this will be. Speaking as though it had already happened, he notes that war was made against the Saints and that the wicked had power to prevail "until the Ancient of days came, and judgment was given to the saints of the most High; and the time came that the saints possessed the kingdom" (7:21–22, KJV). The prophet appears to have had in mind the great future gathering at Adam-ondi-Ahman. At that time Adam, the Ancient of days, will appear, as will the Savior. An account will be given to the Lord, and he will then begin to personally orchestrate all events from that point (see D&C 116).[19] Very likely the events in Revelation 8 and 9 will take place after this event.

How long after the Millennium begins will it take for the Lord to come? "The hour and the day no man knoweth, neither the angels in heaven, nor shall they know until he comes" (D&C

49:7). But it will likely be some time after the seventh seal is opened. For the present, we of the sixth seal are to watch for the signs the Lord has given and wait in faith. In this way we prepare ourselves to receive the Savior's mark, because of which we will have no need to fear the millennial-day horrors.

CHAPTER 10

THE LITTLE SCROLL

(AN ANALYSIS OF REVELATION 10)

ANOTHER MIGHTY ANGEL (vv. 1–7)

1 And I saw another mighty angel come down from heaven, clothed with a cloud: and a rainbow was upon his head, and his face was as it were the sun, and his feet as pillars of fire:

2 And he had in his hand a little book open: and he set his right foot upon the sea, and his left foot on the earth,

3 And cried with a loud voice, as when a lion roareth: and when he had cried, seven thunders uttered their voices.

4 And when the seven thunders had uttered their voices, I was about to write: and I heard a voice from heaven saying unto me, Seal up those things which the seven thunders uttered, and write them not.

5 And the angel which I saw stand upon the sea and upon the earth lifted up his hand to heaven,

6 And sware by him that liveth for ever and ever, who created heaven, and the things that therein are, and the earth, and the things that therein are, and the sea, and the things which are therein, that there should be time no longer:

7 But in the days of the voice of the seventh angel, when he shall begin to sound, the mystery of God should be finished, as he hath declared to his servants the prophets.

John has prepared his reader to expect in chapter ten the final trumpet blast to fill the air the final woe to be hurled against the wicked. But it does not happen. The seventh angel does not appear; the trumpet remains mute. Instead, the picture shifts and a new vision opens. In this way, John dramatically introduces another interlude, a moment of instruction and insight before the resolution of the crisis.

As the new vision opens, John sees another angel, mighty and radiant, descending from heaven, holding a little scroll in his hand. This angel stands in sharp contrast to the star that introduced chapter nine: The star fell to earth; the angel descends of his own accord. The star had to receive the key to the pit; the angel possesses the book. Thick black smoke boiled from the star's abyss, while brilliant spectral light emanates from the angel's face. The star drove the demonic horde; the angel governs cosmic phenomena—cloud, rainbow, sun. One stands as a prince of darkness; the other as a prince of light.[1] One is Satan, the father of lies; the other, the revealer of truth. Thus, John demonstrates the vast difference between the two beings.

Once again the image of the rainbow is present, sign of God's covenant not only with mankind, but also with all living creatures. It surrounds the angel's head like a many-colored diadem beaming around a face full of celestial glory prepared to bestow favor and blessings. It reminds one of the invocation that Aaron bestowed upon Israel saying, "The Lord bless thee, and keep thee: the Lord make his face shine upon thee, and be gracious unto thee: the Lord lift up his countenance upon thee, and give thee peace" (Num. 6:24–26, KJV). The Palestinian Targum adds Aaron's plea that the people may be guarded against demons and malignant spirits.[2]

This vision stands in sharp contrast to the one that just closed. There God turned his face, that is his favor, away from the wicked. In consequence, evil smote the malevolent souls (cf. Ps. 33:17; Lev. 17:10; Ezek. 14:8; 15:7).[3] The angel reflects not only the glory, but also the magnanimity of God whose face is ever toward John. Therefore, with the rest of the faithful, John is beneficiary of the promise: "The Lord God is a sun and shield: the Lord will give grace and glory: no good thing will he withhold from them that walk uprightly" (Ps. 84:11, KJV).

The angel places his feet on the land and the sea. The "foot" symbolizes the power of possession; just as conquerors often placed their feet on the necks of the defeated (see, e.g., Josh.

10:24), whatever he places it upon, he subordinates. The angel's stance indicates that all earth is subject to him, "sea and land" being the Hebrew formula for mastery of the terrestrial order (see Ex. 20:11; Ps. 68:22; cf. Mark 6:48; Matt. 14:28–36). From this position the angel gives a mighty shout to which the "voices" of seven thunders respond. However, John gives neither the content of the angel's cry nor the thunders' message. In fact, God specifically commands him to seal up the message.

This is the only place in all Revelation where disclosure is forbidden, but insight may be gained from John's Gospel. As the Savior approached the hour of atonement, he prayed for strength to glorify the Father. "Then came there a voice from heaven, saying, I have both glorified it, and will glorify it again. The people therefore, that stood by, and heard it, said that it thundered: others said, An angel spake to him. Jesus answered and said, This voice came not because of me, but for your sakes. Now is the judgment of this world: now shall the prince of this world be cast out" (John 12:28–31, KJV). The "thunder" bore testimony not for the sake of the Savior but for those who heard. In doing so, however, it placed the world in a position to be judged and the stronghold of the prince of darkness to be overthrown. This may be the message of the thunders. The declaration of the angel supports this view. He said, "In the days when the seventh angel is about to sound [his trumpet], the mystery of God will be finished, just as he declared to his servants the prophets" (v. 7, AT).

In the New Testament, God's dealings in history are a mystery because one can recognize and understand them only through revelation to the prophets. Before then they are hidden. The sounding of the seventh trumpet makes God's designs from the beginning fully known. These include the overthrow of the kingdom of darkness and the full establishment of the kingdom of God on the earth. In Revelation 11:15, following the sounding of the seventh trumpet, a heavenly chorus proclaims, "The kingdoms of this world are become the kingdoms of our Lord, and of his Christ; and he shall reign for ever and ever" (KJV). As Elder McConkie has stated:

It appears from the added and clarifying knowledge revealed to Joseph Smith that the seven thunders which here utter their voices are the seven angels reciting in some detail that which is to be in each of the thousand year periods of the earth's temporal continuance. In the very nature of things, lest men become as God, knowing the end from the beginning, John was forbidden to record these hidden things.

It also appears that John's vision prefigured what is to be when the events occur and that the promised proclamations shall yet be made when the hour for Millennial peace actually arrives.[4]

Lifting his hand to the sky, the omnipotent angel then swears a solemn oath "that there should be no further delay" (v. 6, AT). The word *chronos* here is not to be equated with time. When a thousand years of temporal existence yet remain, it seems unreasonable to have the angel declare that time is at an end from the moment the seventh trumpet sounds. Besides, it seems unnecessary for the angel to swear an oath just to make a statement about the nature of eternity. The sense of the term here seems to be one of delay. The angel swears that delay will not be permitted. All things will move according to God's dictates from this moment on. God's will is about to be fully executed, and nothing can stop it. The day of repentance is past.

THE LITTLE SCROLL (vv. 8–11)

8 And the voice which I heard from heaven spake unto me again, and said, Go and take the little book which is open in the hand of the angel which standeth upon the sea and upon the earth.

9 And I went unto the angel, and said unto him, Give me the little book. And he said unto me, Take it, and eat it up; and it shall make thy belly bitter, but it shall be in thy mouth sweet as honey.

10 And I took the little book out of the angel's hand, and ate it up; and it was in my mouth sweet as honey: and as soon as I had eaten it, my belly was bitter.

11 And he said unto me, Thou must prophesy again before many peoples, and nations, and tongues, and kings.

In this context John receives the commandment to take a little scroll that the angel held open in his hand. Following Ezekiel 3:1–3, the angel instructs John to eat the scroll with the understanding that, though it would be sweet to the taste, it would make his stomach bitter. The reason is made clear. The scroll contains his role or mission particularly as it relates to the latter days. His specific task is "to gather the tribes of Israel; behold, this is Elias, who, as it is written, must come and restore all things" (D&C 77:14). John is an Elias.

His job includes active participation in restoring the gospel and priesthood blessings to scattered Israel. He did this in part when he moved in concert with Peter and James in restoring the Melchizedek order of the priesthood to Joseph Smith and Oliver Cowdery (see D&C 27:12–13; 128:20). Presently, he is actively involved in fulfilling the rest. In June conference, 1831, the prophet Joseph Smith stated "that John the Revelator was then among the Ten Tribes of Israel who had been led away by Salmanasser, king of Assyria, to prepare them for their return from their long dispersion."[5]

Just why his mission would contain bitterness is unknown. In Ezekiel's case, the parchment he figuratively ate contained woes, lamentations, and judgments (see 2:9–10). Because it was the word of God, it pleased Ezekiel, but because it was harsh it pained him. Note too how God's word is considered sweet in Psalm 119:103 and Jeremiah 15:16. Perhaps John's mission is somewhat the same. The angel told him that "thou must prophesy again before many peoples, and nations, and tongues, and kings" (v. 11, KJV). The formula used seven other times by John is changed here, "kings" replacing "tribes." John's commission includes testifying not just to peoples but to heads of state. The term "many" suggests the vastness of the field; not just to one empire but to a multitude. But by witnessing the gospel, John participates directly in damning rebellious nations. Therefore, their rejection of his message, in part, brings upon them the horrible judgments he saw while on the Isle of Patmos.

CONCLUSION

This interlude helps explain why John received the Patmos vision. He was to play an active role in the events he recorded. Thus, God commanded him to devour the scroll, symbolic of mental digestion, and thereby internalize its contents. The Seer did so, and by this means made a complete appropriation of his mission and the message he was to bear. This done, he was ready to act. The degree to which he internalized the message is illustrated by the book of Revelation itself. The vision rings with clarity and purpose. It had become a part of John. Only after this point does John becomes a participant in, not just an observer of, what goes on. His first official act opens chapter eleven.

CHAPTER 11

THE SEVENTH TRUMPET

(AN ANALYSIS OF REVELATION 11)

JOHN'S COMMISSION (vv. 1–2)

1 And there was given me a reed like unto a rod: and the angel stood, saying, Rise, and measure the temple of God, and the altar, and them that worship therein. 2 But the court which is without the temple leave out, and measure it not; for it is given unto the Gentiles: and the holy city shall they tread under foot forty and two months.

As chapter eleven opens, the seventh trumpet remains mute; tension continues. Before it breaks, John must perform a task growing out of the commission he received in chapter ten. He is given a measuring rod or surveyor's rule, probably made from the "giant reed" (*arundo donax*) that grows in the swampy areas of Mediterranean lands and can reach heights of twenty feet.[1] John is instructed to measure the sanctuary (Greek *naos*) but not the outer court. He probably has either the Tabernacle or Solomon's temple in view rather than Herod's, for both of the former had two courts whereas the latter had four.[2] Since John draws so much of his imagery from the Old Testament, it is likely that he envisions Solomon's Temple. That it is not the tabernacle is suggested by association of the edifice with Jerusalem. However, with the Lord's propensity to adapt images for his own use, John may have had none of these in mind.

Certainly, the picture he builds includes a temple proper with its altar and an outer court.

John's instructions leave no doubt about the fate of the outer court: "It has been given unto the Gentiles: and the holy city shall they tread under foot forty and two months" (v. 2, AT). Therefore, the angel forbids John to measure the court, and further, it, along with the Holy City, is to be "cast out" (Greek, *ekballō*)[3] because both have lost divine favor. Thus, the phrase "it has been given" (Greek, *edothē*) carries the idea that God has already determined how far the destruction will go.

Measuring is God's symbolic means of noting that protective power will not allow the sanctuary to be profaned. The background appears to be Ezekiel 40–42 where the prophet sees the temple measured with great care. Zechariah 1:16, where Israel is saved in association with a measuring line, shows that protection is symbolized.[4] For those outside those limits, there is no celestial shelter. Proximity will not be good enough. The outer court will be in no better position than the city itself. There is a message here. It appears that the sanctuary is itself a symbol of the Lord's people, those who are the living temple of God wherein his Spirit dwells (see 1 Cor. 3:16–17; 2 Cor. 6:16; Eph. 2:19–22). If that is the case, then the outer court is those who are just outside the reach of the Spirit. They are not antagonistic to God, but they are not fully committed to him either. They are the lukewarm, and, as God has said, "I will spue thee out" (Rev. 3:15–16, KJV).

THE TWO WITNESSES (vv. 3–14)

3 And I will give power unto my two witnesses, and they shall prophesy a thousand two hundred and threescore days, clothed in sackcloth.

4 These are the two olive trees, and the two candlesticks standing before the God of the earth.

5 And if any man will hurt them, fire proceedeth out of their mouth, and devoureth their enemies: and if any man will hurt them, he must in this manner be killed.

6 These have power to shut heaven, that it rain not in the days of their prophecy: and have power over waters to turn them to blood, and to smite the earth with all plagues, as often as they will.

7 And when they shall have

finished their testimony, the beast that ascendeth out of the bottomless pit shall make war against them, and shall overcome them, and kill them.

8 And their dead bodies shall lie in the street of the great city, which spiritually is called Sodom and Egypt, where also our Lord was crucified.

9 And they of the people and kindreds and tongues and nations shall see their dead bodies three days and an half, and shall not suffer their dead bodies to be put in graves.

10 And they that dwell upon the earth shall rejoice over them, and make merry, and shall send gifts one to another; because these two prophets tormented them that dwelt on the earth.

11 And after three days and an half the Spirit of life from God entered into them, and they stood upon their feet; and great fear fell upon them which saw them.

12 And they heard a great voice from heaven saying unto them, Come up hither. And they ascended up to heaven in a cloud; and their enemies beheld them.

13 And the same hour was there a great earthquake, and the tenth part of the city fell, and in the earthquake were slain of men seven thousand: and the remnant were affrighted, and gave glory to the God of heaven.

14 The second woe is past; and, behold, the third woe cometh quickly.

The Revelation makes clear the means by which the righteous will be preserved. Human agents with divine power act for God. "They are two prophets that are to be raised up to the Jewish nation in the last days, at the time of the restoration, and to prophesy to the Jews after they are gathered and have built the city of Jerusalem in the land of their fathers" (D&C 77:15). Two is the canonical number necessary to sustain a charge at court (see Deut. 19:15; 2 Cor. 13:1; cf. Deut. 17:6; Num. 35:30). The two witnesses will provide the dual testimony against their antagonists that will bring down the full wrath of God.

"These two shall be followers of that humble man, Joseph Smith," states Elder McConkie, "through whom the Lord of Heaven restored the fulness of his everlasting gospel in this final dispensation of grace. No doubt they will be members of the Council of the Twelve or of the First Presidency of the Church."[5] John symbolically notes their high position with God. They stand before Him as two olive trees, and two lampstands. This reflects Zechariah 4:12–14. Here the two are anointed ones who stand next to the Lord, thus showing the position of preeminence. Note that they not only uphold the light (i.e., the Savior), but that the substance of the light, the Holy Spirit, also flows through them.

The witnesses combine the powers of Moses and Elijah. The latter caused a three-and-one-half-year drought upon Israel (see 1 Kgs. 17:1; Luke 4:25; James 5:17), and on two occasions fire consumed troops sent to arrest him (2 Kgs. 1:9–12; cf. 2 Ezra 13; Jer. 5:14); while the former held authority over water (see Ex. 7:20; cf. Ps. 105:29) and brought plagues against Egypt (see Ex. 7–11). During the course of their ministry, the two latter-day prophets will be absolutely indestructible. Those who attempt to stop the two witnesses will be smitten, so powerful will be the Spirit of the Lord upon them.[6] As the Lord said to Jeremiah, so it will be with these prophets: "I will make my words in thy mouth fire, and this people wood, and it shall devour them" (5:14, KJV). Note, too, that Jeremiah wrote, after he attempted to refrain from bearing witness, God's "word was in mine heart as a burning fire shut up in my bones, and I was weary with forbearing, and I could not stay" (20:9). On this basis, the fire issuing from the mouth of the two prophets is testimony that condemns the heathen to destruction.

John gives the active ministry of these prophets as forty-two months. This corresponds to 1260 days (see 11:3; 12:6), "time, and times, and half a time" (12:14), and three-and-one-half years, if each month is computed as thirty days based on a lunar calendar.[7] However, it may be best not to take John too literally here. The message probably lies behind the symbol. Three and one-half, half of seven (see Rev. 11:9, 11), denotes what is arrested midway in its normal course. The apocalyptic usage of this number goes back to Daniel 7:25 (cf. 9:27; 12:7). Bear in mind that the period from the persecution of Antiochus Epiphanes to the rededication of the Temple was about three and one-half years, from 168–67 to 164–63 B.C..

The number six also connotes deficit, a failure to attain the completeness of seven, while eight designates superabundance. Symbolically forty-two is pejorative, since, as one scholar has pointed out, "it is the result of six multiplied by seven, i.e. 'perfection missing the mark.' "[8] The number is used again in

Revelation 13 where it personifies complete imperfection. In apocalyptic material it designates a limited period in which evil is allowed free reign.[9] The Seer's use of it underscores the idea that the period of the witnesses, of divine protection upon the Saints, and of vehement antagonism toward righteousness are all concurrent.[10] During his mortal ministry the Lord had stated: "Jerusalem shall be trodden down of the Gentiles, until the times of the Gentiles be fulfilled" (Luke 21:24, KJV). When that time is fulfilled, wickedness will end. The ministry of the two prophets marks the moment.

To seal their sure witness (Greek, *marturia*), these two great prophets will be martyred. Thus, their testimony will join with those of the fifth seal to cry against the world of wickedness. Just how these two will die is unknown. John notes that it will come only when they have finished their ministry, and that the beast that ascends from the pit in the abyss will attack and overpower them. But there has not been any previous mention of a beast from the pit. However, in chapter nine Abaddōn, or Satan, is called the king of the pit. We may assume then that Satan and the beast are one and that he will inspire his minions to renewed fury against the prophets. Those within the camp of the witnesses may engineer their death since the enemies outside have been held in abeyance for years. This is suggested through the association of their death with that of the Lord, killed by his own people. Moreover, the witnesses shall lie in the streets of Jerusalem (termed Sodom and Egypt to reflect its corruption and rebellion), not in the camps of the enemy.

The death of the two prophets causes ecstasy among the wicked. The Revelator pictures the whole area involved in a frenzy of joy, the people sending presents to one another and generally making merry "because these two prophets had been a torment to those who dwell on the earth" (v. 10, AT).[11] The nature of that torment, of course, had been their invincible testimony. The brilliant light of truth had burned the eyes and scorched the hearts of the people who had grown to love darkness. With the prophets' deaths, there appears to be nothing to stop the victory of evil. The beast from the abyss has overcome. He has proved himself more mighty than God. No wonder his lackeys rejoice. This is the moment of triumph; death and hell are victorious. But are they?

For three-and-a-half days the bodies, serving as war trophies, remain unburied. Among ancient people, such treatment was a means of mocking and generating great shame toward the unburied, their families, and all they stood for. The time reference, three-and-one-half days, seems symbolically fitting, for this is the period when evil rules unchecked. However, revelries are suddenly cut short; celebrations turn to shock. In an instant, before the carousing multitudes, the spirit of life enters into the bodies of the witnesses, and they are called into heaven. John's phrase parallels that of Ezekiel 37 when the breath of life entered into the dry bones and they arose and stood on their feet. John continues to shadow Moses and Elijah. The witnesses have the same manner of ascension: a chariot and horses of fire catch up Elijah and mount on a whirlwind (see 2 Kgs. 2:11). Moses, according to Clement of Alexandria, was removed from the sight of followers by a cloud.[12] The result is consternation such as has seldom been seen on this planet. What appeared to be total triumph suddenly becomes complete defeat.

Murder is the last resort of the wicked. What happens when the murdered do not stay dead? The ultimate power of the unrighteous fails, and with it all other forms of coercion and intimidation. With this act, God begins to move directly onto the historical stage. No longer working behind the scenes, he shows that he has final authority over life and death.

As the wicked watch the ascension, a great earthquake rocks the area, "and a tenth of the city collapse[s]; seven thousand people [are] killed" (v. 13, AT). For the third time, the Seer evokes the picture of an earthquake. Here it further reveals God's direct intervention. The damage is selective. A tenth of the city falls. This is the Lord's portion—his tithe that he will demand of the wicked. The number ten indicates, among other things, the whole of a part. The ten plagues were the whole of that portion of God's wrath brought against Egypt, but not the fullness of his wrath. The number ten represents all the tribes taken into captivity, but not all of the house of Israel, nor all of any one tribe.[13] Thus, it may be that the Seer indicates that the judgment came at the moment of ascension, upon all the wicked who fought against the witnesses.

That John uses the figure seven thousand as the number devoted to death lends support to this idea. The number is probably not to be taken literally. Rather, it signifies, as in other places, fullness and completeness. Thus, the specific number doomed to death all died during this judgment.

But there are many spared. These may represent the less wicked, the court followers but not the actual doers of evil. Certainly, they do not appear to be the righteous. The effect of the appalling judgment on the city does not lead these survivors to repentance and faith. However, in fright they give "glory to the God of the heaven" (v. 13, KJV). But note, they do not invite him among them. They reverence him as the God of *heaven* because that keeps him at a distance. But John already stated that the two prophets bore witness of "the God of the *earth*" (v. 4, KJV; italics added). It is God who has right and title to the *earth*. That is the issue in dispute with these recreant people and the beast from the abyss. John insists that God has the unqualified and peremptory title, and he will not debate or forego the issue.[14] Hence God settles the question permanently with one last blast of the trumpet.

THE SEVENTH TRUMPET
AND THE LAST WOE (vv. 15–19)

15 And the seventh angel sounded; and there were great voices in heaven, saying, The kingdoms of this world are become the kingdoms of our Lord, and of his Christ; and he shall reign for ever and ever.

16 And the four and twenty elders, which sat before God on their seats, fell upon their faces, and worshipped God,

17 Saying, We give thee thanks, O Lord God Almighty, which art, and wast, and art to come; because thou hast taken to thee thy great power, and hast reigned.

18 And the nations were angry, and thy wrath is come, and the time of the dead, that they should be judged, and that thou shouldest give reward unto thy

servants the prophets, and to the saints, and them that fear thy name, small and great; and shouldest destroy them which destroy the earth.

19 And the temple of God was opened in heaven, and there was seen in his temple the ark of his testament: and there were lightnings, and voices, and thunderings, and an earthquake, and great hail.

With the ascension of the two prophets, the second woe is fulfilled and, at last, the seventh trumpet sounds. Instantly angelic voices proclaim, "The kingdom of the world has become the kingdom of our Lord and of his Christ, and he will reign for ever and ever" (v. 15, AT). The issue of ownership is settled. The twenty-four elders exclaim, "We give thanks to you Lord God Almighty, who is and who was, because you have taken your great power and have begun to reign" (v. 17, AT). Although included in the KJV, the phrase "who is to come" is not in the Greek and does not appear again in Revelation. This is probably because the moment awaited for has now arrived. God has come. Now as he reigns, all is set for "destroying the destroyers of the earth" (v. 18, AT).[15] The destruction of the wicked remnant is the last woe. All heaven prepares for this last assault that God himself will direct.

In preparation, the temple of heaven opens and displays the ark of the covenant. Few things could better symbolize the covenant that God made with Israel. At this moment, when all that was promised is about to come about, the heavenly host enter the Holy of Holies and receive their eternal rest. In Hebrews 9:1–11 Paul notes that the opening of the temple symbolizes that all may now enter God's rest.[16] But not all is done. The world's wicked must still stand judgment. So from the temple issue flashes of lightning, rumblings, peals of thunder, an earthquake, and a great hailstorm. All these are sent against the earth once more.

CONCLUSION

Chapter eleven moves through the second woe and introduces the third. But it only introduces the third. There is no description of the final onslaught, no explanation of how God will wrest control of the world, no judgment. Instead, it focuses on the praise and glory of God as he begins to reign and prepares for the destruction of the wicked. Certainly there must be more to come. Indeed, the Seer does give a preview that justice is about to be meted out. A crescendo of disaster, greater than that shown, is about to usher in the great and terrible day of the Lord.

However, that must wait while John rounds out the picture with additional information. So John breaks the narrative just at the point where God begins his reign. With chapter twelve, John starts anew, and this time he uses a different point of view to disclose additional details of the same scenes. In doing so, he more clearly portrays the foundation, beginning, development, and final end of the antagonism between good and evil.

Some may be concerned because the day of the Lord is filled with destruction. But it has its purpose. Nothing unclean, that is, unjustified, can enter into the Lord's presence and survive (see Nahum 1:2–8; Moses 6:57). The glory of God is about to sweep the earth so that the Holy City can be established. Therefore, evil must come to an end.

Note that by the time the Lord comes, very little evil will be left to put to an end. Throughout Revelation we have seen the self-destructive nature of wickedness. But God cannot allow such self-destruction to act as an impersonal nemesis, an independent self-operating moral law sweeping away all in its path. To do so would allow the powers of evil to carry all the inhabitants of the earth down with them to utter ruin. God would be left with a hollow, Pyrrhic victory that resembled defeat far more than victory. Since God's victory must also be man's victory, it must be won through righteous human agents exercising faith in God. Evil must be allowed to combine its nefarious forces against the Savior's people and then be forced back in utter defeat through the faith, trust, and loyalty of the Lord's disciples.[17]

This is what the second woe is all about. As the third comes, the Saints ride with their Christ on the clouds and move against the remnant of evil in total faith toward victory. Those whose souls have lain beneath the altar will find that they are not only vidicated but also that they are the vindicators. As it states in Joseph Smith–History 1:37, "The day cometh that shall burn as an oven, and all the proud, yea, and all that do wickedly shall burn as stubble; for they that come shall burn them, saith the Lord of Hosts."[18]

THE DRAGON, THE WOMAN, AND THE CHILD

(AN ANALYSIS OF REVELATION 12)

A NEW SERIES OF VISIONS

With the angelic rejoicing caused by the blast of the seventh trumpet, the vision of the seven seals closes. But the revelation does not end. Immediately another series of visions begins. These, however, do not take up where the old series left off. Chapter twelve breaks the flow of the vision and introduces new elements and explanations. Flashing back to John's day, it develops the whole story again, this time continuing on to the end of time.

The second half of Revelation has far fewer scriptural guides than the first half. Doctrine and Covenants 77, very helpful up to this point, contains no information on material after the eleventh chapter of Revelation. The JST, however, remains useful. In it we see that Joseph Smith made more changes in chapter twelve than in any other portion of Revelation with the possible exception of chapter one. However, a careful examination of these changes shows that the amount of actual material added is small. Most of the changes constitute little more than switching verses. The result, unfortunately, is not very helpful.[1]

Joseph Smith, breaking from total silence on the subject, gave three discourses on the beasts of Revelation, two on 2 April

1843 and one on 8 April 1843. The speeches were recorded in brief in Joseph Smith's diary by his scribe Willard Richards and more extensively by William Clayton. Franklin D. Richards made a few notes on points of interest to him. Unfortunately all these accounts are so abbreviated that a great deal of ambiguity exists. These speeches do provide some assistance and will be used in reconstructing John's message in this and the following chapter.[2]

THE WOMAN AND THE MAN CHILD (vv. 1–2, 5)

1 And there appeared a great wonder in heaven; a woman clothed with the sun, and the moon under her feet, and upon her head a crown of twelve stars: 2 And she being with child cried, travailing in birth, and pained to be delivered.

5 And she brought forth a man child, who was to rule all nations with a rod of iron: and her child was caught up unto God, and to his throne.

John introduces this section, according to the KJV, with the words: "And there appeared a great wonder in heaven." Here "wonder" would be better translated as "sign" (Greek *sēmeion*). A wonder is a surprise of great magnitude, but a sign is replete with meaning and points to a definite subject or object. The word denotes an optical impression through which one gains confirmations.[3] John's use of the word is consistent. It foreshadows a coming event and thus serves as a prophetic or anticipatory omen. The JST notes that the sign in heaven was "in the likeness of things on the earth," (v. 1), making it clear that the heavenly vision symbolized earthly conditions.

The adjective "great" is used six times in this chapter, suggesting the importance of the themes covered. The first of the great signs, in order but not in eminence, is the woman. John describes her as being "clothed with the sun, and the moon under her feet, and upon her head a crown of twelve stars" (KJV). The woman, according to the JST, represents the Church (see v. 7). On her head are the victor's laurels (*stephanos*) garnished with twelve stars. These symbolize the twelve apostles, or priesthood authority, who stand at the Church's head.

Celestial glory surrounds her as a garment, showing that

the power of God is upon her. The Greek word used here, *peribebēmenē*, "having been clothed," suggests that the woman wears the glory as a garment but that it does not belong to her. It is reflected by her. Thus, she manifests the light of Christ but is not the source of that light. There is also a secondary meaning of the Greek verb *periballō*, translated "clothed," that is very likely at play here. The word means "to throw up a rampart around" (cf. Luke 19:43). John's imagery could, therefore, represent the glory of God acting as a bulwark to protect the Church.[4]

The woman is in travail. Her pangs suggest creative suffering, a suffering that ends in joy as she brings forth a son. The Old Testament often associates such suffering with the suffering that precedes the establishment of Zion (cf. Isa. 13:8; 26:17; 66:7–8; Jer. 4:31; 13:21; Micah 4:10). These references suggest that the imagery represents the coming forth of the New Israel or the New Jerusalem. J. Massyngberde Ford notes that the woman is the antithesis of the harlot exposed in chapter eighteen and thus is the symbol of the New Jerusalem.[5] She is not far from the mark. As will be shown below, the child represents the political kingdom of God whose laws will come forth from Zion. John's vision suggests that this nearly became a reality during the apostolic ministry. The book of Acts shows that the earliest Saints practiced, albeit briefly, a kind of law of consecration and enjoyed immense spiritual power and unity (see 2:41–47; 4:31–37).

However, the child, according to the JST, does not represent Zion per se but a particular aspect of God's work in establishing Zion. The child, "who was to rule all nations with the rod of iron" (v. 3), is "the kingdom of our God and his Christ" (v. 7). Insights from modern prophets make it clear that John's "man child" represented a real political kingdom that was to be established by God to govern the whole earth.[6] Brigham Young taught that this political power actually grows out of the Church.[7] Speaking of the latter-day event, he explained, "The Church of Jesus Christ will produce this government, and cause it to grow and spread, and it will shield round about the church.

And under the influence and power of the Kingdom of God, the church will rest secure and dwell in safety, without taking the trouble of governing and controlling the whole earth."⁸ Elder Joseph Fielding Smith stated:

> After Christ comes, all the peoples of the earth will be subject to him, but there will be multitudes of people on the face of the earth who will not be members of the Church; yet all will have to be obedient to the laws of the kingdom of God, for it will have dominion upon the whole face of the earth. These people will be subject to *the political government,* even though they are not members of *the ecclesiastical kingdom which is the Church.*
>
> *This government which embraces all peoples of the earth, both in and out of the Church, is also sometimes spoken of as the kingdom of God,* because the people are subject to the kingdom of God which Christ will set up.⁹

John's account suggests that the early Church endeavored to establish the political kingdom in the meridian of time. The attempt proved unsuccessful.¹⁰ Such an institution would have shaken the very powers of hell as it overmastered the world and protected the Church. Little wonder that the manifestation of the woman and the child is followed by another portent showing Satan's opposition to the kingdom.

THE GREAT RED DRAGON (vv. 3–4, 6)

3 And there appeared another wonder in heaven; and behold a great red dragon, having seven heads and ten horns, and seven crowns upon his heads.

4 And his tail drew the third part of the stars of heaven, and did cast them to the earth: and the dragon stood before the woman which was ready to be delivered, for to devour her child as soon as it was born.

6 And the woman fled into the wilderness, where she hath a place prepared of God, that they should feed her there a thousand two hundred and threescore days.

The second sign John sees is that of a great red dragon—not the winged and fire-breathing creature of fairy tales, though just as ferocious and evil. The Greek word (*drakōn*) signifies a serpent or sea monster, but it is best understood as the personification of seething chaos, often represented as the dark primeval waters, which oppose not only God but all that is holy.[11] It is no minor power. Indeed, in the Old Testament it represents that force which only God can subdue.[12] The distinguishing feature of the beast is its insatiable cruelty.[13] It is demonic in its genesis and intent and, as such, is the perfect type of Satan at his worst.[14]

John sets this symbol against that of the woman, who represents poise, harmony, beauty, and life-giving creation. In this context the significance of the dragon's color is heightened. It is fiery red, the color of what engulfs and consumes.[15] The color seems to suggest the despiteful, violent, and murderous means by which Satan, the dragon, brings about his ends. Jesus said of his adversaries, "Ye are of your father the devil. . . . He was a murderer from the beginning" (John 8:44).

The dragon has seven crown-wearing heads and ten horns. Note the inconsistency. There are either too many or too few horns for the heads. But God is not creating an image to be pictured but is rather communicating through symbols the nature of the thing he describes.[16] Both numbers are significant. The seven crowns are not the laurels of victory (stephanos), which the woman wears, but diadems (diadēma), symbols of political domination. The scriptures never depict Satan wearing laurels because he wins no permanent victories.[17] The seven crowned heads suggest the universality of his rule as the king of chaos. They represent Satan's pseudoclaim to royalty set against that of the King of kings and the Lord of lords, whom John describes as wearing "many diadems" (Rev. 19:12—"crowns" in KJV).[18]

The horns seem to denote the dragon's all-pervasive false sovereignty. Horns symbolize power. As discussed previously, ten represents the whole of a part but not the whole itself. Thus, the dragon has great power, but John shows that he does not have all power; some portion is lacking. This is not true of the Lamb whom John depicts with seven horns, the symbol of fullness (see 5:6). Thus, John's metaphors subtly show that the Lamb has all power and can overmaster the dragon.

In this episode, John depicts Satan as a tremendous and frightening spiritual force working against the Church of God.

But he does not work alone. John states that his mighty tail "draws a third part of the stars of heaven" (AT), symbolic of his fallen minions. The tense John chooses, contrary to that shown in the KJV, is present.[19] By this means John shows that the dragon draws his lackeys with him by clutching them in the coils of his tail. John has the dragon rise against God's earthly authority by attempting to destroy God's agent the moment he is born into the world. This hostile act symbolizes Satan's attempt to become king of the earth.[20] Once again, the Seer emphasizes the issue of sovereignty and authority. The Church during the meridian of time briefly challenged Lucifer's domain by bringing forth the kingdom of God. The old dragon had to act with all his fury, bringing the entire legion of demons with him, to stop this threat to his kingdom.

Though Satan failed in his attempt to destroy the man child, he was partially successful. He did prevent the kingdom of God from being permanently established. According to the JST, "the dragon stood before the woman which was delivered, ready to devour her child after it was born" (v. 4), but the "child was caught up unto God and his throne" (v. 3). Thus it appears that God took the fledgling kingdom—that is, the political keys and authority given to the apostles and other leaders—to heaven, where it was safe from the dragon, until the restoration in the in the latter days. Frustrated because he could not destroy the child, the dragon turns on the woman herself, but she escapes by fleeing into the wilderness (see v. 6).

THE WAR IN HEAVEN (vv. 7–12)

7 And there was war in heaven: Michael and his angels fought against the dragon; and the dragon fought and his angels,

8 And prevailed not; neither was their place found any more in heaven.

9 And the great dragon was cast out, that old serpent, called the Devil, and Satan, which deceiveth the whole world: he was cast out into the earth, and his angels were cast out with him.

10 And I heard a loud voice saying in heaven, Now is come salvation, and strength, and the kingdom of our God, and the power of his Christ: for the accuser of our brethren is cast down, which accused them before our God day and night.

11 And they overcame him by

the blood of the Lamb, and by the
word of their testimony; and they
loved not their lives unto the
death.

12 Therefore rejoice, ye heavens, and ye that dwell in them.

Woe to the inhabiters of the earth
and of the sea! for the devil is come
down unto you, having great
wrath, because he knoweth that
he hath but a short time.

At this point, John chooses to do a flashback to the war in
heaven, probably to show that the conflict between the Church
and the dragon had its genesis in the premortal world. I am
cautious on when this battle occurred. Depending on how it is
read, the JST may suggest that the war in heaven was not the
premortal conflict. The JST notes that the devil did not win the
battle "against Michael, neither the child, nor the woman, which
was the church of God, who had been delivered of her pains,
and brought forth the kingdom of our God and his Christ" (v.
7). Further, it notes how Lucifer was overcome: "For they [the
righteous] overcame him by the blood of the Lamb, and by the
word of their testimony; for they loved not their own lives, but
kept the testimony even unto death" (v. 11). Placing these two
passages in a premortal context is difficult for two reasons: first,
the battle takes place *after* the man child is taken into heaven,
and second, those who overcame Satan did so by giving their
lives. Since righteous immortals do not die any form of death,
the context suggests mortal martyrs.

It would be easy to see the changes in the JST reordering
the events recorded in the KJV in such a way that those in chapter
twelve continue the story in chapter eleven. This would give
chapter twelve a nineteenth-century context. The woman would
be the Church, which went into the wilderness; the child would
be the kingdom of God, which the early brethren tried to establish but could not, the keys of which are presently dormant;
and the battle, a representation of the spiritual conflict between
the forces of good and evil continuing from that time forth. The
problem with this view is that the JST places the woman in the
wilderness for an extended period (1,260 years, v. 5), which
does not fit a contemporary setting; furthermore, the dragon is
cast out of heaven (see vv. 8, 11), an event associated directly

with the war in heaven. Because of the ambiguity in our modern work, I have elected to follow the ancient Greek text.

John reveals that the central figure in the premortal battle was Michael, who led the angels of God against Satan and his minions. There victory resulted in banishment of the Devil from heaven but not from the world: the old dragon "was cast out into the earth, and his angels were cast out with him" (v. 9, KJV). On the earth the battle was renewed, and the Church in John's day felt the brunt of it.

The Seer's account gives insight into the nature of the heavenly war. He states that Lucifer, the accuser (Hebrew, *satan*), "accused [the brethren] before God day and night" (v. 10). (One wonders what the nature of those accusations were. Perhaps that the gospel would fail, that the Savior would back away from the wracking pain of the Atonement, or that the priesthood would crumble under the pressure of mortality.) The vision emphasizes the powers that overcame Satan: faith and testimony—faith that the Redeemer would make the Atonement, and willingness to proclaim it to all who would hear. Courageously, these Saints of the spirit world put their eternal lives on the line. Their witness won many souls and assisted in overthrowing the great enemy.

With the defeat of the dragon, John hears a voice proclaim, "Now is come salvation, and strength, and the kingdom of our God, and the power of his Christ" (v. 10, KJV). The exclamation suggests that much was at risk during the great war. Satan sought to introduce modifications in God's plan of salvation through which Satan himself would take the honor, or power, of God (see Moses 4:1–3; D&C 29:36). Apparently Lucifer's intent was to replace Elohim. The victory secured God's authority over the rest of the children and firmly established his kingdom in heaven. Further, it confirmed the power of the Savior.

But heaven's win was earth's loss. Thus the angel laments, "Woe to the inhabiters of the earth and of the sea! for the devil is come down unto you, having great wrath, because he knoweth that he hath but a short time" (v. 12, KJV). Satan has lost. However, the prison prepared for him and his angels, Gehenna, yet stands empty. Gehenna comes from the Hebrew through the Greek and represents the place of misery for rebellious souls. The term is often used as a synonym for hell but is more expressive of perdition. It is briefly described in Doctrine and Covenants 76:44–48. Satan has a little season in which to operate before God freezes him into eternal impotence, but this fact only serves to anger him. He is not out to win. He can't, and no one knows it better than he. But driven by his insane wrath, he seeks the misery of God's children for as long as he can (see 2 Ne. 2:27).

THE DRAGON AND THE WOMAN (vv. 13–17)

13 And when the dragon saw that he was cast unto the earth, he persecuted the woman which brought forth the man child.

14 And to the woman were given two wings of a great eagle, that she might fly into the wilderness, into her place, where she is nourished for a time, and times, and half a time, from the face of the serpent.

15 And the serpent cast out of his mouth water as a flood after the woman, that he might cause her to be carried away of the flood.

16 And the earth helped the woman, and the earth opened her mouth, and swallowed up the flood which the dragon cast out of his mouth.

17 And the dragon was wroth with the woman, and went to make war with the remnant of her seed, which keep the commandments of God, and have the testimony of Jesus Christ.

The war in heaven serves as the background for understanding the attack on the man child and the woman. Satan exercised his energy first on the organization of the kingdom. Once he had chased off that threat to his earthly sovereignty—the greater threat—he turned on the woman. However, she received divine assistance and escaped into the wilderness. "The two great wings of an eagle" (v. 14, AT) symbolize this assistance. The insertion of the definite article, omitted in the KJV, underscores the explicitness of the action.

The wings have a double meaning: rapid motion or flight and divine deliverance. The idea of divine protection grows out of the reference to eagles' wings in Jehovah's past care of his people and deliverance from impending danger. Note Deuteronomy 32:10–11, where the care of God for Jacob is compared to a mother eagle fluttering over her young, where she "spreadeth abroad her wings, taketh them, beareth them on her wings" (cf. Ex. 19:4). In Isaiah 40:31 the prophet promises that those who wait upon the Lord "shall mount up with wings as eagles."

With these wings the woman flees into the wilderness, symbolic of spiritual refuge.[21] Both the Old and the New Testaments represent the desert as a place of provisional safety, of discipline, of waiting for the promises of God. It was thus of the Exodus period (cf. Deut. 8:2–10). Twice Elijah withdrew to the wilderness (see 1 Kgs. 17:2–3; 19:3–4). Jehovah attracted his bride there that she might find comfort (see Hos. 2:14). In Song of Solomon, the litter and bride of Jehovah come from there (see 3:6–8; 8:5). In Revelation 12, the desert illustrates that the church has become inaccessible to humans.[22]

As the woman flees to her place of refuge, the dragon makes a last desperate attempt to destroy her. Casting out water, his primary weapon, from his mouth he endeavors to sweep her away in a flood of destruction. But the earth assists the woman by swallowing the vast tide. Just what John intended is difficult to assess. Satan is the father of lies, that much is known for sure. In one way or another, everything that issues from his mouth conveys deception. Perhaps with a deluge of lies, not unlike those that the modern Church faces from its detractors, he tried to destroy the early Church.

But John could have had other ideas in mind. Flood waters are a common metaphor in the Old Testament for tribulation as well as overwhelming evil (see Ps. 18:4; Isa. 43:2). The term is used to denote oppressive nations such as Assyria (see Isa. 17:12–14, cf. 8:5–8), Egypt (see Jer. 46:7–8), and Babylon (see Jer. 51:55), as well as hostile nations generally (see Ps. 18:14–15; 46:1–3).[23] Oppression may be what John alludes to, especially in light of the heightened persecution of Rome against the Christian people at the time of the Seer's writings. Further, the waters represent chaos, the result of unchecked iniquity. Satan, once the kingdom of God was gone, secured his place as prince of the world. Unchecked iniquity characterizes his reign.[24]

Perhaps Satan tried through tribulation and unbridled wickedness to destroy the Church. Conceivably, he attempted to seduce and threaten, or wear out, the true saints. Just how the earth assisted in saving the woman is unknown. The metaphor echoes Numbers 16:32 where Korah's rebellion against Moses ended when "the earth opened her mouth, and swallowed them up, and their houses, and all the men that appertained unto Korah, and all their goods" (KJV).[25] Somehow the earth absorbed Satan's lies and malice long enough to allow the Church time to secure what was most precious before fleeing to the safety that awaits the righteous in God.

The wilderness, as the Revelator makes clear, was a place of protection where the woman would be nurtured. The period of her rest would be one thousand two hundred and sixty days, or three-and-one-half years. (Verse five of the JST changes "days" to "years," probably to suggest that the stay in the wilderness would be of long duration.) This number, as has been shown earlier, represents a period of tremendous trial. The trial comes because it is the period of Satanic rule. Since three and one-half, half of seven, which is the symbol for perfection, represents the fullness of imperfection, it describes the period of Satan's rule. However, in each case where the number is used, the period ends in total victory for God. Thus the woman, though forced to flee from the earth to heaven where men would have no access to her, would triumph in the end.

For a time the Church's progress ceased. But it may be fair to ask, what church? Since the temporal church fell into apostasy, what church did God preserve and place in safe-keeping? Likely John refers to the Church of the Firstborn spoken of in the Doctrine and Covenants. There the Savior states, "I was in the beginning with the Father, and am the Firstborn; and all those who are begotten through me are partakers of the glory of the same, and are the church of the Firstborn" (93:21–22). How one is begotten is clearly spelled out in Doctrine and Covenants 76:50–70: faith, baptism, and reception of the Holy Ghost are prerequisite. Then one must be sealed through continuous good works by the Holy Spirit of Promise. Those who do so become the Church of the Firstborn, being "priests and kings, who have received of his [God's] fulness, and of his glory" (D&C 76:56).

In John's day, this group constituted those who had ears to hear what the Spirit was saying to the churches. Upon their death, they carried the keys back to heaven where they could be restored to the earth in the latter-days. Thus, God frustrated Satan in his attempt to destroy this church. Having failed to rid the earth of the Church, the dragon turned upon the few remaining faithful—those who continued to resist the forces of apostasy in their own lives—and made war on them.

CONCLUSION

John seems to have written the book of Revelation during the period portrayed in chapter twelve. The external church was on the defensive, and John warned her of what would happen if she failed to resist the floods of evil and persecution that Satan was loosing upon her. But to those who were true and faithful, the Lord held out hope. Indeed, the inner church, during the period of John's writing, was already escaping—sometimes through the assistance of Roman persecution—to a place prepared by God where it would be secure until God needed the keys to begin the work again.

CHAPTER 13

THE BEASTS OF REVELATION

(AN ANALYSIS OF REVELATION 13)

THE BEAST FROM THE SEA (vv. 1–10)

1 And I stood upon the sand of the sea, and saw a beast rise up out of the sea, having seven heads and ten horns, and upon his horns ten crowns, and upon his heads the name of blasphemy.

2 And the beast which I saw was like unto a leopard, and his feet were as the feet of a bear, and his mouth as the mouth of a lion: and the dragon gave him his power, and his seat, and great authority.

3 And I saw one of his heads as it were wounded to death; and his deadly wound was healed: and all the world wondered after the beast.

4 And they worshipped the dragon which gave power unto the beast: and they worshipped the beast, saying, Who is like unto the beast? who is able to make war with him?

5 And there was given unto him a mouth speaking great things and blasphemies; and power was given unto him to continue forty and two months.

6 And he opened his mouth in blasphemy against God, to blaspheme his name, and his tabernacle, and them that dwell in heaven.

7 And it was given unto him to make war with the saints, and to overcome them: and power was given him over all kindreds, and tongues, and nations.

8 And all that dwell upon the earth shall worship him, whose names are not written in the book of life of the Lamb slain from the foundation of the world.

9 If any man have an ear, let him hear.

10 He that leadeth into captivity shall go into captivity: he that killeth with the sword must be killed with the sword. Here is the patience and the faith of the saints.

Foiled in his attempt to destroy the church of God, the dragon moves to the seashore and there summons assistance. There are two manuscript traditions for verse one. One has John standing on the seashore (the KJV follows this one); the other, the dragon (as seen in the RSV and the NIV). The JST solves the problem by noting that the monster from the sea was what stood upon the sandy shore.

"I saw another sign," states the JST, "in the likeness of the kingdoms of the earth; a beast rise up out of the sea, and he stood upon the sand of the sea, having seven heads and ten horns; and upon his horns ten crowns" (v. 1). In this way John introduces the first of two agents through whom the dragon will carry out his seduction of the earth over the next two millennia. This appears to have been the period seen by Nephi when he saw "among the nations of the Gentiles the formation of a great church." This church, or institution, was, according to an angel, "most abominable above all other churches, which slayeth the saints of God, yea, and tortureth them and bindeth them down, and yoketh them with a yoke of iron, and bringeth them down into captivity." Further, Nephi notes, "I saw the devil that he was the founder of it" (1 Ne. 13:4–6).

Satan, though the very personification of evil, must, as with God, carry out his work through people and human institutions—the great and abominable church and the kingdoms of the earth. Joseph Smith notes that Daniel saw the image of a beast but not an actual beast, but that John saw real beasts in heaven.[1] The prophet's statement, however, was not referring to chapters twelve and thirteen but rather to chapters four and five. In chapter thirteen God uses a metaphor, as it were, to describe the organized wickedness that Lucifer will use to promote his purposes. Joseph Smith taught that "the beast that rose up out of the sea [in Rev. 13:1] should be translated the image of a beast, as I have referred to it in Daniel's vision."[2] He also said, "The beasts are spoken of to represent the kingdoms of the world, the inhabitants whereof were beastly and abominable characters; they were murderers, corrupt, carnivorous, and brutal in their dispositions."[3] But precise identity of these kingdoms remains unknown.

"The beast," states Elder McConkie, "is being used to symbolize certain unnamed kingdoms on earth and to show their dealings toward the saints and the cause of righteousness." Further, "the beast does not represent all the world, but only selected 'kingdoms.' "[4] Taking his text from the Seer's statement that "all the world wondered after the beast," Joseph Smith asked: "If the beast was all the world, how could the world wonder after the beast?" Then answering, he stated, "It must have been a wonderful beast to cause all human beings to wonder after it; and I will venture to say that when God allows the old devil to give power to the beast to destroy the inhabitants of the earth, all will wonder."[5] Ambiguity also surrounds the meaning of the word "kingdom," though "political entities" seems to best fit the context.

Though the exact identity of these kingdoms remains unknown, their nature and disposition do not. What symbolizes them comes out of the sea. The home of the beast as well as its features bring to mind Daniel 7–8. But other Old Testament themes come to play as well. Echoes of Jehovah's battles with the sea monsters Leviathan and Rahab are heard. These monsters, which only God could subdue, were the epitome of the forces of chaos, death, and sterility. Order, fertility, and life won the victory through their defeat.[6] From certain Old Testament uses, clearly the sea often portrays unsettled political and social conditions, the kind of stormy circumstances from which revolution and tyranny arise (see Dan. 7).[7] The Revelator sees in the oceans the peoples of the world, those nations and institutions that will originate during and after his day to carry on a work of darkness. For this reason, all should exercise caution against identifying one group, one nation, or one institution as the beast.

And yet, there is a commonality. These organizations were and are grounded on a common philosophy, seek specific objectives, and use a similar methodology. All possess an air of superiority anchored in pride, ambition, vanity, and a lust for power. However, the fuel that drives their collective engine is derived neither from human ego nor from human spirit but from Lucifer.

The Bible uses the term *beast* to translate three Greek words: *zōon, ktēnos,* and *thērion. Zōon* describes living creatures, often those connected with God like the seraphim of Isaiah 6:2–3 and the four living beings in Revelation 4:6–9. *Ktēnos* refers to domesticated animals, especially beasts of burden and animals used for food as in Revelation 18:13. *Thērion,* on the other hand, characterizes wild beasts, especially beasts of prey.[8] John calls the sea monster *thērion,* and the term aptly fits. The beast's three components—leopard, bear, and lion—are all untameable and flesh-devouring.

This beast has seven heads and ten horns each crowned with a diadem. At first glance the image is that of the dragon, but there is an important difference. The old serpent had but seven diadems that he wore upon his heads. The beast on the other hand has its ten crowns placed upon its horns, suggesting that its power rests upon brute force.[9] The beast, however, does not overshadow the dragon in either power or rule. The number of crowns reveals that the beast actually has less power than the dragon, seven representing a whole with ten representing only a portion. Thus, the beast comes under the authority of the dragon, drawing its power from him. Even so, the likenesses cannot be overlooked. This beast of prey is thoroughly diabolic: he possesses the power, authority, and very image of the devil, and his objective is to devour men spiritually.[10]

A curious aspect of the beast, from which has risen no end of speculation, is that one of its heads had been mortally wounded yet the beast survived (v. 3).[11] One of the most popular views is that the head represents the Roman emperor Nero or Domitian. The former started the pogroms against the Christians, and the latter resurrected them, as it were, thus negating Nero's death at the time of John's writing. A major problem with this view is that it confines the beast and its activities to the Roman period. Further, it was the beast, not the head, that survived the wound (v. 14).[12]

The wound unto death echoes that of the Lamb in chapter five. Comparing the beast and the Lamb allows us to surmise what the Seer had in mind. As the dragon is the antithesis of God, the beast is the converse image of Christ. Satan bestows on the beast his throne, power, and great authority. The Savior shares these same privileges with the Father. The beast receives authority over every nation, tongue, tribe, and people (see v. 7); the Lamb holds this same domain. In 17:8, John states that the beast "was and is not and is to come" (AT). This mimics the description of the Savior in Revelation 1:4 as he "which is, and which was, and which is to come" (KJV). The Lamb is Lord of lords and King of kings, and the beast seeks the same positions. In short, the beast is the spiritual antithesis of Christ and his kingdom. Thus, the beast not only wears the name of blasphemy upon its heads, it embodies the name by counterfeiting the attributes and position of deity.[13]

In light of this evidence, the beast, together with its heads and horns, represents kingdoms and organizations opposed to Christian principles. However, the beast also seems to be something else, something that undergirds and supports governments and leagues in their antireligious movements. Its broad influence and wide domain suggest that this beast should be understood as a philosophical system and political ideology inspired by satanic ideals. The revelation shows that the influence of this monster is so great that all the world, except the righteous, begin to revere it and its initiator. But the world's song of praise belies its sincerity and devotion to this master: "Who is like unto the beast? who is able to make war with him?" (v. 4, KJV). The motive for worship is not reverent awe generated by moral greatness, but rather amazement generated by fear of brute force.[14]

The beast speaks great blasphemies. One target is God and his name. Of the other target, the manuscript tradition varies. Some manuscripts state that the beast also blasphemes God's tabernacle and those who dwell in heaven. The problem may be resolved in John's use of the Greek word *skēnē,* translated "tabernacle." John's usage suggests that the *skēnē* is God's heavenly dwelling place among men, a kind of heaven on earth (see 7:15; cf. 21:3). In verse six *skēnē* seems to denote God's tabernacling presence upon the earth that overshadows and protects the Saints. It could be against these — God's temple or heavenly home on earth, and the Saints who are worthy to enter therein — that the beast rails.[15]

The beast's authority and power lasts for a restricted period: forty-two months, or three-and-one-half years. Once again John uses the symbol denoting the period of temporary victory for Satan, the time when he and his minions prevail and the righteous suffer. However, because the beast had to receive authority and power to blaspheme, it is, in all its ferocity, a dependent being. Though Satan gives the beast his throne, Satan himself is restricted and can move only when allowed. Thus, the real authority of the beast derives from God alone. It exists only by divine permission, and it speaks and acts within the bounds the Lord has set. Bounded by God, the beast is destined to assist, against its own desires, with God's grand strategy.[16]

Even so, the period of its rule will cause great distress among the righteous, and that period sweeps from John's time to the latter days. But its meanest work was done during the mortal ministry of the Seer. That was the period of the tribulation of the Saints when patience and faith were enjoined. In verse ten John warns: "If any one is destined for captivity, he will go into captivity. If anyone kills with the sword, with the sword he must be killed" (AT).[17] The statement echoes that of the Savior in Matthew 26:52: "All they that take the sword shall perish with the sword" (KJV). The first phrase of the couplet taught the Saints that they must accept and endure what God had ordained, the second that they must not take the offensive in any war against the beast.[18] That was not to say the Saints should not work against the monster, but that they should work by promoting the gospel of Jesus Christ and its objectives.

THE BEAST FROM THE LAND (vv. 11–17)

11 And I beheld another beast coming up out of the earth; and he had two horns like a lamb, and he spake as a dragon.

12 And he exerciseth all the power of the first beast before him, and causeth the earth and them which dwell therein to worship the first beast, whose deadly wound was healed.

13 And he doeth great wonders, so that he maketh fire come down from heaven on the earth in the sight of men,

14 And deceiveth them that dwell on the earth by the means of those miracles which he had power to do in the sight of the beast; saying to them that dwell on the earth, that they should make an image to the beast, which had the wound by a sword, and did live.

15 And he had power to give life unto the image of the beast, that the image of the beast should both speak, and cause that as many as would not worship the image of the beast should be killed.

16 And he causeth all, both small and great, rich and poor, free and bond, to receive a mark in their right hand, or in their foreheads:

17 And that no man might buy or sell, save he that had the mark, or the name of the beast, or the number of his name.

The first beast does not work alone. John sees a second beast "coming up out of the earth; and he had two horns like a lamb, and he spake as a dragon" (v. 11, KJV). The second monster is unlike the first, and perhaps even more dangerous because of its deceptively harmless appearance. It stands as a deliberate counterfeit of the Lord. The two beasts with their master, the dragon, "constitute an unholy trinity of malicious evil."[19]

The lamb is Antichrist working miracles and teaching false doctrines in the name of salvation. Later in the revelation this lamb is called the "false prophet" (16:13; 19:20; 20:10, KJV) and uses counterfeit prophetic knowledge as a means of deception. The two horns represent feigned benevolent authority. Note John's words carefully. He says that the beast had horns "like a lamb," not like *the* Lamb. Therefore, the second beast, the fraudulent Christ, imitates the Lord.

But the Lord works through mortal agents, and the two most prominent are those already met in chapter eleven. These witnesses testify of Christ and bring men to worship him. The beasts similarly imitate this relationship; the second beast testifies and affirms the first. Like the witnesses, the second beast uses miracles, especially control over fire, to validate its authority (see Matt. 24:24; 2 Thes. 2:9).[20] In fact, this becomes the primary means by which it is able to deceive the nations into worshipping the first beast.

With the coming of the false prophet, a wolf in lamb's clothing, the evil triumvirate stands complete. Now they can imitate by deception the true Godhead. As the Son has his two witnesses, so too the dragon has his two monsters; as the Son draws his power from the Father, so too the first beast draws authority from the dragon; as the Holy Ghost glorifies the Son, so too the evil lamb glorifies the first beast.[21] There is little doubt but that John exposes them in symbolic terms as the counterfeit godhead, the beguiling revelators, the false law-givers whose powers will rule through the last days.

The second beast never comes fully into view but remains in the background, the deceptive distance catching those who might not otherwise be attracted to the first beast, and in this way it betrays people into the worship of the latter. Indeed its whole function seems to be to seduce mankind into this false worship. And what is the objective of this worship? In a word, materialism: the ability to buy and sell and to get gain.

John lays before the reader the terrifying prospect of an economic system completely dominated by what has been called "the Mahanic principle." Satan, who stands as initiator of this system, first revealed its great secret to Cain, who in turn revealed it to his followers (see Moses 5:29–31). Satan "did plot with Cain and his followers from that time forth" (Hel. 6:27). And what was the objective of all that plotting? To learn the trade of turning human life into property. Evil and conspiring men formed the secret combination that then swept across oceans and survived through time. And Satan "doth hand down their plots, and their oaths, and their covenants, and their plans of awful wickedness, from generation to generation according as he can get hold upon the hearts of the children of men" (Hel. 6:30).

The Seer shows that this power will stoke the destructive forces of the latter days. Slowly genuine humility and brotherliness will be suppressed under a vast and complex coercion of sophisticated and bewitching propaganda and the brutality of pragmatism and unrestrained egoism.[22] We may not know exactly who the beasts are — Elder McConkie has noted that "the identity of these powers remains to be revealed"[23] — but whatever they are, the only reason the beasts can gain control is because of the fallen and spiritually degenerate state brought about by evil being able to impose itself on mankind because of indifference and ambivalence toward the good.

The real issue is one of worship. The battle is for the hearts and minds of mankind. The objective of the false lamb is to get men to worship the beast. Thus, the false prophet takes on a priestly role with pseudoreligious authority. A false religion drives the people. Blinded by selfishness and lust, they worship secular power that is able to explain away real miracles. The result is the universal victory of secular humanism in which God is denied and mankind is exalted.[24] Out of this philosophy and its worldliness come the "miracles" of the age. Such miracles have deceived many into false faith and blinded many into a false security. Willingly, the deluded follow the ways of the first beast.

The second beast commands those "who dwell upon the earth," that is, the unregenerate among mankind, "to make an image for the beast" (v. 14, AT). The dative is used here, which marks the possessor. In other words, the false lamb creates an image that then belongs to the beast. In verse fifteen the Greek use of the genitive is possessive, so the phrase "image of the beast" should be understood as the image that belongs to the beast rather than the image that looks like the beast.

Here we see the false prophet acting as minister of propaganda for the beast, causing men to yield to it all that it desires. The false prophet is able to engender this submission by those miracles he has power to do "in the sight of the beast" (v. 14, KJV). As the two witnesses in chapter eleven stand before the Lord and have power over fire, so the false prophet performs miracles as he stands before his lord.[25] Both God and Satan have their servants upon the earth working miracles. Many who refuse to follow those whom God has appointed will fall under the spell of those whom Satan has.

THE MARK OF THE BEAST (v. 18)

18 Here is wisdom. Let him number of a man; and his number that hath understanding count the is Six hundred threescore and six. number of the beast: for it is the

Those who worship the beast receive the right to wear its mark. Verses fifteen through eighteen underscore the idea that only through the act of worship can one receive the mark. Since refusal to wear the mark results in death, the only way to escape is to venerate the beast.[26] But such homage does not bring peace or happiness. John states that those who worship the beast "have no rest day nor night" (14:11, KJV). Though looking to a future state, John well describes the restless, nervous, and nearly exhausted existence of individuals who sell themselves to the idol of materialism.

The mark of the beast has intrigued many. The Seer uses the Greek term *charagma,* which denotes a stamp, etching, engraving, or impression. It also describes the brand upon an animal or a slave. And it must not be overlooked that it also describes the mark left by a serpent's bite.[27] The objective of the beast is that "all, both small and great, rich and poor, free and bond" receive the mark "in their right hand, or in their foreheads" (v. 16, KJV). No one is to be free of the mark. This mark stands in contrast to and is the converse of the seal placed upon the faithful followers of the other Lamb. As such it signifies those who are slaves of the Adversary.

The mark of the monster consists of the letters of its name written in its numerical equivalent. Most ancient people did not have a separate numbering system and alphabet, so letters also served as numbers. Generally the first nine letters of the alphabet stood for numbers one through nine, the next nine for numbers ten through ninety, and so on. In one kind of riddle, a name was translated into its numerical equivalent. For example a line of graffiti from Pompeii reads, "I love her whose number is 545."[28] Among the Jews the practice was known as gematria. Many Rabbis looked for esoteric meanings in the numbers found in the Old Testament. For example, Abraham is said to have taken 318 trained men to rescue Lot from his captors (see Gen.

14:14). That number translates into "Eliezer," Abraham's chief servant.[29]

Verse eighteen has caused no end of speculation. There John gives the challenge, "Let him that hath understanding count the number of the beast" (KJV), and then gives the number as 666. Scholars and amateurs both have suggested many ingenious solutions ranging in possibilities from single individuals to whole institutions.[30] Some popular suggestions include, for an individual, the emperor Titus (Greek *teitan*, where t = 300, e = 5, i = 10, t = 300, a = 1, n = 50); for a nation, the Romans (Greek *lateinos*, where l + o = 100, a = 1, t = 300, e = 5, i = 10, n = 50, s = 200). There are other names that work as well, like the man's name *Euanthas*.[31] Significantly *thērion*, the word John uses for the beast, also equals 666.

One popular suggestion is that the number refers to the Catholic Church because the Greek forms *Italika ekklēsia* (Italian Church) and *hē letana basileia* (the Latin Church) both add up to 666. Further, some claim that the inscription on the mitre of the Pope also yields the same number. If such an inscription exists, the *Catholic Encyclopedia* and other reference works on religious vestments used by the Catholics do not disclose it. The view that the beast is a church seems narrow, if not bigoted, especially since the idea behind the beast seems more state than church. The Adversary would probably like the wrong kingdoms to be pegged.

The whole problem is fraught with difficulties. First, there are two manuscript traditions. The majority give the number 666, but others give 616. Second, the meaning may require the use of the *digamma*, an archaic letter out of use in the Greek alphabet before John's day but sometimes retained for use as the number "six."

Taking the Greek as it stands, John's riddle points to "a man," that is, a single individual. Historically, the one man who has left his mark as the arch persecutor of the Christians is Nero, whom many have argued for as the man John had in mind. To derive the number, Nero's name is transliterated into Hebrew *nron ksr*. The breakdown is n = 50, r = 200, o = 6, n = 50, k =

100, s = 60, r = 200. Though the solution is ingenious, it is hard to believe that John would have put his readers through so much trouble. Also, Nero had been dead for nearly a quarter century before John wrote. However, in John's day there was another who bore the spiritual nature of Nero. This was Domitian. As emperor, he sought to exterminate the church of God. To John he may have seemed to be Nero reincarnate.

But a specific historical entity may not be what John had in mind. It may be that he was portraying a spiritual condition. As noted above, the mark and the worship of the beast cannot be separated. The mark stands for the beast. In such a case, the number six would stand in contrast to the number seven, God's number. Six would then be what comes the closest to perfection but falls short in each of its digits. The three digits could thus represent a trinity of imperfection: the dragon, the beast, and the false prophet. Partaking of the mark signifies spiritual devotion to the beast. It designates those who throughout time have been bitten by the serpent from the sea and who carry its venom in their veins.[32]

CONCLUSION

There is much in chapter thirteen that awaits further revelation. When it is important for the Latter-day Saints to know specifics, the prophet will reveal them from God. In the meantime, an understanding of the message underlying the chapter sheds a little light. John's major concern is the question of worship, that is, to whom will men give their loyalty. Herein lies the message for those living in the last days when the beast will again actively recruit souls.

The monster is not Satan but the result of the unchecked work of Satan within institutions, communities, and countries. Wherever men refuse to be controlled by God or governed by truth, Satan rules; this is the danger of drive without humility. All spiritual aberrations are rooted here and are a result of the greatest of moral evils—pride. President Benson has warned the Saints against pride. "The central feature of pride," he instructs, "is enmity — enmity toward God and enmity toward our fellow-men. *Enmity* means 'hatred toward, hostility to, or a state of opposition.' It is the power by which Satan wishes to reign over us." He goes on to state that "the proud cannot accept the authority of God giving direction to their lives. (See Hel. 12:6.) They pit their perceptions of truth against God's great knowledge, their abilities versus God's priesthood power, their accomplishments against His mighty works." The prophet further states that the proud man gets no joy out of having anything but only out of having more than others.[33]

Thus, pride is competitive. It drives men on and on, never allowing satisfaction, all the while twisting their minds and souls into eternal selfishness. "I am the greatest," such insist, "therefore, what *I* want should happen. I'll step on anyone or anything that will not bow to my will." Sooner or later, such souls become saturated with the same poison that turned the son of the morning into the devil himself. Affected by the bite of the serpent from the sea, they carry his mark always with them. It affects both their labor (the mark on the hand) and their thought (the mark on the forehead). To these prideful, perverted souls, all men must eventually become slaves. Those who refuse are considered the enemy and soon become the persecuted. Since God will not submit to their program, will not follow their agenda, he becomes their ultimate enemy.[34]

The beast does not work alone. He teams up with the false lamb, a treacherous religious system pushed by pseudoprophets. The two beasts have produced the philosophical base and theological foundation for the satanic doctrine upon which the world feeds. The promise is always easy salvation, that property exists for the taking, that man can rejoice in sins and find joy. The doctrine is clearly enunciated by such men as Sherem (see Jacob 7:1–18), Nehor (see Alma 1:3–5), and Korihor (see Alma 30:6–16). Each taught what was "pleasing unto the carnal mind," and they "had much success" (Alma 30:53). But a lesson awaited each of these men.

There is an old saying that "you can't get something for nothing." But the truth behind the beasts is that you get nothing for something. That is Satan's method of operation. His minions make satanically inspired but empty promises ("ye shall not surely die" — Moses 4:10), and then extract their payment. Note that it is neither the monster nor the false prophet who makes the image for the beast. The people do that. The image is made from the salt of their sweat, their toil, their tears, and even their blood. But in their hour of need, the beast will quickly abandon them; "and thus we see that the devil will not support his children at the last day, but doth speedily drag them down to hell" (Alma 30:60).

CHAPTER 14

THE WINEPRESS OF THE WRATH OF GOD

(AN ANALYSIS OF REVELATION 14)

THE VIRGINS (vv. 1–5)

1 And I looked, and, lo, a Lamb stood on the mount Sion, and with him an hundred forty and four thousand, having his Father's name written in their foreheads.

2 And I heard a voice from heaven, as the voice of many waters, and as the voice of a great thunder: and I heard the voice of harpers harping with their harps:

3 And they sung as it were a new song before the throne, and before the four beasts, and the elders: and no man could learn that song but the hundred and forty and four thousand, which were redeemed from the earth.

4 These are they which were not defiled with women; for they are virgins. These are they which follow the Lamb whithersoever he goeth. These were redeemed from among men, being the firstfruits unto God and to the Lamb.

5 And in their mouth was found no guile: for they are without fault before the throne of God.

Chapter fourteen serves as yet another interlude. It presents a message of hope and encouragement just before vivid descriptions of destruction. Here it is sandwiched between the great persecutions carried on by the two beasts and the judgment of God upon both them and the world they have created. The central, though less obvious, message of this section is a plea for the Saints to follow the Lord even during periods of distress.[1]

The message is relevant for this chapter brings the reader into the present age.

The chapter divides into three sections, each starting with the phrase "I looked" or "I saw" (vv. 1, 6, 14, KJV). The first scene is of the Lamb and the Saints in Zion, the second of the three angels who both warn and comfort, and the last of the harvest of the earth. The final section is further divided into two parts: first, the ingathering of the righteous—the period of the harvest; and second, the destruction of the wicked—the time of the vintage.

This chapter echoes the interlude between the sixth and seventh seals where the 144,000 were introduced (chapter 7). In this chapter John sees them standing with the Lamb on Mount Zion. Unlike the earlier vision, this one depicts their earthly station at the time judgment commences in earnest.

The vision has prepared the reader for the onset of a great battle, but, as usual, God throws in a twist. The figure standing on Mount Zion is not a terrible warrior-king garbed in battle array, but instead, a lamb, the symbol of meekness and peace. Further, harmony and joy reign over all those in John's view. These people do not know worry, distress, or the threat of war. The harmony of sweet music fills the region, reaching a climax as the heavens explode into the rhapsody of a new song—new not only because it has never been sung before, but also because it could never have been sung before. It signals a total victory that only now has become possible. For this reason, only the 144,000—representing the sealed, those who have won the battle—are able to sing it.

Doctrine and Covenants 84:96–102 provides the setting for and content of such a song. In it the Lord states:

> For I, the Almighty, have laid my hands upon the nations, to scourge them for their wickedness. And plagues shall go forth, and they shall not be taken from the earth until I have completed my work, which shall be cut short in righteousness—until all shall know me, who remain, even from the least unto the greatest, and shall be filled with the knowledge of the Lord, and shall see eye to eye, and shall lift up their voice, and with the voice together sing this new song, saying:

The Lord hath brought again Zion;
The Lord hath redeemed his people, Israel,
According to the election of grace,
Which was brought to pass by the faith
And covenant of their fathers.

The Lord hath redeemed his people;
And Satan is bound and time is no longer.
The Lord hath gathered all things in one.
The Lord hath brought down Zion from above.
The Lord hath brought up Zion from beneath.

The earth hath travailed and brought forth
     her strength;
And truth is established in her bowels;
And the heavens have smiled upon her;
And she is clothed with the glory of her God;
For he stands in the midst of his people.

Glory, and honor, and power, and might,
Be ascribed to our God; for he is full of mercy,
Justice, grace and truth, and peace,
Forever and ever, Amen.

Here we understand the triumphant nature of the song. The plagues of judgment have cleansed the earth. Only the redeemed remain. God and his Saints have won the day, and Zion stands supreme.

The focus of this part of the vision is on the 144,000 servants of God. As has been suggested, the term symbolizes priesthood authority in its fullness. The term *virgin* (Greek *parthenos*) used by John to describe them emphasizes a spiritual quality. The image of "virgin" as applied to males was probably related to Israelite military practices. Soldiers were required to maintain ritual purity, including sexual abstinence, before going into battle. This state of ceremonial cleanliness for those engaged in war seems to be an excellent symbol for the moral purity that the Saints must maintain during the spiritual war against the beasts (on conducting holy war, see Deut. 20; 23:9–10; cf. 1 Sam. 21:5; 2 Sam. 11:11).[2] For this reason there should be neither concern for the epithet "virgins" pertaining to males, nor the idea that John is espousing celibacy.

The scriptures use the image of the virgin to represent the

church and frequently portray her as the Lord's bride. In reality, the term reflects the state of individual members of the Lord's earthly kingdom who have kept themselves from defilement by the world (see 2 Kgs. 19:21; Jer. 18:13; Hosea 2:5; 2 Cor. 11:2). Thus, John states that they "follow the Lamb whithersoever he goeth" (v. 4, KJV).

John makes the point that "in their [the virgins'] mouth was found no guile" (v. 5, KJV). The Greek word translated "guile" (*pseudos*) means "falsehood" in a broad sense, thus encompassing both lying and deceiving. However, John uses the term with a specific meaning. For him it is neither error nor lying but an active contesting against truth.[3] Thus, the 144,000 are the antithesis of the beast and the false prophet. The Seer's context suggests that the men represented by the 144,000 are the true prophets. The whole picture captures the fidelity to Jehovah that the Saints of God espouse.[4]

THE MESSAGE OF THE THREE ANGELS (vv. 6–11)

6 And I saw another angel fly in the midst of heaven, having the everlasting gospel to preach unto them that dwell on the earth, and to every nation, and kindred, and tongue, and people,

7 Saying with a loud voice, Fear God, and give glory to him; for the hour of his judgment is come: and worship him that made heaven, and earth, and the sea, and the fountains of waters.

8 And there followed another angel, saying, Babylon is fallen, is fallen, that great city, because she made all nations drink of the wine of the wrath of her fornication.

9 And the third angel followed them, saying with a loud voice, If any man worship the beast and his image, and receive his mark in his forehead, or in his hand,

10 The same shall drink of the wine of the wrath of God, which is poured out without mixture into the cup of his indignation; and he shall be tormented with fire and brimstone in the presence of the holy angels, and in the presence of the Lamb:

11 And the smoke of their torment ascendeth up for ever and ever: and they have no rest day nor night, who worship the beast and his image, and whosoever receiveth the mark of his name.

Having shown the nature of the latter-day church, the vision dramatically switches scenes. John sees an angel in the midst of heaven "having the everlasting gospel to preach unto them that dwell on the earth" (v. 6, KJV). Modern revelation bears directly on the interpretation of this verse. To the world the Lord has declared:

> I have sent forth mine angel flying through the midst of heaven, having the everlasting gospel, who hath appeared unto some and hath committed it unto man, who shall appear unto many that dwell on the earth. And this gospel shall be preached unto every nation, and kindred, and tongue, and people. And the servants of God shall go forth, saying with a loud voice: Fear God and give glory to him, for the hour of his judgment is come; and worship him that made heaven, and earth, and the sea, and the fountains of waters (D&C 133:36–39).

On one hand, the angel apparently symbolizes Moroni and those events connected with the coming forth of the Book of Mormon. The Lord states that he sent Moroni "to reveal the Book of Mormon, containing the fulness of my everlasting gospel, to whom I have committed the keys of the stick of Ephraim" (D&C 27:5). On the other hand, the angel seems to represent the Church members serving in their callings as missionaries who will take the teachings of that book and a warning message to all the nations of the earth.[5] Of this period the Lord has said:

> Through their administration the word may go forth unto the ends of the earth, unto the Gentiles first, and then, behold, and lo, they shall turn unto the Jews. And then cometh the day when the arm of the Lord shall be revealed in power in convincing the nations, the heathen nations, the house of Joseph, of the gospel of their salvation. For it shall come to pass in that day, that every man shall hear the fulness of the gospel in his own tongue, and in his own language, through those who are ordained unto this power, by the administration of the Comforter, shed forth upon them for the revelation of Jesus Christ (D&C 90:9–11).

We are living in the day when more missionaries preach the Savior's word to greater and greater portions of the earth in native tongues. The Lord has prophesied that "the poor and the meek shall have the gospel preached unto them, and they shall be looking forth for the time of my coming, for it is nigh at hand—and they shall learn the parable of the fig-tree, for even now already summer is nigh" (D&C 35:15–16; cf. 45:37–39).

However, along with the message of comfort, there is a message of warning: "The hour of his judgment is come" (Rev. 14:7, KJV). The Greek word John uses (*krisis*), translated "judgment," was originally a legal term often meaning "condemnation" and including the punishment associated with it. But there was a medical application denoting that point when it was uncertain whether or not the patient would recover.[6] Thus, the cry of the angel places the world in a position to respond to either life or death. It is truly a moment of crisis. The rejection of the gospel will immediately bring condemnation upon the world. Accordingly, the voice of the first angel is followed by that of the second proclaiming, "Babylon is fallen, is fallen" (v. 8, KJV). The angel proclaims his joyful message in the present tense. There is good reason. The advent of the gospel sounds the death knell of the kingdom of Satan, a composite of the first and second beast and named Babylon. (Further discussion of this subject appears in chapters seventeen and eighteen.)

Note that the first angel invites all men to worship God the creator. Our Lord is not the destroyer of the universe — man is. God merely allows (usually through inaction) men to receive the results of their own lawlessness. The book of Revelation shows the result: the four horsemen, the burning mountain, the star Wormwood, the angel Apollyon, and, in the end, the beasts. These are the destroyers of the earth (see 6:1–8; 8:8–11; 9:7, 18). But judgment grows from the clear pronouncement of the gospel; it removes these destroyers so that the God of life may reign. For this reason the second angel, who proclaims the fall of Babylon, follows the first.[7]

The reason Babylon must fall is clearly given: "Because she made all nations drink of the wine of the wrath of her fornication" (v. 8, KJV). The translation of the last phrase is difficult. The term given as "wrath" (Greek *thumos*) carries the meaning of "wrath," "rage," or "anger" pushed with a passion. Those who drink the wine of whoredom must yet drink from another cup. This too will be a cup of unbridled passion, but this time of anger—a just God's anger meted out in its full strength, entirely undiluted and untempered by either mercy or grace.[8]

The passion against Babylon, the great whore, results from the seduction of the nations through her use of intoxicating philosophies and corrupting power.[9] However, the nations did not have to partake; they chose to be deceived. The truth, a sharp but refreshing antidote to Babylon's sweet wine, was available, but they refused it. In this light the prophetic warning of the third angel takes on meaning. Anyone who partakes of Babylon's favors, or in other words, who worships "the beast and his image, and [receives] his mark in his forehead, or in his hand," comes fully under the condemnation of God (v. 9, KJV). The Seer paints a graphic picture of the hellfire suffered by those who worship the beast and carry his mark (see vv. 10–11). By this symbolic means, John conveys the state of the burning conscience where the soul is racked "with eternal torment" and "tormented with the pains of hell," where the "very thought of coming into the presence of . . . God" racks the "soul with inexpressible horror" (Alma 36:12–14).

A MESSAGE AND PROMISE TO THE SAINTS (vv. 12–13)

12 Here is the patience of the saints: here are they that keep the commandments of God, and the faith of Jesus.

13 And I heard a voice from heaven saying unto me, Write, Blessed are the dead which die in the Lord from henceforth: Yea, saith the Spirit, that they may rest from their labours; and their works do follow them.

Verses twelve and thirteen contain the heart of this chapter. It is an interlude within the interlude and allows John to petition the Saints to forbear and "keep the commandments of God, and the faith of Jesus" (v. 12, KJV). This applies to Saints living in any era but especially during the time when the beasts will make a living hell on earth—before divine judgment will free the Saints from the tyranny of Babylon and before Zion will protect them from the wrath in store for the world. For those who continue faithful, their state will be blessed, for they will "rest from their labours; and their works do follow them" (v. 13, KJV). Note the shift in tense that accurately follows the Greek. The future state of the Saints will be glorious because good deeds follow them; that is, the effects of a good deed do not pass away. The consequence of many good deeds results in a future reward.

Joseph Smith is also reported to have taught that the phrase "their works do follow them" should be translated "they shall continue their work." Understood in this way, Revelation teaches that the Saints continue the work of the gospel into the next life.[10] In either interpretation, notice that this message follows the dual emphasis in John's vision on the faith of the Saints and their good works.

THE HARVEST OF THE WORLD (vv. 14–20)

14 And I looked, and behold a white cloud, and upon the cloud one sat like unto the Son of man, having on his head a golden crown, and in his hand a sharp sickle.

15 And another angel came out of the temple, crying with a loud voice to him that sat on the cloud, Thrust in thy sickle, and reap: for the time is come for thee to reap; for the harvest of the earth is ripe.

16 And he that sat on the cloud thrust in his sickle on the earth; and the earth was reaped.

17 And another angel came out of the temple which is in heaven, he also having a sharp sickle.

18 And another angel came out from the altar, which had power over fire; and cried with a loud cry to him that had the sharp sickle, saying, Thrust in thy sharp sickle, and gather the clusters of the vine of the earth; for her grapes are fully ripe.

19 And the angel thrust in his sickle into the earth, and gathered the vine of the earth, and cast it into the great winepress of the wrath of God.

20 And the winepress was trodden without the city, and blood came out of the winepress, even unto the horse bridles, by the space of a thousand and six hundred furlongs.

At the close of the interlude, the scene swiftly shifts. John beholds a white cloud upon which is seated "one . . . like unto the Son of man" (v. 14, KJV). The imagery is taken from Daniel 7:13–14 and appears to be a reference to the resurrected Lord coming in the fulness of his power. On his head sits the golden wreath (*stephanos*) of victory, and in his hand the sickle of judgment readied for the harvest. The day of judgment has fully come "for the harvest of the earth is ripe" (v. 15, KJV). It is the ripeness that determines the timing of the reaping. The Lord expresses this idea in a parable of harvest:

> In the last days, even now while the Lord is beginning to bring forth the word, and the blade is springing up and is yet tender—behold, verily I say unto you, the angels are crying unto the Lord day and night, who are ready and waiting to be sent forth to reap down the fields; but the Lord saith unto them, pluck not up the tares while the blade is yet tender (for verily your faith is weak), lest you destroy the wheat also. Therefore, let the wheat and the tares grow together until the harvest is fully ripe; then ye shall first gather out the wheat from among the tares, and after the gathering of the wheat, behold and lo, the tares are bound in bundles, and the field remaineth to be burned (D&C 86:4–7).

The first harvest, the harvest of the Lord, is the ingathering of the wheat. That time is now and the time is urgent. To his Saints the Lord declared: "Ye are called to lift up your voices as with the sound of a trump, to declare my gospel unto a crooked and perverse generation. For behold, the field is white already to harvest; and it is the eleventh hour, and the last time that I shall call laborers into my vineyard" (D&C 33:2–3). In this light the Lord admonishes: "Whoso desireth to reap let him thrust in his sickle with his might, and reap while the day lasts, that he may treasure up for his soul everlasting salvation in the kingdom of God" (D&C 11:3). Now is the time when the wheat must be gathered in. Those who participate are the Lord's sickle. The Lord will reward the effort of his laborers with the wonders and peace of Zion.

Through the efforts of the laborers, the world will hear the gospel. But when the world openly rejects goodness and turns against God's people, then another sickle will begin to do its terrible work. Note 2 Nephi 28:15–20 with Alma 37:30–31, which teach that the world is fully ripe when it both rejects and fights against goodness. That will be the day when the voice of God will utter "out of heaven, saying:"

> Hearken, O ye nations of the earth, and hear the words of that God, who made you. O, ye nations of the earth, how

often would I have gathered you together as a hen gathereth her chickens under her wings, but ye would not! How oft have I called upon you by the mouth of my servants and by the ministering of angels, and by mine own voice, and by the voice of thunderings, and by the voice of lightnings, and by the voice of tempests, and by the voice of earthquakes, and great hailstorms, and by the voice of famines and pestilences of every kind, and by the great sound of a trump, and by the voice of judgment, and by the voice of mercy all the day long, and by the voice of glory and honor and the riches of eternal life, and would have saved you with an everlasting salvation, but ye would not! Behold, the day has come, when the cup of the wrath of mine indignation is full (D&C 43:23–26).

This scripture seems to depict the period of the second sickle, when all attempts to redeem the world have failed and the harvest is ripe for judgment and destruction. The harvest of ruin will be carried out not by the Lord but by an angel of destruction. His target is not the fields but the vineyards. His instrument is the *drepanon* ("sharp sickle," KJV), an all-purpose blade used for pruning, cutting clusters of grapes, and harvesting grains. Its roughly foot-long curved blade made it easy to handle with clean cutting power. The angel is to "gather the clusters of the vine of the earth; for her grapes are fully ripe" (v. 18, KJV). Further, he is to cast the fruit "into the great winepress of the wrath of God" (v. 19, KJV). His authority comes from the angel of the altar, probably the one already met in 8:3–5 who cast fire upon the earth. As noted elsewhere, the altar is connected with the prayers of the Saints. John may again be suggesting that the faithful play a significant role in bringing about the harvesting of the wicked.[11]

This part of the vision does not seem to depict the final judgment that belongs to God alone (see 20:11–15) but the time of the return of the victorious Son, who has overcome all things and who takes his place as God of the earth. Upon his return, later in chapter nineteen, he will tread "the winepress of the fierceness and wrath of Almighty God" (19:15, KJV).

If John intended the first harvest to denote the time of separation of the wheat from the tares (see Matt. 13:30; D&C 86:1–6), or the wheat from the chaff (cf. Luke 3:17), the second denotes unmitigated judgment. The association of the angel of the altar with the temple suggests that he is God's agent, *the* destroying angel given full authority for this awesome task.[12]

God executes judgment outside the city. John probably has Jerusalem in mind, following the imagery of Joel 3:12–14 (which also uses the dual symbols of vintage and harvest). The judgment upon the nations takes place in the valley of Jehoshaphat, a name meaning "Jehovah is judge" (see Joel 3:2, 12). According to tradition, this is synonymous with the Kidron valley between Jerusalem and the Mount of Olives[13] and was near the place where the Son of Man suffered so that all who would come to him would not need to suffer (see John 19:20; Heb. 13:12; D&C 19:16–18).

Those who refuse this first suffering will feel the full effect of the second. In graphic and appalling terms, John symbolizes the slaughter: blood flowing for 1600 furlongs (about 184 miles). Geographically, this is about the maximum length of Palestine. Symbolically, the number is the square of four, denoting geographical completeness, multiplied by the square of ten, the number denoting all of a part. Taken together, the number suggests that God's judgment actually involves all John's world, not just those who are around Jerusalem, and that all those who belong to that portion outside the protecting power of God will be directly affected.[14]

John's vision seems to take in the same geographical area as that of Jeremiah 25:15–26 and Ezekiel 38:1–7. It is essentially central Europe, western and southern Russia, the Near East including Egypt, and much of North Africa. If other nations play any role in the battle at all, Revelation does not note it. Very likely conditions in the rest of the world will be such that regional problems will take up the time, energies, and resources of all the other nations.

CONCLUSION

John continues to use the pattern that shows first the protected state of the righteous and the indefensible position of the wicked. In this chapter, he symbolically shows that the gospel will be preached in all the world before the end comes; furthermore, he indicates that this preaching dooms Babylon. This is the time when the Church will move "out of the wilderness of darkness, and shine forth fair as the moon, clear as the sun, and terrible as an army with banners" (D&C 109:73). The onslaught of this mighty kingdom of righteousness will be invincible. But for a time, conditions will be rough and opposition heavy.

When the true Saints are strong in the faith, when all peoples have clearly had a chance to hear the gospel proclaimed in their own tongue, when missionaries and Church officers are within reasonable reach of every soul, when temples dot the face of the lands, then the preparation for the first harvest will be complete. The actual harvest will commence in earnest when the world turns against the truth, actively persecuting righteousness because it is righteous, attacking the Saints of God and all who are good. The Son of Man will then gather the righteous out from among the wicked. Simultaneously the second harvest will begin. The angel of destruction will wield his sickle and cast those ripe in iniquity into the "great winepress of the wrath of God" (v. 19, KJV). Chapters fifteen through nineteen describe that harvest.

CHAPTER 15

THE SEVEN ANGELS

(AN ANALYSIS OF REVELATION 15)

THE GREAT AND MARVELOUS SIGN (v. 1)

1 And I saw another sign in heaven, great and marvellous, seven angels having the seven last plagues; for in them is filled up the wrath of God.

Chapter fourteen closes with a description of carnage. The harvest of the earth has begun. Chapter fifteen opens with a new vision. Once again John sees a sign in the heavens. Seven angels, having the seven last plagues, prepare to do their work against the wicked. The vision is moving irresistibly toward its climax. John reveals the full extent of God's wrath as it is vented against the wicked.

The Seer's view changes from its perspective in the earlier part of the vision. It becomes much narrower. He sees the seven plagues neither as they affect the whole earth (as in chapter eight), nor as they molest mankind in general (as in chapter nine). Here only the wicked are in view. Thus, John says of the angels' plagues, "In them is filled up the wrath of God" (v. 1, KJV). The term translated "filled up" (Greek *teleō*) means to reach a consummation or perfection as well as to carry out, accomplish, perform, or fulfill. The Seer's use of the word suggests that in these judgments the wrath of God achieves its goal.[1]

166

THE SAINTS OF GOD (vv. 2–4)

2 And I saw as it were a sea of glass mingled with fire: and them that had gotten the victory over the beast, and over his image, and over his mark, and over the number of his name, stand on the sea of glass, having the harps of God. 3 And they sing the song of Moses the servant of God, and the song of the Lamb, saying, Great and marvellous are thy works, Lord God Almighty; just and true are thy ways, thou King of saints. 4 Who shall not fear thee, O Lord, and glorify thy name? for thou only art holy: for all nations shall come and worship before thee; for thy judgments are made manifest.

As already noted, John has a pattern of describing the peaceful condition of the faithful before presenting the horrors unleashed against the ungodly. His pattern continues here as he briefly mentions the blessed condition of the Saints before the vials of wrath are poured out upon the earth. The vision centers on the final glorious reward of the victorious Saints as they "stand on the sea of glass, having the harps of God" (v. 2, KJV). We have already learned that the sea of glass represents the celestialized earth. John assures us that the Saints will come through the fiery trials — which will destroy the wicked — to their eternal glory. Thus, appropriately they sing a new song. As did the Israelites who overcame Pharaoh and his army through faith in God, so these victorious Saints celebrate their triumph in song. But because they won through no other weapon than the blood of the Lamb, the song is appropriately called the song of the Lamb.

While their song echoes a number of Old Testament doxologies, John has combined them in such a way as to amplify the Christian hope.[2] The song, praising God and the Lamb who give victory, is sung by those who were delivered from the wrath of the dragon and who prevailed in their testimony of Christ. The song focuses on the works and the ways of God. His deeds amaze men in two ways: in their magnitude and in their unpredictability. At the same time they consist of two attributes: they are perfectly just and totally proper. Because of these, God is worthy of praise and honor.

Though the song is a celebration of victory, it does not

mention God's judgment upon his enemies. Rather, it concentrates on the rightness of his redemptive acts through which "all nations shall come and worship before thee" (v. 4, KJV).[3] The phrase "King of the saints" as rendered in verse three of the KJV is highly questioned. The term *saints* is replaced by either *ages* (*aionion*) or *nations* (*ethnon*) in most ancient manuscripts. Because of a near parallel verse in Jeremiah 10:7, the favored translation is "King of nations." The point of the praise is in the last clause of verse four, "for thy judgments are made manifest." Nothing can stop the will of God from being done. He executes it through the course of history—thus, constructing that history. In the end, justice will be done, and judgment will have its total sway.

THE SEVEN ANGELS (vv. 5–8)

5 And after that I looked, and, behold, the temple of the tabernacle of the testimony in heaven was opened:

6 And the seven angels came out of the temple, having the seven plagues, clothed in pure and white linen, and having their breasts girded with golden girdles.

7 And one of the four beasts gave unto the seven angels seven golden vials full of the wrath of God, who liveth for ever and ever.

8 And the temple was filled with smoke from the glory of God, and from his power; and no man was able to enter into the temple, till the seven plagues of the seven angels were fulfilled.

John again looks and sees the heavenly tabernacle. Once before he has seen this celestial shrine (see 11:19); however, that time the vision focused on the ark that held the covenant. The covering of the ark was called the mercy seat (see Ex. 25:22; Lev. 16:2), and there the mercy of God shone forth. This time the ark is not what occupies the Seer's attention but the "tabernacle of the testimony" (v. 5, KJV). The covenant and the law stand center. Mercy has had its day. The time for the execution of the law has arrived.[4] That John focuses on judgment, flowing not from the throne but from the temple, dramatically changes the nature and purpose of the scourge. The more severe course of chastisement does not derive from God's sovereignty but from his righteousness and holiness.[5]

God designates seven angels to enforce the judgment. Again the symbolism is important. All heaven combines in this great moment to see that God's will is fully executed. The ministers of justice are angels of high rank, as suggested by the golden girdles they wear like that of the Son of Man (see 1:13). One of the living creatures hands each of the angels of doom a vial, or bowl (Greek *phialē*), filled with God's wrath. At the same time John sees God's glory and power fill the heavenly temple, "and no man was able to enter into the temple, till the seven plagues of the seven angels were fulfilled" (v. 8, KJV). Thus, John depicts the ominous moment. No one can enter the temple. No blood of expiation can be sprinkled as the High Priest had done on the Day of Atonement to bring renewal of the covenant of peace and mercy between God and Israel. No one can enter and make peace until judgment has had its way.

Note the contrast between the seven seals, seven trumpets, and seven bowls. The seals announce the designs of God, the trumpets sound the voice of warning, and the bowls execute his judgment. The bowls and trumpets strikingly correspond. In the first four of each series, the sphere of operation is the same, namely, earth, sea, rivers, fountains, and sun. But in the trumpets the area touched is somewhat restricted. The change produced under the bowls is different and of a more severe character. Further, the fifth, sixth, and even seventh trumpets correspond in general respects to the last three bowls. But in the latter, the range of the various plagues is in no way limited to a fourth (see 6:8) or third part (see chap. 8) of the prophetic earth. All evil is searched out and destroyed.[6] From this point on, there is neither turning back nor remorse. God has clearly stated: "If ye walk contrary unto me, and will not hearken unto me; I will bring seven times more plagues upon you according to your sins" (Lev. 26:21, KJV). During this time of ultimate justice, any show of mercy would be wickedness.

CONCLUSION

This chapter celebrates not the God of mercy but the God of justice. John shows that justice must have its day. "For behold, justice exerciseth all his demands" (Alma 42:24). They who "bring forth evil fruit . . . must be hewn down and cast into the fire" (Jacob 6:7). This "according to the power of justice, for justice cannot be denied" (v. 10) because "on such the plan of redemption could have no power, for the works of justice could not be destroyed, according to the supreme goodness of God" (Alma 12:32). John has aptly shown that the world has had its chance to repent but refused. As a result of its recalcitrance, the world forfeited mercy. Now according to the "goodness of God," justice must be satisfied.

Chapter fifteen makes two points: first, that the plagues are inexorable once they commence; and second, that God executes them in justice and vengeance upon the world. Though punishment comes without mitigation, it is both just and righteous. In modern times the Lord has declared that the testimony of his witnesses "shall also go forth unto the condemnation of this generation if they harden their hearts against them; for a desolating scourge shall go forth among the inhabitants of the earth, and shall continue to be poured out from time to time, if they repent not, until the earth is empty, and the [wicked] inhabitants thereof are consumed away and utterly destroyed by the brightness of my coming" (D&C 5:18–19). Further, he has warned: "Lo, vengeance cometh speedily upon the ungodly as the whirlwind; and who shall escape it? The Lord's scourge shall pass over by night and by day, and the report thereof shall vex all people; yea, it shall not be stayed until the Lord come; for the indignation of the Lord is kindled against their abominations and all their wicked works" (D&C 97:22–24).

Once the plagues begin, there is no way to stop them. But what of the Saints? The Lord has both warned and promised them: "Nevertheless, Zion shall escape if she observe to do all things whatsoever I have commanded her" (D&C 97:25). Here the Lord states his conditions: obedience will bring safety and security, disobedience will bring wrath. No unrighteousness is exempt even if found within the Church. The Saints must never forget the Lord's declaration:

Vengeance cometh speedily upon the inhabitants of the

earth, a day of wrath, a day of burning, a day of desolation, of weeping, of mourning, and of lamentation; and as a whirlwind it shall come upon all the face of the earth, saith the Lord. And upon my house shall it begin, and from my house shall it go forth, saith the Lord; first among those among you, saith the Lord, who have professed to know my name and have not known me, and have blasphemed against me in the midst of my house, saith the Lord (D&C 112:24–26).

Under the power of judgment, the mask of pretended righteousness will be ripped off and all hypocrisy fully revealed. The rebellious Latter-day Saint will not escape the justice of God.

CHAPTER 16

THE SEVEN BOWLS

(AN ANALYSIS OF REVELATION 16)

THE VOICE FROM THE TEMPLE (v. 1)

1 And I heard a great voice out of the temple saying to the seven angels, Go your ways, and pour out the vials of the wrath of God upon the earth.

The revelation of chapter fifteen forms the backdrop for that of sixteen. John has already seen the victorious Saints sing their song of triumph. In this way, the Seer assures his readers that they will eventually be victorious and that they have nothing to fear from the vials to be poured out against the wicked. This assurance steels them for the doom that grips the ungodly as the vision continues.

Chapter fourteen closed with the picture of wrath contained in the symbolism of the harvest of the vintage. Why does sixteen go through the whole thing again? Probably because of the need to emphasize both the intensity and finality of the coming judgment.[1] This suggests why the Lord chose symbols different from those he used in chapters eight and nine to depict the same judgments. In those chapters the purview took in all the earth. There judgment was mitigated. Here he concentrates only on the wicked: "the men which had the mark of the beast, and . . . worshipped his image" (v. 2, KJV).

Some commentators see the plagues of chapter sixteen as

172

additional to those in chapters eight and nine. In this view the plagues are seen as the fulfillment of the final trump. The reasons are primarily three in number. First, the trumpet plagues are partial while the bowl plagues are total; second, the trumpet plagues are viewed as a call to repentance while the bowls leave no room for remorse; and finally, mankind is not affected but indirectly by the first four trumpets while the bowls blast right at him.[2] I believe that these reasons do not take into account the different focus of the two visions. The trumpets are universal and, taken in the aggregate, many people will survive, whereas the bowls are specifically directed at wickedness, which shall utterly be destroyed.

From the temple "filled with smoke from the glory of God, and from his power" (Rev. 15:8, KJV) comes the voice of command. "Go your ways," it directs the seven angels, "and pour out the vials of the wrath of God upon the earth" (16:1, KJV). The imagery echoes Isaiah 66:6: "a voice from the temple, a voice of the Lord that rendereth recompense to his enemies." The content of the vials, or bowls, renders the recompense. The term translated "vial" (Greek *phialē*) means "bowl," especially one used in making sacred offerings. In this context John probably envisioned the bowl used to catch the blood of the sacrificial animal. In making the sacrifice, the priest splashed the blood against the altar (e.g., Lev. 1:5; 3:8). Here the content of the bowls is not blood but that which will shed blood. It is the wrath of God poured out in its fullness against the wicked.

THE FIRST THREE BOWLS (vv. 2–7)

2 And the first went, and poured out his vial upon the earth; and there fell a noisome and grievous sore upon the men which had the mark of the beast, and upon them which worshipped his image.

3 And the second angel poured out his vial upon the sea; and it became as the blood of a dead man: and every living soul died in the sea.

4 And the third angel poured out his vial upon the rivers and fountains of waters; and they became blood.

5 And I heard the angel of the waters say, Thou art righteous, O Lord, which art, and wast, and shalt be, because thou hast judged thus.

6 For they have shed the blood

of saints and prophets, and thou
hast given them blood to drink;
for they are worthy.

7 And I heard another out of

the altar say, Even so, Lord God
Almighty, true and righteous are
thy judgments.

The voice dispatches the first angel to pour out his bowl against
the followers of the first beast. These have proudly worn the
beast's mark; now they will wear the sign of God's wrath.[3] Foul
and angry sores come upon them. The KJV states that they are
"noisome" and "grievous." *Noisome* (from *kakos*) is often translated "evil." The word emphasizes the pernicious and destructive nature of the sores that plague the mind as well as the
body.[4] *Grievous* (from *ponēros*) suggests their virulent and serious
nature. The sores themselves are open abscesses or ulcers echoing those of the sixth Egyptian plague brought by Moses (see
Ex. 9:8–12; see also Job 2:7–8, 13).[5]

The second angel pours out the wrath of God upon the sea,
while the third directs his vial toward the rivers and springs of
waters. The result is that all became as blood, and "every living
soul died in the sea" (v. 3, KJV). Here the sea, as part of creation,
suffers as a result of sin. Speaking of the last days the Lord has
stated: "There are many dangers upon the waters, and more
especially hereafter; for I, the Lord have decreed in mine anger
many destructions upon the waters" (D&C 61:4–5). Further, "I,
the Lord, in the beginning blessed the waters; but in the last
days, by the mouth of my servant John, I cursed the waters.
Wherefore, the days will come that no flesh shall be safe upon
the waters. And it shall be said in days to come that none is
able to go up to the land of Zion upon the waters, but he that
is upright in heart" (D&C 61:14–16). Note that only the righteous
can transverse the waters during this period. All others, the
wicked, die.

In verse three, the Lord incorporates an important symbol
in constructing his message. In chapter thirteen, the first monster arose from the sea. There the term *sea* denoted a large
segment of society out of whose upheavals the beast came. In
17:15 an angel states that the waters "are peoples, and multitudes, and nations, and tongues" (KJV). Here, in verse three,

the sea may have a double connotation: the real sea, and a spiritually dead society that has abandoned itself to idolatry and immorality. As one scholar has noted: "In such a society, morals decline to the lowest level; the family collapses, schools breed anarchy and rebellion, business ethics are forgotten, entertainment becomes base and sordid, and printing presses exude smut and filth, until the whole is strangled in its own death blood and suffocated by its own stench."[6]

What fuels the furnace and drives the engines of such a society is the spirit of idolatry. According to the Doctrine and Covenants, this evil spirit "has been growing stronger and stronger, and is now the very mainspring of all corruption, and the whole earth groans under the weight of its iniquity" (D&C 123:7).

The angel of the water, speaking for the other seven, proclaims the righteousness of God "because [he has] judged thus" (v. 5, KJV).[7] The execution of the sentence reveals and underscores the justice of God. John shows that this justice is a cosmic force that acts as a heavenly flame. When this consuming fire contacts something that is not itself just, conflagration occurs. Corruption must fall to the flame: "When the veil of the covering of my temple, in my tabernacle, which hideth the earth, shall be taken off, and all flesh shall see me together. And every corruptible thing, both of man, or of the beasts of the field, or of the fowls of the heavens, or of the fish of the sea, that dwells upon all the face of the earth, shall be consumed" (D&C 101:23–24). Nothing that has basked and gloried in corruption shall escape the justice of God.

However, it should be noted that the bowls of wrath are not designed to destroy the natural order, but rather to enlist it in the service of divine recompense. Thus, the whole of creation becomes a means by which the wicked are punished. But, as was shown in chapter nine, the most important determinant is man's own malicious disregard for man.

Throughout Revelation (except 11:1), judgment and altar are inseparable (see 6:9; 8:3–5; 9:13; 14:18; 16:7). God inextricably interweaves two principles: sacrifice and judgment. Thus, echoing the angel of the water, the angel of the altar declares the absolute justice of God in executing his judgments. One hears reverberations of the song of Moses and the Lamb (see 15:3–5) as the angel declares, "True and righteous are thy judgments" (16:7, KJV). God's actions are in absolute accordance with truth and justice. The execution of God's will enacted by the pouring out of the first three bowls ends in the declaration of his justice. The next two bowls focus on men's reactions to that justice.

THE FOURTH AND FIFTH BOWLS (vv. 8–11)

8 And the fourth angel poured out his vial upon the sun; and power was given unto him to scorch men with fire.

9 And men were scorched with great heat, and blasphemed the name of God, which hath power over these plagues: and they repented not to give him glory.

10 And the fifth angel poured out his vial upon the seat of the beast; and his kingdom was full of darkness; and they gnawed their tongues for pain,

11 And blasphemed the God of heaven because of their pains and their sores, and repented not of their deeds.

The fourth angel pours out his bowl upon the sun. Scorching heat results. Very likely this symbolizes the turmoil and unremitting strife of the times. It stands in sharp contrast to the condition of the sealed where they "hunger no more, neither thirst any more; neither shall the sun light on them, nor any heat" (7:16, KJV; cf. Ps. 121:5–7). With the righteous, there is peace, security, and love; where the beast rules, anxiety, unrest, and turmoil.

But the pressure does not let up. The fifth angel releases the power of his bowl upon the seat of the beast. The result is darkness—not a cool and relieving penumbra but a smothering and suffocating blanket. The smoke of the pit in the abyss produces the darkness (see 9:2). Its purpose is to expel light and truth. The result reflects the warning from the Almighty: "The Lord shall smite thee with madness, and blindness, and astonishment of heart: and thou shalt grope at noonday, as the blind gropeth in darkness, and thou shalt not prosper in thy ways: and thou shalt be only oppressed and spoiled evermore, and no man shall save thee" (Deut. 28:28–29, KJV; cf. Ex. 10:21–23). Now has come the time when "all things shall be in commotion; and surely, men's hearts shall fail them; for fear shall come upon all people" (D&C 88:91). This is the day of the locusts, those engines of destruction associated with heat and fire (see 9:3–12). As darkness swallows the kingdom of the first beast, the whole movement underscores one theme: finality.

The core of the Seer's message centers on the reaction of men to the plagues. They recognize God as the one who controls the plagues, and they curse him because of their pains and anguish, but they do not repent (see 9:20–21). Instead, they blaspheme their maker. This point is significant. Before, only the beast has spoken blasphemy. In chapter sixteen, men are the ones who thrice curse God (vv. 9, 11, 21). John seems to be showing that these men have wholly taken on the character of the beast they serve. The mark of the monster has become indelible not only on their bodies, but also upon their souls, resulting in a sickness that can only reap the reward for which it has blindly sought: reprobation and annihilation (see 14:10–11; 20:15; 21:8; 22:15).[8]

THE SIXTH BOWL (vv. 12–16)

12 And the sixth angel poured out his vial upon the great river Euphrates; and the water thereof was dried up, that the way of the kings of the east might be prepared.

13 And I saw three unclean spirits like frogs come out of the mouth of the dragon, and out of the mouth of the beast, and out of the mouth of the false prophet.

14 For they are the spirits of devils, working miracles, which go forth unto the kings of the earth and of the whole world, to gather them to the battle of that great day of God Almighty.

15 Behold, I come as a thief. Blessed is he that watcheth, and keepeth his garments, lest he walk naked, and they see his shame.

16 And he gathered them together into a place called in the Hebrew tongue Armageddon.

The sixth angel prepares the world for war. As he pours out his bowl, the Euphrates River dries up. The idea of waters being dried up for God's purposes is common in the Old Testament (see Ex. 14:21; Josh. 3:13–17; Isa. 11:15–16; 44:27; Jer. 51:36; Zech.

10:11).[9] The locusts of chapter nine have been waiting for the directive to come out of the darkness. The sixth plague sounds the command. With it, everything that held back the war, symbolized by the great river, is removed. The nature of the symbols used in this chapter, as in others, suggests that they reflect actual conditions.[10] Bizarre weather patterns, scorching heat, large rivers drying up, famine, and plague reveal nature itself working with God in his recompense upon wickedness gone mad.

There is an irony in the sixth plague. On at least two other occasions, waters were dried up in the service of God's people: the first time was the Red Sea (see Ex. 14:21); and the second, the Jordan River (Josh. 3:14–17). This time the dry waters allow horror to sweep the land. But the engines of destruction are in reality the tool of the Almighty. "I, the Lord, am angry with the wicked," he proclaims, and "I am holding my Spirit from the inhabitants of the earth. I have sworn in my wrath, and decreed wars upon the face of the earth, and the wicked shall slay the wicked, and fear shall come upon every man; and the saints also shall hardly escape" (D&C 63:32–34).

The war results from a great delusion. The dragon, the beast, and the false prophet spin lies into webs that captivate the nations. John pictures their pervasive and persuasive philosophy as frogs working among men. Leviticus classifies frogs as unclean (see 11:10). That these three originate from the unholy triumvirate suggests the deceptive nature of their propaganda. Its effectiveness results in the unconditional surrender by men to the cause of evil.[11]

From the visions recorded in chapter twelve on, John had watched the dragon and his beasts in the act of working their lies. Filth had already spewed from their mouths: from the dragon came a river of lies (see 12:15), from the beast came blasphemies (see 13:5), and from the false prophet came seductive propaganda that enticed the world to follow the ways of the beast (see 13:14).[12] In the last days all three send forth their agents.

Here John stops to identify the symbolism of the frogs. They are evil spirits that work counterfeit signs to deceive the nations.

The KJV states that the frogs are "spirits of devils" (16:14). The phrase translates the Greek *eisin gar pneumata daimonin*. The phrase should be translated "demonic spirits" or "spirits, that is, demons." The genitive is one of apposition or definition. Devils have no spirits, being themselves spirits.[13] The purpose of the evil spirits is totally satanic, that is, to gather the forces of evil in an effort to annihilate the good. Thus, the object of the unclean spirits is to muster the forces of the kings of the earth "to the battle of that great day of God Almighty" (v. 14, KJV).

Through the machinations of the frogs, nations will be seized with a passion for war. But the battle will be God's, for this is the great day when he will reckon with the wicked nations of the world (see Ezek. 38–39; Zech. 14).[14] John's vision goes beyond nationalistic limits as he views the entire Mediterranean area moved to battle. This is no mere skirmish, nor merely another war. John depicts nothing less than the end of the telestial world order caused by the abrupt coming of God himself.[15]

At this point John makes an interjection. Paraphrasing Matthew 24:42–46, he notes the Lord's admonition that he will come as a thief in the night and that one must be constantly prepared. The warning just at this point is very appropriate. As the forces of the beast gather, the crises will not bypass the Saints. They must respond to the moment in faith, with constant alertness, or else they will be as a soldier who, because he has misplaced his rifle, must flee to his shame at the first sound of alarm.[16] Having given the warning, John returns to the narrative.

The army gathers, but who musters it? John states, "He gathered them together" (v. 16, KJV). The singular pronoun suggests it was neither the frogs nor the evil triumvirate. Most likely the reference is to God, for everything is proceeding exactly as he has planned. The evil host is gathered to one spot where he can more easily dispose of it.

John calls this place "Armageddon." Just what he had in mind is unclear due to ambiguity with the term. The Greek form is *Harmagdōn*. John states that this is a transliteration of a Hebrew word, but he does not supply the word. Many feel it should be "har-magedon," meaning "the mount of Megiddo." If this is the case then the reference would be to an ancient fortress that guarded one of the major highways going through the Jezreel valley to and from Jerusalem. Megiddo was the site for a number of famous battles, perhaps the most celebrated being the defeat of Sisera and his army when "the stars in their courses fought against Sisera" (Judg. 5:19–20). Also in the valley Esdraelon (Jezreel), Gideon's three hundred soldiers roundly defeated the Midianites (see Judg. 7); Saul and Jonathan met their end (see 1 Sam. 31:1–6); and king Josiah fought Pharaoh Neco and was killed (see 2 Kgs. 23:29–30).

A problem arises in that there is no reference to a "Mount Megiddo" in any ancient writing. Scriptural references abound for Megiddo and its three small towns (see Josh. 17:11; Judg. 1:27),[17] to "the waters of Megiddo" (Judg. 5:19, KJV), and even to "the valley of Megiddo" (2 Chr. 35:22, KJV; Zech. 12:11), but there is not a whisper about a mount with the name Megiddo. In John's day, the site of the city would have been little more than seventy feet above the plain. That hardly qualifies for the epithet "mountain."

Other scholars have suggested that "Har" identifies Mount Carmel and "Megadon" as the citadel Megiddo, both being alluded to in the same breath. Others translate the expression as the mount of assembly mentioned in Isaiah 14:13; or "his [Jehovah's] fruitful field," or "the desirable city" meaning Jerusalem, still others as the "marauding mountain" paralleling Jeremiah's destroying mountain (see 51:25).[18]

Whatever John had in mind, one thing seems clear: as with his other names, the intent is symbolic. The final battle is not to end in northern Israel but at Jerusalem. Zechariah connects Jerusalem and Megiddo in this context (see 12:10–11). The mountain that is the object of the battle must be the Mountain of the Lord's House, for, as has been shown, the battle is essentially religious: one ideology and theology against another. Therefore, the beast must eventually destroy the Mountain of the Lord's

House, the seat of God's power on earth, if he is to reign supreme.[19]

THE SEVENTH BOWL (vv. 17–21)

17 And the seventh angel poured out his vial into the air; and there came a great voice out of the temple of heaven, from the throne, saying, It is done.

18 And there were voices, and thunders, and lightnings; and there was a great earthquake, such as was not since men were upon the earth, so mighty an earthquake, and so great.

19 And the great city was divided into three parts, and the cities of the nations fell: and great Babylon came in remembrance before God, to give unto her the cup of the wine of the fierceness of his wrath.

20 And every island fled away, and the mountains were not found.

21 And there fell upon men a great hail out of heaven, every stone about the weight of a talent: and men blasphemed God because of the plague of the hail; for the plague thereof was exceeding great.

With the seventh bowl, the voice emanating from both the temple and the throne declares, "It is done" (KJV). The combining of both the throne and temple suggests the absolute authority by which God accomplishes his will. He invokes both kingly and priestly authority. The pouring out of the seventh bowl fully executes the will of God. As John said in 11:18, the time has come to destroy those who destroyed the earth.

In vivid language, John describes the power God unleashes against the wicked: thunder, lightning, tumult, and finally an earthquake of unprecedented proportions (cf. Dan. 12:1). "For, with you saith the Lord Almighty, I will rend their kingdoms; I will not only shake the earth, but the starry heavens shall tremble" (D&C 84:118). In reality, all this is nothing less than the preparation of the earth for its paradisiacal state.

> He shall utter his voice out of Zion, and he shall speak from Jerusalem, and his voice shall be heard among all people; and it shall be a voice as the voice of many waters, and as the voice of a great thunder, which shall break down the mountains, and the valleys shall not be found. He shall command the great deep, and it shall be driven back into the north countries, and the islands shall become one land; and the land of Jerusalem and the land of Zion shall be turned back into their own

place, and the earth shall be like as it was in the days before it was divided. And the Lord, even the Savior, shall stand in the midst of his people, and shall reign over all flesh (D&C 133:21–25).

The earthquake causes the fall of the cities of the nations: "The great city was divided into three parts" (v. 19, KJV). The focus appears to be on Babylon, divided into thirds, symbolic of the fullness of the divine wrath that strikes her to her destruction. Men have long stood in fear of the power of the earthquake. Here the force of God rocks the lands, and entire civilizations fall at the blow. Babylon herself comes down, her division becoming a mortal wound.

Associated with the seventh bowl, John sees one last plague of tremendous proportions. As was the earthquake, this one is not directed at the cities and nations under the power of spiritual Babylon. The new threat is directed at the people who inhabit those cities: "There fell upon men a great hail out of heaven, every stone about the weight of a talent" (v. 21, KJV). From the days Moses brought this plague upon Egypt, hail has served as both the symbol and reality of God's judgment upon hardened mankind (see, e.g., Ex. 9:18–26; Ps. 78:47; 105:32; Josh. 10:11).[20]

Here the weight of each stone is between 60 to 80 pounds. Through this symbol, John describes the pounding power that will bring all men to their knees. But it will not bring penitence. Once again John notes how hardened these men have become who can only curse God and wish to die and who never for a second consider repentance. Little wonder that the angels declared that God's judgments against the wicked were entirely true and just.

CONCLUSION

After bringing his reader three times to the point of judgment, John finally shows its execution. Sandwiched between all the symbolically graphic material is a warning to the Saints: watch and be prepared (see v. 15). Now is the time to set that watch. The Lord has charged his prophets to "prepare the saints for the hour of judgment which is to come; that their souls may escape the wrath of God, the desolation of abomination which awaits the wicked, both in this world and in the world to come" (D&C 88:84–85). To the Saints, he commands: "Entangle not yourselves in sin, but let your hands be clean, until the Lord comes. For not many days hence and the earth shall tremble and reel to and fro as a drunken man. . . . [For] after your testimony cometh wrath and indignation upon the people" (D&C 88:86–88).

The world must respond to the cry of repentance or face the consequences. Chapter sixteen describes what will happen to those who will not repent. Ironically, their refusal to repent is the very thing that continues the plagues. They curse God when they should be blaming themselves. God is not the cause of their misery—they are. But they are too blinded, too hardened, too spiritually dead to see it. They bring upon themselves the fires of Hades even in mortality. Yet while they hate it, their minds have become so perverted that the filth of hell seems better than the purity of heaven. And thus they die.

CHAPTER 17

BABYLON THE GREAT

(AN ANALYSIS OF REVELATION 17)

THE WOMAN AND THE BEAST (vv. 1–3)

1 And there came one of the seven angels which had the seven vials, and talked with me, saying unto me, Come hither; I will shew unto thee the judgment of the great whore that sitteth upon many waters:

2 With whom the kings of the earth have committed fornication, and the inhabitants of the earth have been made drunk with the wine of her fornication.

3 So he carried me away in the spirit into the wilderness: and I saw a woman sit upon a scarlet coloured beast, full of names of blasphemy, having seven heads and ten horns.

To John, an angel cries: "Come hither, I will shew unto thee the judgment of the great whore" (v. 1, KJV). With those words, the angel invites John to take a microscopic view of the destruction of that prepossessing evil "that sitteth upon many waters." The imagery rests on Jeremiah 51:13, where the prophet describes ancient Babylon as the city that "dwellest upon many waters, abundant in treasure" (KJV). The waters the woman sits upon represent "peoples, and multitudes, and nations, and tongues" whom the harlot rules (v. 15, KJV). Little wonder that the angel calls her "great," an adjective denoting quantity not quality.

To find the harlot, they go into the wilderness. The last time John viewed the wilderness, a different woman was there — the virtuous mother, the pure church of God. Now upon his return,

184

that woman is gone, and in her place sits another "upon a scarlet coloured beast, full of names of blasphemy, having seven heads and ten horns" (v. 3, KJV). The great woman reeks of prostitution and revels in sin as she urges the beast forward. But the harlot is not the master of the beast. They form a union, a mutual bond of assistance. Indeed, the beast supports and sustains the woman while the woman seduces men to honor the beast.

Some commentators speculate that the immoral woman represents the true church become apostate through the seduction of the philosophy and propaganda of the beast. They base this argument on the idea that the harlot and the woman are both in the same place, the wilderness. However, the assumption does not necessarily hold. The wilderness has a dual symbolism in the scriptures. On the one hand, it denotes a place of discipline and protection where the Lord "made his own people to go forth like sheep, and guided them in the wilderness like a flock" (Ps. 78:52, KJV). Indeed, his people "shall dwell safely in the wilderness, and sleep in the woods" (Ezek. 34:25, KJV). On the other hand, those who are not his people shall find their habitation "a desolation, and dry like the wilderness," full of wild beasts, and the haunt of scavengers. (Zeph. 2:13.) Therefore, the wilderness may be the abode of peace, protection, and divine schooling with God's assistance, or it may be the place of desolation, desertion, and death without him. The Church is in the first place, the whore exists in the second.[1]

The close connection between the two women, however, seems deliberate. The harlot with her beast is the reverse image of the woman with the man child. Herein stands an interesting contrast: the Church produces the kingdom of God, a heavenly society, while conversely, the kingdom of the devil produces and sustains Babylon, the degenerate society. Unlike the virtuous woman, the whore has no son; indeed, one of her most striking features is her perpetual barrenness. All her glitter and ornamentation do not hide the reality; she personifies sterility and death.[2]

John views the period just before the end time when nearly all the world follows after the whore, committing economic, political, and religious immoralities for both pleasure and gain. By promoting her objectives, society purchases her favors; and as flatterers and sycophants, they yield to her whims. No class of society is without representation; all have become intoxicated with her lusts. As Isaiah prophesied, "They are drunken, but not with wine; they stagger, but not with strong drink" (29:9, KJV). The Old Testament uses harlotry as a symbol for inordinate wealth-getting that arises through commerce and trade. Ezekiel blasts Israel with the words: "Thou hast played the whore also with the Assyrians, because thou wast unsatiable; yea, thou hast played the harlot with them, and yet couldest not be satisfied. Thou hast moreover multiplied thy fornication in the land of Canaan unto Chaldea; and yet thou wast not satisfied herewith" (16:28–29, KJV). In the last days, the inebriating wine of materialism and unchastity fills their souls; the liquor of selfishness dissipates them.

Nephi notes that the great and abominable church had its genesis just before the Lord's apostles died. Its members, called the children of the devil, removed plain and precious parts from the Bible. The purpose was to entrap the unwary in Satan's snare. They were largely effective, for Nephi sees that "an exceedingly great many do stumble, yea, insomuch that Satan hath great power over them" (1 Ne. 13:29). Then looking at the last days, Nephi notes that this same institution will dig a great pit, a kind of doorway to hell, for the destruction of men. At the same time God will work a great work "which shall be everlasting, either on the one hand or on the other — either to the convincing of them unto peace and life eternal, or unto the deliverance of them . . . to the captivity of the devil" (1 Ne. 14:7). Nowhere does he identify the historical name of the great and abominable church or any of the institutions that support it.

The beast that supports the woman appears to be the monster that came up from the sea. Its color, horns, and heads are the same as the dragon's, but it is more closely associated with blasphemy. In chapter thirteen John states that the monster wore "upon his heads the name of blasphemy" (v. 1, KJV) and that he "opened his mouth in blasphemy against God, to blaspheme his name" (v. 6, KJV). The beast in the wilderness is "full of the names of blasphemy" (17:3, AT). Clearly the beast that supports the mistress has become the embodiment of sacrilege.

This does not mean that it merely defiles and reviles the name of God. It goes even further by claiming the very attributes of deity; indeed, of being deity itself. Second Thessalonians 2:3–4 tells us that the "son of perdition . . . opposeth and exalteth himself above all that is called God, or that is worshipped; so that he as God sitteth in the temple of God, shewing himself that he is God" (KJV). The special form this blasphemy takes is the claim of savior. But the salvation the dragon offers is the momentary thrill—the cheap pleasure of the prostitute that is fleeting, empty, and immoral. The beast's seductive promises are anchored solely in the illusion that one can find happiness and security in iniquity.

Scarlet radiates from the beast and the dress of the woman. The blush reflects the essence of the dragon from which both monster and rider receive their power. But it is not the same color as that of the dragon. John described the old serpent as *purros*, fiery red. The color here is *kokkinos*, crimson blended with dark blue. A ribbon of this color, representing the sins of Israel, was tied round the neck of the scapegoat on the Day of Atonement before it was driven into the wilderness to its death.[3] It became indirectly associated with harlotry and the deep sins of ungodly conduct. (See Isa. 1:18; Ps. 51:7.) The color stands in contrast to the white robes of the redeemed and of the gown of the bride of the Lamb (see 19:8).[4]

THE GREAT WHORE BABYLON (vv. 4–6)

4 And the woman was arrayed in purple and scarlet colour, and decked with gold and precious stones and pearls, having a golden cup in her hand full of abominations and filthiness of her fornication:

5 And upon her forehead was a name written, MYSTERY, BAB-YLON THE GREAT, THE MOTHER OF HARLOTS AND ABOMINATIONS OF THE EARTH.

6 And I saw the woman drunken with the blood of the saints, and with the blood of the martyrs of Jesus: and when I saw her, I wondered with great admiration.

Since God directs his total wrath against the harlot, understanding what she represents is important. First and foremost, she reeks with the stench of gross immorality. The figure of the harlot is used consistently in the Old Testament to represent spiritual apostasy, the deliberate and willful rebellion against God and his covenants. This disobedience results in a kind of false worship that draws strength, momentum, and addiction from selfishness and pride.

The harlot drinks from a golden cup filled with abominations and corruption (cf. Jer. 7–8). This stands in contrast to the golden chalice held by the Levitical high priest and used in the temple for making a wine offering to God.[5] But this is not the only imitation of holy things that John associates with the woman. Purple and scarlet comprise her clothing. These colors, along with white and blue, dominate the fabric of the veils and interior of the temple as well as the vestments of the high priest. Further, the high priest wore a mitre. Engraven upon a golden plate fastened to it were the words "Holiness to the Lord," identifying the priest as the Lord's own. The whore also wears an inscription upon her brow proclaiming her threefold status as "MYSTERY, BABYLON THE GREAT, THE MOTHER OF HARLOTS AND ABOMINATIONS OF THE EARTH" (v. 5, KJV). Unlike the high priest, she belongs to no one. No covenant ties her to one order or loyalty. She is faithful only to herself.

Through these images, John paints the picture of a priestess-harlot standing as a counterfeit high priest.[6] The woman, therefore, represents more than rulers or nations with their attendant power (the beast's heads and its horns do that). The woman epitomizes a religious-philosophical or theological system through which men are seduced to worship the dragon. For this reason she combines elements of both the first and second beast but more especially those of the false prophet.

She bears the name: "MYSTERY." Significantly, the word not only makes up part of her name, but also stands as the leading element. The term generally refers to the most holy teachings and doctrines of God kept from the profane world. Paul speaks of the Apostles as "stewards of the mysteries of

God" (1 Cor. 4:1, KJV). Only "the power of the Holy Ghost" reveals these mysteries (1 Ne. 10:19), which remain in the temple and constitute in large measure the mysteries of God. The woman represents counterfeit ordinances with their secret oaths and binding covenants, a kind of pseudoworship containing "secret combinations of murder and all manner of secret works of darkness" (2 Ne. 9:9). These are "the combinations of the devil, for he is the founder of all these things" (2 Ne. 26:22). These combinations constitute the "ABOMINATIONS OF THE EARTH" (Rev. 17:5, KJV; cf. 3 Ne. 5:6). They also form the last part of the harlot's titles.

In the Bible the term *abomination* describes those things so vile that they rouse the instant wrath of God. In their worse form, they are called "the abomination of desolation" and are associated with the corruption of the temple (cf. Dan. 11:31; Matt. 24:15). Their presence in the temple causes God's spirit to withdraw, leaving the sanctuary fully exposed to destruction. In particular, the Greek form of the word *bdelugma* denotes idolatry and harlotry, especially when combined to create a maleficent worship (see Deut. 29:26; 2 Chr. 28:3).[7]

This worship has its objectives: the acquisition of wealth and luxury at the expense of righteousness and decency. The whore represents those forces that move the world to wholesale adoption of the Mahanic principle. For this reason, it stands counter to the Christian objectives of service, virtue, and love. In self-defense born of a seared conscience, the whore mocks, derides, and openly persecutes the Church of God. So severe is her hatred that she is only satisfied when she can glut herself on the wine of their tears and blood.

John also identifies the woman as "Babylon." This image will be discussed more fully in chapter eighteen, but note here that the ancient city had the reputation of being the first where men combined against God with the deliberate goal of frustrating and wresting control from him. It was where a false theological system fought against the true (see Gen. 11:1–9). In the first and last books of the Bible, Babylon incarnates arrogance, pride, and insatiable corruption in opposition to God and his kingdom. It stands in contrast to the heavenly city, the New Jerusalem, where the law of God thrives.

In this image Babylon represents a real historical organization. Nephi saw the devil establish it among the nations and kingdoms of the Gentiles (see 1 Ne. 13:4–6), and he traced its continual existence into the present (see 1 Ne. 13:26–29; 14:1–17). That prophet makes it clear, however, that it is composed of more then one entity. He notes that "*they* have taken away from the gospel of the Lamb many parts which are plain and most precious. . . . And all this have *they* done that *they* might pervert the right ways of the Lord" (1 Ne. 13:26–27, italics added). Seeing spiritual Babylon as only one association, either at its inception or today, would therefore be wrong. It symbolizes all leagues that may be properly called Antichrist, that pervert the right way of the Lord, and that promote antichristian principles and life-styles.[8]

The term *Antichrist* seems to fit well with the whore in the form of Babylon. The term comes out of the writings of John (1 Jn. 2:18, 22; 4:3; 2 Jn. 1:7) where it takes the form of a collective order. Babylon is the symbol for this group. The historical reality takes first the form of false teachers moving out from the true church with the purpose of deception, and then the leagues that base themselves upon and promulgate these falsehoods.

John's two motifs make apparent two major aspects of the same phenomenon: the figure of the city portrays the historical bodies, the figure of the woman the essence of their souls.[9] Both operate among the nations of the world. Taken together they symbolize a kind of state-cult that combines with local and national governments to impose its sham religious system upon men.[10] Such a system can be either theistic or atheistic. As one scholar put it, "The whore provides the theory; government provides the muscle."[11] Both together compose the state-church.

THE MYSTERY OF THE BEAST (vv. 7–13)

7 And the angel said unto me, Wherefore didst thou marvel? I will tell thee the mystery of the woman, and of the beast that carrieth her, which hath the seven heads and ten horns.

8 The beast that thou sawest was, and is not; and shall ascend out of the bottomless pit, and go into perdition: and they that dwell on the earth shall wonder, whose names were not written in the book of life from the foundation of the world, when they behold the beast that was, and is not, and yet is.

9 And here is the mind which hath wisdom. The seven heads are seven mountains, on which the woman sitteth.

10 And there are seven kings: five are fallen, and one is, and the other is not yet come; and when he cometh, he must continue a short space.

11 And the beast that was, and is not, even he is the eighth, and is of the seven, and goeth into perdition.

12 And the ten horns which thou sawest are ten kings, which have received no kingdom as yet; but receive power as kings one hour with the beast.

13 These have one mind, and shall give their power and strength unto the beast.

The greatness of the woman's power causes John to feel nothing short of consternation (see v. 6). The Greek word *thaumazō*, translated "admiration" in the KJV, means to be amazed, to wonder, to be astonished. The common element seems to be incredulous surprise.[12] The context dictates the positive or negative sense of the word. Here the context suggests the translation "consternation," rather than "admiration" as used in the KJV. Seeing John's reaction, the angel asks, "Why didst thou marvel? I will tell thee of the mystery of the woman and of the beast" (v. 7, AT).

The messenger begins with the monster. It is the same beast John depicted in chapter thirteen. As noted there, the description shows that it is a counterfeit of the Lamb of God: "The beast that thou sawest was, and is not; and shall ascend out of the bottomless pit" (v. 8, KJV). As noted earlier, this statement stands in contrast to the description of the Savior as "the Lord, which is, and which was, and which is to come" (1:8, KJV). The Savior is the great Jehovah who exists from everlasting to everlasting (see D&C 20:17; 61:1). The beast is, at best, only a momentary reality. John's statement that he "is not" suggests his shadowy nature. He seems to have suffered death, but in reality he is but momentarily in the abyss, waiting to arise.[13]

Again a backhanded parallel emerges. This satanically inspired power imitates the resurrecting power of the divine Lamb who died and came back to life. The beast returns to hurl itself in fury against the kingdom of God. This resiliency causes those who "dwell on the earth" to wonder "when they behold the beast that was, and is not, and yet is" (v. 8, KJV). John can see that the beast is neither dead nor gone, it is only hidden; it still pulls the strings and will do so until the day it emerges full force from the abyss.

The last of its descriptive phrases, "and yet is" (Greek *kai parestai*), has the same root as the Greek word *parousia*, a technical term used to describe the arrival of an emperor and used consistently for the second coming of the Lord. The word appears in 1 Thessalonians 4:15–17 and 2 Thessalonians 2:1, where it is translated in the KJV with the phrase "the coming of the Lord." It is also used as a title for the Lord in Revelation 1:8. Here in 17:8 the angel connects it with the ascent of the beast out of the abyss. As the Savior will have his second coming, so too the monster will have its diabolical parousia.[14] This will not be long lasting, for, from the moment it arises, it shall move relentlessly toward its final destiny—perdition.

The beast, as viewed in chapter seventeen, is thus not a particular political organization but a composite entity working from a common ideology that pits government against true religion. Mutual support therefore exists between the beast, its heads, and its horns. In this light John states, "These have one mind," which is the mind of the beast, and they "shall give their power and strength unto the beast" so that his perverse theology may be imposed upon all (v. 13, KJV).

John begins the interpretation of the heads and horns with an admonition, "Here is the mind which hath wisdom" (v. 9, KJV). John seems to be warning his reader that the reality behind the symbols is not obvious. The amount of scholarly generated speculation accentuates this. Unfortunately, Latter-day Saints have no better understanding than the rest of the world. No prophetic or scriptural commentary exists to help decipher this portion of John's revelation. Though Nephi seems to have seen the historical period covered in this part of Revelation, he focuses only on the great whore. He tells us nothing about the kings or other institutions that support and sustain her. Even so, there are a few generalities that can be said about her adherents.

John states that "the seven heads are seven mountains, on which the woman sitteth" (v. 9, KJV). The allusion to seven hills best fits Rome, which was called the city of seven hills[15] and certainly manifested the spirit of the great beast in John's day. However, Rome itself stands as a symbol of the archetypal Babylon. As the number for completeness, seven not only symbolizes the power exercised by Rome in John's day, but it also denotes the political powers of the latter days.[16]

Associated with the hills are seven kings. More than likely they represent Roman rulers contemporary with John. A number of schemes have been created to identify these rulers. None, however, have found universal acceptance.[17] John states that the beast "is the eighth, and is of the seven" (v. 11, KJV). It has been speculated at great length, due to a myth circulating among the Romans in the last half of the first century, that the eighth emperor represents Nero. In spite of knowledge of his death in A.D. 68, a rumor persisted that he had actually escaped to Parthia in the east and would return to recapture the empire. Many feel that the beast represents this Nero *redivivus*. The problem is that such a view leaves the prophecy of John unfulfilled. Others argue that the eighth is Domitian, who embodied the evil disposition of Nero against the Christians.[18] Note that the monster is not one of the seven (the Greek reads *kai ek ton hepta estin*) but encapsulates all of them, for they all play the same role.

Affiliated with these are certain kings, probably representing institutions that would come into being after the period of Roman rule, for John states that they "have received no kingdom as yet" (v. 12, KJV). John uses the number ten to describe them, symbolically representing the whole of a part. As applied to the kings, it suggests that they represent all those kingdoms and rulers whom the great whore seduces and who, therefore, adopt her philosophy and manner. But they do not represent all kingdoms. The kingdom of God particularly, as John has shown, stands apart.

The beast is ever present but holds greatest hegemony in

the latter days, the period of the ten kings. At that time, he will be able to make many nations subservient to his will. Taking up his banner, the nations will war against the Messiah.[19] But the time of their rule will be short, for they "receive power as kings one hour with the beast" (v. 12, KJV). Here, John also notes that their kingly authority is derived. Whoever gives the authority can set the limits and strength of the power. Once again, the Seer subtly shows that God controls all. The machinations of both the kings and the beast work God's will, to their total frustration. Indeed, the Lord will win, "for he is Lord of lords, and King of kings" (v. 14, KJV), unlike the rulers of the earth who are but pseudokings. John is perfectly consistent with the Bible and Jewish apocalyptic literature in applying the superlative title "Lord of lords and King of kings" to deity (see, e.g., Deut. 10:17).[20]

THE FALL OF THE HARLOT (vv. 14–18)

14 These shall make war with the Lamb, and the Lamb shall overcome them: for he is Lord of lords, and King of kings: and they that are with him are called, and chosen, and faithful.

15 And he saith unto me, The waters which thou sawest, where the whore sitteth, are peoples, and multitudes, and nations, and tongues.

16 And the ten horns which thou sawest upon the beast, these shall hate the whore, and shall make her desolate and naked, and shall eat her flesh, and burn her with fire.

17 For God hath put in their hearts to fulfil his will, and to agree, and give their kingdom unto the beast, until the words of God shall be fulfilled.

18 And the woman which thou sawest is that great city, which reigneth over the kings of the earth.

The beasts gather the Babylonian portion of mankind into a great war. The frogs of chapter sixteen efficiently spread their seductive propaganda (see v. 14). A great army forms in response and moves forth with one objective: destruction. Of this period, Ezekiel proclaimed:

> After many days thou [Gog of Magog] shalt be visited: in the latter years thou shalt come into the land that is brought back from the sword, and is gathered out of many people, against the mountains of Israel, which have been always waste:

but it is brought forth out of the nations, and they shall dwell safely all of them. Thou shalt ascend and come like a storm, thou shalt be like a cloud to cover the land, thou, and all thy bands, and many people with thee.

Thus saith the Lord God; It shall also come to pass, that at the same time shall things come into thy mind, and thou shalt think an evil thought: and thou shalt say, I will go up to the land of unwalled villages; I will go to them that are at rest, that dwell safely, all of them dwelling without walls, and having neither bars nor gates, to take a spoil, and to take a prey; to turn thine hand upon the desolate places that are now inhabited, and upon the people that are gathered out of the nations, which have gotten cattle and goods, that dwell in the midst of the land (Ezek. 38:8–12, KJV).

But things do not go as planned.

At the same time when Gog shall come against the land of Israel, saith the Lord God, that my fury shall come up in my face. For in my jealousy and in the fire of my wrath have I spoken, Surely in that day there shall be a great shaking in the land of Israel; so that the fishes of the sea, and the fowls of the heaven, and the beasts of the field, and all creeping things that creep upon the earth, and all the men that are upon the face of the earth, shall shake at my presence, and the mountains shall be thrown down, and the steep places shall fall, and every wall shall fall to the ground.

And I will call for a sword against him throughout all my mountains, saith the Lord God: every man's sword shall be against his brother. And I will plead against him with pestilence and with blood; and I will rain upon him, and upon his bands, and upon the many people that are with him, an overflowing rain, and great hailstones, fire, and brimstone. Thus will I magnify myself, and sanctify myself; and I will be known in the eyes of many nations, and they shall know that I am the Lord (Ezek. 38:18–23, KJV).

Thus, a kind of civil war will erupt that brings down the whore with all her power. John makes it clear, despite the apparent chaos, that God designed the whole thing to happen this way. Nephi seems to have had this same period in mind when when he prophesied: "I beheld that the great mother of abominations did gather together multitudes upon the face of the earth, among all the nations of the Gentiles, to fight against the Lamb of God. And it came to pass that I, Nephi, beheld the power of the Lamb of God, that it descended upon the saints of the church of the Lamb, and upon the covenant people of the Lord, who were scattered upon all the face of the earth; and they were armed with righteousness and with the power of God in great glory" (1 Ne. 14:13–14). The enemy cannot win against the power of the Lamb. In frustration and rage, the nations will turn upon the whore who drove them to the fight and "shall hate the whore, and shall make her desolate and naked, and shall eat her flesh, and burn her with fire" (Rev. 17:16, KJV; cf. Ezek. 23:25–30). The attackers carry the seeds of their own destruction.

The task of the Saints is to rely on God and continue in the faith unto the end. Apparently, the Saints do not fight though they are present. They do not need to: rather than physical, their weapons are spiritual, that is, being faithful and bearing witness. John identifies them as the "called, and chosen, and faithful" (Rev. 17:14, KJV). Though there is a Jewish tradition that the righteous take direct part in the destruction of the wicked, this is not an act of revenge but the fulfillment of righteous retribution.[21]

CONCLUSION

The prominence of the whore in the drama of the latter days shows that when men cease to worship God, they do not cease to worship. They turn to a false form of religion to establish meaning and direction in life. The whore provides them with a "priestess" counter to God's true priests, with false rites in contrast to God's saving ordinances and with useless sacrifices in opposition to the Lord's effective ones. Both God and the beast demand a lot, but the beast renders nothing in return while the Lord blesses with everything.

The Seer casts the great evil of the last days in a double form. One is that of the seductive and shameless harlot, reveling in the slaughter of the righteous. The other is that of the great city Babylon, mother of abominations, dominating kings and kingdoms while crushing truth, virtue, and love. The image of the harlot and the city, taken together, represents the formation of a kind of state religion that is able to impose its will on the people. During this period the warning words of John hold true: "Here is the patience and faith of the Saints" (13:10, KJV; cf. 14:12). Indeed, this is the time—as with the Saints in John's own day, waiting, forbidden to take the offensive against the whore, concerned with doing nothing but good works—when the Saints need great faith and patience most. In the end, these attributes will prove to be the very tools of victory.

The Fall of Babylon the Great

(AN ANALYSIS OF REVELATION 18)

SINS THAT REACH UNTO HEAVEN (vv. 1–8)

1 And after these things I saw another angel come down from heaven, having great power; and the earth was lightened with his glory.

2 And he cried mightily with a strong voice, saying, Babylon the great is fallen, is fallen, and is become the habitation of devils, and the hold of every foul spirit, and a cage of every unclean and hateful bird.

3 For all nations have drunk of the wine of the wrath of her fornication, and the kings of the earth have committed fornication with her, and the merchants of the earth are waxed rich through the abundance of her delicacies.

4 And I heard another voice from heaven, saying, Come out of her, my people, that ye be not partakers of her sins, and that ye receive not of her plagues.

5 For her sins have reached unto heaven, and God hath remembered her iniquities.

6 Reward her even as she rewarded you, and double unto her double according to her works: in the cup which she hath filled fill to her double.

7 How much she hath glorified herself, and lived deliciously, so much torment and sorrow give her: for she saith in her heart, I sit a queen, and am no widow, and shall see no sorrow.

8 Therefore shall her plagues come in one day, death, and mourning, and famine; and she shall be utterly burned with fire: for strong is the Lord God who judgeth her.

Chapter eighteen fulfills the promise of the angel that he would show to John "the judgment of the great whore" (17:1, KJV).

John sees an angel radiant with power and glory descend from heaven, "and the earth was lightened with his glory" (18:1, KJV). The imagery parallels that found in Ezekiel. In a grand vision, that prophet saw the heavens open and a restoration commence in which the glory of the Lord returned to his temple and overspread his people, "and the earth shined with his glory" (Ezek. 43:2, KJV). From this we gather that the angel John sees, in spite of the gloomy nature of his dirge that "Babylon the great is fallen" (Rev. 18:2, KJV), bears the power of the gospel. He does not exult over the overthrow of the woman but proclaims the triumph of the good. God has fully realized his purposes, and his people at last are ready to enjoy liberation from all oppression.[1]

The angel's proclamation describes the fallen city of Babylon as the great keep for devils, unclean spirits, and hateful birds. The latter inhabitants seem out of place with devils and spirits. In the Mosaic law, fowls that ate carrion were considered unclean (see Lev. 11:13–20). However, it is unlikely that John had this image in mind. The Old Testament associates fowl with the judgment of God upon a rebellious people. Out of this grew the association of something feeding upon the souls of men (see, e.g., Deut. 28:26; 1 Sam. 17:44; 1 Kgs. 14:11; Ps. 79:2; Isa. 18:6; Jer. 16:4; Ezek. 29:5). The birds thus probably symbolize in general those incorporeal forces that destroy the souls of men.

The fallen Babylon becomes a shattered palace and wretched prison for abomination because of the role she played with the leaders of the world, seducing them to partake without measure of her fornications. In this chapter the angel makes clear the true nature of her power of seduction—the allure of wealth. While earthly lords were guilty of economic dalliance, the merchants committed idolatry through the worship of mammon. The term *mammon* (Greek *mammonas*) means money in any form. It symbolizes avarice deified.

The leaders had ample opportunity: Babylon offered it all — for a price. She had cargos of gold, silver, precious stones, and pearls; clothiers who produced fine linen, purple, silk, and scarlet cloth; furniture makers and home decorators who used citron wood and made articles of ivory, costly wood, bronze, iron, and marble. The list goes on. She was the great supermarket carrying cinnamon and spice, incense, myrrh, frankincense, wine, oil, fine flour and wheat, cattle and sheep; her transportation department included horses and carriages.

Finally, she offered as slaves the very souls of men (see vv. 12–13). The word translated "slaves" is literally "bodies" (Greek *sōma*). Babylon seeks to reduce people to flesh that can be bought and sold for profit. In the conquest, men are dehumanized by the consorts of Babylon. This idea is brought out by the last phrase, "souls of men." This is an old Hebrew phrase depicting men as "little more than human livestock."[2] This last commodity shows the spiritual depth of Babylon's wickedness: she sold human beings, both old and young, male and female. Their lives were to be drained away to provide more for those whose fortunes were already so vast that not even the most lavish expenditures could deplete them.

John shows that Babylon's seductive power tempts almost everyone. In the face of this reality the angel gives a command and warning: "Come out of her, my people . . . that ye receive not of her plagues" (v. 4, KJV). The Saints in the latter days have received the same warning: "The voice of the Lord is unto you: Go ye out of Babylon; gather ye out from among the nations, from the four winds, from one end of heaven to the other" (D&C 133:7). And more explicitly: "Go ye out from among the nations, even from Babylon, from the midst of wickedness, which is spiritual Babylon" (D&C 133:14). The Lord means the Saints to take him seriously; he warns: "After today cometh the burning—this is speaking after the manner of the Lord—for verily I say, tomorrow all the proud and they that do wickedly shall be as stubble; and I will burn them up, for I am the Lord of Hosts; and I will not spare any that remain in Babylon" (D&C 64:24).

So great is the total of her iniquities that it has reached, as it were, into heaven. And heaven pays her back for all her mischief. But the payback is not one for one—it is two for one, for she must satisfy the full measure of God's judgment. Therefore, that which she rendered shall be rendered to her doubled. Sins of commission *and* omission must both be accounted for.

John's vision shows a consistent belief in the *lex talionis,* the idea that punishment should match the crime. However, this is modified in two instances. The first modification affects those who refuse to come out of the great city. Her punishment, thereby, becomes their punishment. Because they have been warned, they will have to answer not only for their own sins, but for hers as well. The second alteration concerns those who do come out of her. Angels keep books of judgment in heaven (see 20:12). But what the books contain is a matter of what God chooses to remember, *not* what he chooses to forget. He has promised that, when his people repent and become one with him, "I will remember their sin no more" (Jer. 31:34, KJV). As one scholar noted, what "God forgives, he also forgets; and what God forgets is blotted for ever from the record (Jer. xxxi.34)."[3] When men and women forsake Babylon, God forgets they were ever there.

One of the great sins of Babylon is that she glorifies herself. "I sit a queen, and am no widow," she exults (v. 7, KJV; cf. Isa. 47:7–8). Her fault is twofold: boastful arrogance, and total faith in her boundless resources without a whisper of conscience.[4] Her death shall be swift, "in one day," and full, "she shall be utterly burned with fire" (v. 8, KJV). Her fate is significant. John's harlot is no commoner. As has been noted earlier, she represents a priestly class. The Levitical punishment for adultery or harlotry for the daughter of a priest was burning (see Lev. 21:9). For the nonpriestly class, the less torturous punishments of strangulation or stoning were employed. Babylon, as apostate — even idolatrous religion — deserves her fate.[5]

THE THREE DIRGES (vv. 9–19)

9 And the kings of the earth, who have committed fornication and lived deliciously with her, shall bewail her, and lament for her, when they shall see the smoke of her burning,

10 Standing afar off for the fear of her torment, saying, Alas, alas, that great city Babylon, that mighty city! for in one hour is thy judgment come.

11 And the merchants of the

earth shall weep and mourn over her; for no man buyeth their merchandise any more:

12 The merchandise of gold, and silver, and precious stones, and of pearls, and fine linen, and purple, and silk, and scarlet, and all thyine wood, and all manner vessels of ivory, and all manner vessels of most precious wood, and of brass, and iron, and marble,

13 And cinnamon, and odours, and ointments, and frankincense, and wine, and oil, and fine flour, and wheat, and beasts, and sheep, and horses, and chariots, and slaves, and souls of men.

14 And the fruits that thy soul lusted after are departed from thee, and all things which were dainty and goodly are departed from thee, and thou shalt find them no more at all.

15 The merchants of these things, which were made rich by her, shall stand afar off for the fear of her torment, weeping and wailing,

16 And saying, Alas, alas, that great city, that was clothed in fine linen, and purple, and scarlet, and decked with gold, and precious stones, and pearls!

17 For in one hour so great riches is come to nought. And every shipmaster, and all the company in ships, and sailors, and as many as trade by sea, stood afar off,

18 And cried when they saw the smoke of her burning, saying, What city is like unto this great city!

19 And they cast dust on their heads, and cried, weeping and wailing, saying, Alas, alas, that great city, wherein were made rich all that had ships in the sea by reason of her costliness! for in one hour is she made desolate.

The smoldering ashes of Babylon become the smoke signals of her own destruction. As they ascend upward in tribute to the omnipotence of God, her lovers' lamentations also rise. The kings of the earth (vv. 9–10), the merchants (vv. 11–17), and all those in the maritime trades (vv. 17–19) sing dirges.[6] Each has his special reason for sorrow. The kings lament because they have lost their mistress, she who provided them with such great satisfaction. The merchants weep and mourn because suddenly their overstocked wares are worthless. Finally, the sailors "cast dust on their heads" (v. 19, KJV) and weep and wail because the appetite of Babylon was what made them wealthy.

The Seer shows that without the false values of Babylon, the merchants and sea lords cannot foist their goods upon mankind. The whole of their marketing enterprise is built upon a pretense sustained by the creation of artificial needs. They do this by simple tricks of marketing through which warmth becomes mink; shelter becomes marble and brass; food becomes escargot and caviar. And when the bottom falls out of the market, the kings are left without taxes, armies, or treasuries, and the merchants with rotting cargos and glutted stockpiles that no one will buy.

THE GREAT REJOICING (vv. 20–24)

20 Rejoice over her, thou heaven, and ye holy apostles and prophets; for God hath avenged you on her.

21 And a mighty angel took up a stone like a great millstone, and cast it into the sea, saying, Thus with violence shall that great city Babylon be thrown down, and shall be found no more at all.

22 And the voice of harpers, and musicians, and of pipers, and trumpeters, shall be heard no more at all in thee; and no craftsman, of whatsoever craft he be,

shall be found any more in thee; and the sound of a millstone shall be heard no more at all in thee;

23 And the light of a candle shall shine no more at all in thee; and the voice of the bridegroom and of the bride shall be heard no more at all in thee: for thy merchants were the great men of the earth; for by thy sorceries were all nations deceived.

24 And in her was found the blood of prophets, and of saints, and of all that were slain upon the earth.

The command of the angel to "rejoice over her, O heavens, and the Saints, and apostles, and prophets, because God passed your judgment upon her" (v. 20, AT) stands in contrast to the lamentation of the men of the world (see vv. 9–19).[7] Twice John has intimated that the prayers of the Saints greatly influenced the time of the judgment. Here he indicates that more was going on than mere timing. The whore played the role of the great judge against the Saints. Now the tables are turned, and those the harlot once wrongfully judged become the judges.

All this is quite just according to divine law. God had set down two laws that apply — the law of bloodshed, and the law of the spiteful witness. According to the first, the life of a man is required if he slays a fellow man (see Gen. 9:5–6). According to the second, when a witness is found guilty of perjury, he receives the punishment he desired for his fellow (see Deut. 19:16–19). Here God allows the Saints, apostles, and prophets to pass sentence on the harlot. Of course, based on their own experience, they find her guilty of both perjury and murder. Because she brought forth false accusations and then passed the death sentence on holy men and women—"in her was found the blood of prophets, and of saints, and of all that were slain upon the earth" (v. 24, KJV)—she must forfeit her life.

An angel's symbolic act dramatizes the fate of the whore. He hurls a heavy millstone into the sea with the cry, "With violence shall that great city Babylon be thrown down, and shall be found no more at all" (v. 21, KJV). This act represents the complete and final demise of the harlot-city. As the massive stone could never rise again from the depths, so the great city will ever remain buried and lifeless (cf. Jer. 51:61–64).

CONCLUSION

The story of the tower of Babel is no mere myth; it provides historical background for understanding man's rebellion against God. The most impressive symbol of the Babylonian religion was its ziggurats, of which some ruins stand even to this day. As noted earlier in this work, they reveal the quest of base men to compete with the Gods by erecting colossal buildings, counterfeit holy mountains, where men could pretend to know the mysteries of God while promulgating unholy laws and base practices. These mountainlike towers stand in defiance of true faith and emphasize the growing gulf between God and the natural man.

The Book of Mormon testifies of God's wrath upon these people (see Ether 1:33), and what caused it? The arrogant Babylonians combined purely sensual and material principles with the lofty striving within the soul of man. Out of this grew the principle of spiritual fornication. Men mistook lust for joy, sought happiness through passion, and pursued security through materialism. The bit of graffiti, "He who dies with the most toys wins," could have been written as easily in Babylon as in New York, or Las Vegas. Today many still seek to find heaven through drugs, lust, money, success, or power. People continue to try to escape the deadly round of daily life through material and immoral means. The result merely mires them more deeply in the muck that spews from the pit in the abyss.

God has provided a solution: flee Babylon. The command demands a complete severing of relations. God allows no association whatsoever. There is good reason. Babylon is not to be converted but destroyed: "We would have healed Babylon, but she is not healed: forsake her" (Jer. 51:9, KJV). Any that linger in Babylon will be taken with her plagues, "For after today cometh the burning . . . and I will not spare any that remain in Babylon" (D&C 64:24). Therefore, the cry is "deliver thyself, O Zion, that dwellest with the daughter of Babylon" (Zech. 2:7, KJV).

CHAPTER 19

THE KING OF KINGS

(AN ANALYSIS OF REVELATION 19)

IN PRAISE OF A GOD OF JUDGMENT (vv. 1–5)

1 And after these things I heard a great voice of much people in heaven, saying, Alleluia; Salvation, and glory, and honour, and power, unto the Lord our God:

2 For true and righteous are his judgments: for he hath judged the great whore, which did corrupt the earth with her fornication, and hath avenged the blood of his servants at her hand.

3 And again they said, Alleluia. And her smoke rose up for ever and ever.

4 And the four and twenty elders and the four beasts fell down and worshipped God that sat on the throne, saying, Amen; Alleluia.

5 And a voice came out of the throne, saying, Praise our God, all ye his servants, and ye that fear him, both small and great.

Chapter nineteen continues the tempo of rejoicing begun in chapter eighteen. John hears the multitude of heaven joining in one unified act of praise: "Hallelujah; salvation, and glory, the honor, and power belong to our God" (v. 1, AT). The adoration focuses on those aspects of God revealed through his victory over Babylon. Exaltation, authority, and blessing all originate and end in him. Therefore, all honor is due him.

The heavenly host repeat the theme of the nature of God's judgments; they are both "true and righteous" (v. 2, KJV). The idea behind the term *true* (Greek *althēs*) is "exact" or "correct" but goes beyond that. The word conveys the idea of legitimacy.[1]

The term righteous (Greek *dikaios*) denotes what is in keeping with the sovereignty of God, by which his laws are kept inviolate. Out of this grows the rest of the praise: "He hath judged the great whore . . . and hath avenged the blood of his servants" (v. 2, KJV). Judgment always comes. Though God may delay the time in accordance with his designs, it is inevitable. The world will learn that mercy cannot rob justice.

Mankind can have faith in God because before all else he is just. As the Book of Mormon prophet Alma explained to one of his sons: "The work of justice could not be destroyed; if so, God would cease to be God" (Alma 42:13). Further, "there is a law given, and a punishment affixed, and a repentance granted; which repentance mercy claimeth; otherwise, justice claimeth the creature and executeth the law, and the law inflicteth the punishment; if not so, the works of justice would be destroyed, and God would cease to be God" (v. 22). The point is that God gave the law that inflicts the punishment upon those who will not repent. This is totally just. Thus, God "changeth not; if so he would cease to be God; and he ceaseth not to be God" — that is, a God of justice (Morm. 9:19). John shows that the unrepentant world will learn this lesson too late.

During this act of praise, a voice from the throne speaks. When a voice near the altar spoke in a former vision (see 16:7), the focus was on the witness and suffering of the Saints. In the present vision, the Saints suffer no longer. Thus, from the source of government — for God is on his throne — goes forth the call to praise (see v. 5). All the heavenly host join in the anthem. But just at this moment, a shift occurs as a new cause of rejoicing springs forth.

THE MARRIAGE OF THE LAMB (vv. 6–10)

6 And I heard as it were the voice of a great multitude, and as the voice of many waters, and as the voice of mighty thunderings, saying, Alleluia: for the Lord God omnipotent reigneth.

7 Let us be glad and rejoice, and give honour to him: for the marriage of the Lamb is come, and his wife hath made herself ready.

8 And to her was granted that she should be arrayed in fine linen, clean and white: for the fine linen is the righteous-

ness of saints.

9 And he saith unto me, Write, Blessed are they which are called unto the marriage supper of the Lamb. And he saith unto me, These are the true sayings of God.

10 And I fell at his feet to worship him. And he said unto me, See thou do it not: I am thy fellowservant, and of thy brethren that have the testimony of Jesus: worship God: for the testimony of Jesus is the spirit of prophecy.

The multitude thunders its praise: "Alleluia: for the Lord God omnipotent reigneth" (v. 6, KJV). But the cause of joy does not arise solely from God's reign. Rather, it also stems from what develops out of it: the marriage of the Lamb. "Let us be glad and rejoice," sings the host, "and give glory to him: for the marriage of the Lamb is come" (v. 7, AT). The day has arrived when, at last, the Church unites forever with her king. The revelation skillfully weaves together three distinct strands from the Old Testament, all of which have been used before in the New Testament and related literature, but never together. The first is the depiction of the reign of God as a great feast (see Isa. 25:6; cf. Mark 2:19; Matt. 22:1–14; 25:1–13; Luke 14:15–24).[2] The second is the notion of Israel as the bride of Jehovah (see Hosea 2:5; Isa. 1:21; Jer. 2:2; cf. Eph. 5:32). The final is the use of clean garments as a symbol of sanctity (see Gen. 35:2; Isa. 52:1; 61:10; Zech. 3:4; cf. Rev. 3:4; 6:11; 7:14).

The Church as a bride wears a garment both clean and white. John, so that the reader does not miss the meaning of this important symbol, adds, "The fine linen is the righteous deeds of saints" (v. 8, AT). The Greek word used here, *dikaiōma*, focuses on the acts of the righteous rather than on righteousness itself. The Seer's wording in this verse is interesting: "It was granted her to be clothed with fine linen, bright and pure" (AT). The thrust of the verb (*edothē*, from *didōmi* meaning "to give") conveys the impression of an impartation, bestowal, or endowment. The active agent is God; he is the bestower of the garment. All righteousness centers in him. Even man's righteous deeds result from God's goodness in that the spirit and light within man, as well as all law, come from God (see D&C 88:11–13).

The harlot's costume and manner, revealed in chapter seventeen, contrast with the glorious dress and demure behavior of the bride. The great whore, gorgeously arrayed in bright and expensive apparel, insisted that her ornamentation, splendor, and pomp are her full due—a direct result of her own works. The bride's attire is different; her apparel reflects her acknowledged dependence on grace.[3]

At this point an angel commands John to write. The injunction marks the importance and seriousness of the communication. The angel dictates the exact words for the Seer to record: "Blessed are they which are called unto the marriage supper of the Lamb" (v. 9, KJV). The word *called* (Greek *klēsis*) in its religious context denotes an invitation to enter the kingdom of God. Not everyone receives such an invitation, only those who have found the grace of the Lord. John does not separate the called from the chosen as the Savior did in Matthew 22:1–14. The context of Revelation suggests that those who are called are also chosen because, based on the angel's insistence that "these are the true sayings of God" (v. 9, KJV), those who are invited receive the blessings. Therefore, the list is exclusive, containing only the names of those who will have eternal life. God says (and his word will not be altered) that only those who are invited to the marriage supper of the Lord will enter the state of blessedness.

Interestingly, John makes a distinction between the bride and the guests. The former is in more intimate association with the Lamb than the latter: the bride is wed while the guests sup. If the bride represents the Church, then whom do the guests represent? Apparently, John sees the bride as the institution itself—the Church as a whole, composed of both leaders and members. The guests symbolize individual Saints. The bride, then, represents the true and living church in which God's covenant resides. The guests are those who "are priests and kings, who have received of his fulness, and of his glory; and are priests of the Most High, after the order of Melchizedek, which was after the order of Enoch, which was after the order of the Only Begotten Son. Wherefore, as it is written, they are gods, even the sons of God" (D&C 76:56–58). Because this verse focuses exclusively on priesthood authority, it must not be assumed that righteous women, the queens and priestesses of the church, are not there. The gathering is of all the justified. In this light, all the righteous are truly the blessed ones.

At this point, John bows in worship before the divine being who proclaimed the words. Just what brought on this deep expression of awe is not stated. Perhaps it was the angel's declaration that the words he spoke were of God. At any rate the Seer receives a sharp rebuke from the angel: "See thou do it not." The angel goes on to explain, "I am thy fellowservant" (v. 10, KJV), one of those who have the testimony of Jesus. He then commands John to "worship God: for the witness which testifies that Jesus is the Christ is the spirit of prophecy" (v. 10, AT). The last phrase of the verse as interpreted in the KJV "for the testimony of Jesus is the spirit of prophecy" (Greek *hē gar marturia Iēsou estin to pneuma tēs prophēteias*) has been variously understood. Based on John 15:26 and Joseph Smith,[4] I have taken it as an objective genitive, meaning that the testimony *about* Jesus is the common ground of all prophecy.

THE RIDER ON THE WHITE HORSE (vv. 11–16)

11 And I saw heaven opened, and behold a white horse; and he that sat upon him was called Faithful and True, and in righteousness he doth judge and make war.

12 His eyes were as a flame of fire, and on his head were many crowns; and he had a name written, that no man knew, but he himself.

13 And he was clothed with a vesture dipped in blood: and his name is called The Word of God.

14 And the armies which were in heaven followed him upon white horses, clothed in fine linen, white and clean.

15 And out of his mouth goeth a sharp sword, that with it he should smite the nations: and he shall rule them with a rod of iron: and he treadeth the winepress of the fierceness and wrath of Almighty God.

16 And he hath on his vesture and on his thigh a name written, KING OF KINGS, AND LORD OF LORDS.

The command to worship God relates directly to the next vision. At the beginning of his heavenly revelations, John saw "a door . . . opened in heaven" through which he was able to see the throne of God (4:1, KJV); later "the temple of God was opened in heaven" such that the Seer could behold the ark of the testimony (11:19, KJV); afterward, the whole temple opened so that the seven angels with the seven bowls could come out (see 15:5). Now John sees the entire expanse of heaven unfold to make way for the Warrior-king and his army prepared to battle the hosts of darkness.[5]

The Rider, terrible in majesty (cf. D&C 45:74–75) upon his white horse, is the Savior, "called Faithful and True" (v. 11, KJV). These names of Christ, as Elder McConkie points out, "signify that he is the embodiment and personification of these godly attributes. Above all his fellows, he was obedient to the will of the Father and true to every trust imposed upon him."[6] John clearly states the rider's purpose: "In righteousness he doth judge and make war" (v. 11, KJV). War results from his just judgment. Evil must be put down even by force when necessary.

John deliberately contrasts the King with the dragon and the sea beast. While the former two possess seven and ten diadems respectively, the Warrior has "many diadems" (v. 12, AT). The King's true royalty far surpasses the false sovereignty of Satan and his minion. He now rides as "KING OF KINGS, AND LORD OF LORDS" (v. 16, KJV) — and he has acquired his crowns since John last saw him. Although there was no doubt earlier that he was king sitting upon his throne (see 3:21, cf. 1:5), John mentions no crowns. Here they are prominently displayed. They signify that the "kingdoms of this world are become the kingdoms of our Lord, and of his Christ; and he shall reign for ever and ever" (11:15, KJV).[7]

The Rider bears a name "that no man knew, but he himself" (v. 12, KJV). Again Elder McConkie gives insight: "As with all glorified beings, our Lord has a new name in celestial exaltation, a name known to and comprehended by those only who know God in the sense that they have become as he is and have eternal life. See Rev. 2:12–17. Thus, Christ's 'new name' shall be written upon all those who are joint-heirs with him (Rev. 3:12), and shall signify that they have become even as he is."[8]

But the Warrior does have a known name: "The Word of God" (v. 13, KJV). John calls him by this same title at the beginning of his gospel (see John 1:1–3). In Revelation the name emphasizes the authoritative declaration that judges the kings of the world.[9] "In Hebrew thought," states Mounce, "a word is not a lifeless sound but an active agent that achieves the intention of the one who speaks"[10] (see, for example, Gen. 1:3, 7, 9; Heb. 4:12). The Savior is the active agent who executes the word (i.e. the will) of God. That word is now judgment. Thus, the Rider's vestments are blood red for the judgment is one of death (cf. Isa. 63:1–6). According to the Doctrine and Covenants, his appearance will cause consternation among the nations. Many will ask:

> Who is this that cometh down from God in heaven with dyed garments; yea, from the regions which are not known, clothed in his glorious apparel, traveling in the greatness of his strength? And he shall say: I am he who spake in righteousness, mighty to save. . . .
> So great shall be the glory of his presence that the sun shall hide his face in shame, and the moon shall withhold its light, and the stars shall be hurled from their places. And his voice shall be heard: I have trodden the wine-press alone, and have brought judgment upon all people; and none were with me; and I have trampled them in my fury, and I did tread upon them in mine anger, and their blood have I sprinkled upon my garments, and stained all my raiment; for this was the day of vengeance which was in my heart (133:46–51).

Clearly John depicts the moment of vengeance when the Lord will destroy all wickedness by the brightness of his coming (see D&C 5:19). At this moment all nations will come under his authority, "and he shall rule them with a rod of iron" (v. 15, KJV).

THE BATTLE OF THE WARRIOR-KING (vv. 17–21)

17 And I saw an angel standing in the sun; and he cried with a loud voice, saying to all the fowls that fly in the midst of heaven, Come and gather yourselves together unto the supper of the great God;

18 That ye may eat the flesh of kings, and the flesh of captains, and the flesh of mighty men, and the flesh of horses, and of them that sit on them, and the flesh of all men, both free and bond, both small and great.

19 And I saw the beast, and the kings of the earth, and their ar-

mies, gathered together to make war against him that sat on the horse, and against his army.

20 And the beast was taken, and with him the false prophet that wrought miracles before him, with which he deceived them that had received the mark of the beast, and them that worshipped his image. These both were cast alive into a lake of fire burning with brimstone.

21 And the remnant were slain with the sword of him that sat upon the horse, which sword proceeded out of his mouth: and all the fowls were filled with their flesh.

Suddenly the vision changes. John sees an angel bathed in celestial glory. The divine being summons birds of prey to a great feast (cf. Ezek. 39:17–20). This banquet stands in contrast to the banquet at the wedding party of the Lamb. Here the bodies of the rebellious supply the entree. Ignorant of their fate, John sees "the beast, and the kings of the earth, and their armies, gathered together to make war against him that sat on the horse, and against his army" (v. 19, KJV). The purpose of the battle is clear. They fight to decide who is to be the king of the earth. The irony is grim; the outcome is already certain. Before the armies even march, the birds of ruin stand ready.

Though the battle itself is not described, clearly the first to fall are the beast and the false prophet. Under the light of the power of Christ, false political entities and faithless institutions along with pseudoreligious philosophies will fail. No longer supported by these philosophies, the armies of the world will succumb to anarchy. A work of death will result. The legions will be unable to stand against the sword of the Rider. As noted earlier, the sharp sword symbolizes the power of the prophets. In reality it is the word they speak that cuts the wicked to the core because it is the word of God (see Isa. 49:2; Heb. 4:12; Eph. 6:17). The only weapon the prophets need to defeat the enemy hosts and to establish peace upon the earth is the proclamation of the gospel.[11] With false ways exposed and destroyed, nothing can stand in the way of the total victory of righteousness.

CONCLUSION

Chapter nineteen depicts two feasts. One is the feast of the justified, the other the feast of the condemned. The Lord will set both tables. The feast for the birds is called "the supper of the great God" (v. 17, KJV). Thus, the Lord stands as host as he does at the wedding. For the obedient the banquet will consist of "fat things, of wine on the lees well refined, . . . a supper of the house of the Lord, well prepared, unto which all nations shall be invited" (D&C 58:8–9). Those who refuse to come to it may well be the fare of the second meal, for it will consist of "the flesh of kings, and the flesh of captains, and the flesh of mighty men, and the flesh of horses, and of them that sit on them, and the flesh of all men, both free and bond, both small and great" (Rev. 19:18, KJV). What determines to which feast a person will go? It is clearly a matter of worship. Those whom God calls to the wedding supper worship him, those who come to the death feast worship the beast and its image. Blessedness awaits the first gathering, destruction the second.

CHAPTER 20

THE THOUSAND YEARS

(AN ANALYSIS OF REVELATION 20)

SATAN IS BOUND FOR A THOUSAND YEARS (vv. 1–3)

1 And I saw an angel come down from heaven, having the key of the bottomless pit and a great chain in his hand.
2 And he laid hold on the dragon, that old serpent, which is the Devil, and Satan, and bound him a thousand years,

3 And cast him into the bottomless pit, and shut him up, and set a seal upon him, that he should deceive the nations no more, till the thousand years should be fulfilled: and after that he must be loosed a little season.

After the eradication of the false prophet and the beast, John's vision centers on the destruction of the dragon. The importance of Satan's defeat must not be overlooked. Not only must instruments and agents of evil be overthrown, but the father of evil himself must perish. Casting the two monsters into the lake of fire would be insufficient; the dragon, who motivated and empowered them, must share their fate. A lesson grows from this. War will end neither through pacifist or militant means nor by leagues or treaties as long as hatred, malice, and lust for power dominate the hearts of men. Zion will not come by political revolution, only by spiritual renovation. Zion, being the pure in heart, expands only as love dominates society. The fall of Satan, master of hate, must precede the era of millennial peace.[1]

215

John beholds an angel coming down from heaven having the key to the pit in the abyss. The contrast with the "star" of chapter nine is striking: the star fell and the angel descends; while the star was given the key, the angel possesses it on his own. The identity of the angel remains unknown, but he holds the key to seal the pit. This suggests that he ministers directly under the Lord. More than likely he is Michael once again warring with and defeating the lord of darkness. Doctrine and Covenants 88:112 identifies Michael as the seventh angel, and in verses 106–7 the seventh angel proclaims the victory of the Lamb and his angels. Michael is definitely involved in the latter-day overthrow of the satanic kingdom. The book of Daniel may reflect this period when it notes that the Saints of the last days could not prevail over the world until "the Ancient of days [i.e. Michael] came, and judgment was given to the saints of the most High; and the time came that the saints possessed the kingdom" (7:21–22, KJV).

There appears to be no real contest between the adversary and the angel. The archangel seizes, binds, and throws the devil into the pit of the abyss with little if any struggle on Satan's part. The idea of binding Satan goes back to Isaiah, who speaks of him being bound for a brief period in Isaiah 24:22 and forever in 24:23.[2] Though no human eye may witness the event, John makes it clear that the act will be a historical reality (see D&C 43:31; 45:55; 84:100; 88:110–11).

The key and the chain denote God's supremacy over both Satan and his realm. Indeed, the angel incarcerates Satan in the pit. Thus, Satan is not the magistrate of hell, God is. The angel not only locks the dragon away with a key, but he also binds him with chains and seals the pit. The KJV suggests that the devil is the one who has the seal upon him, but the Greek manuscript makes it clear that the pit is what is sealed over him (cf. Dan. 6:17). Thus, the devil's power is triply curtailed. Only when all three bonds are freed will he be able to make mischief again.[3] Through the use of this triple binding, John emphasizes the extent of Satan's impotency during the Millennium when "Satan shall not have power to tempt any man" (D&C 101:28).

One point should not be overlooked. The angel does the binding, not mankind. People do not bring about the millennial condition through some kind of supreme righteous act; God does.[4] However, it would be incorrect to believe that the people play no role in keeping Satan bound. "Because of the righteousness of his people," Nephi proclaimed, "Satan has no power; wherefore, he cannot be loosed for the space of many years; for he hath no power over the hearts of the people, for they dwell in righteousness, and the Holy one of Israel reigneth" (1 Ne. 22:26). Thus, the subjugation of Satan involves teamwork: the Lord's power binds Satan initially, and the righteousness of the Saints keeps him bound.

The purpose of Satan's binding is not yet punitive but precautionary.[5] The Savior and his people must have time to prepare the earth for celestial glory. Satanic delusions are not to get in the way for a season. John spells out precisely the reason for the dark lord's incarceration: "that he should deceive the nations no more" (v. 3, KJV). Satan has used deception as a major tool from the beginning, whispering to Cain and his brethren the Mahanic secret that one could obtain gain by murder and remain forever free. Yet Satan knew full well that "these things are not hid from the Lord" (Moses 5:39; see vv. 29–41). And when Cain faced the wrath of a just God, Satan, with his delusion, discreetly stayed away.

The Seer's use of the term *nations* is significant. Because of Satan's power to deceive the kings of the earth through the glitter of Babylon, one may mistakenly believe that all nations were under the deceptive power of the beast and his false prophet and fought against the Lamb and his people. In verse three, John makes it clear that the "kings of the earth" (Rev. 12:9; 16:12, 14; 17:2; 18:3, 9, KJV) represent a select number of nations and peoples who are deceived by and assist Satan in his cause. Only these will be annihilated during the great battle (see 19:19). Many of those who do not join this cause will survive and come to Christ during the Millennium (see 21:24). Joseph Fielding Smith notes that there will be many within the nations who shall not know of the gospel law yet who shall live terrestrial-quality lives. These will be spared destruction and enjoy the millennial period with the Saints of God. Through a tremendous missionary effort, all will eventually come to worship the Lord.[6]

THE FIRST RESURRECTION AND THE LORD'S REIGN (vv. 4–6)

4 And I saw thrones, and they sat upon them, and judgment was given unto them: and I saw the souls of them that were beheaded for the witness of Jesus, and for the word of God, and which had not worshipped the beast, neither his image, neither had received his mark upon their foreheads, or in their hands; and they lived and reigned with Christ a thousand years.

5 But the rest of the dead lived not again until the thousand years were finished. This is the first resurrection.

6 Blessed and holy is he that hath part in the first resurrection: on such the second death hath no power, but they shall be priests of God and of Christ, and shall reign with him a thousand years.

After the angel binds Satan, John sees the paradisiacal era. Other prophets have focused their attention on the millennial world, where they describe the nature, beauty, and peace of that time (see, for example, Isa. 11:6–9; 65:17–25; Ezek. 34:25–31). Unlike the other prophets, however, the Seer draws the readers' attention to the type of people who will share in that reign. These people worshipped God and not the dragon; they did not fall to Satan's blandishments and false values but actively fought for truth. Having done so, they came under the power of the first resurrection and became kings with the Lamb. "I saw thrones," the Seer states, "and they [who] sat upon them, and judgment was given unto them: and I saw the souls of them that were beheaded for the witness of Jesus, and for the word of God, and which had not worshipped the beast" (v. 4, KJV). John may have viewed two sets of kings: those who suffered martyrdom in his day (see 6:9–11) and those who overcame the beast in the latter day (see 14:4–5).[7] But more than likely he wished to symbolize all who gave their lives in service to the Lamb.

The Seer notes the nature of their reward: "Judgment was

given unto them" (v. 4, KJV). The Greek here (*kai krima edothē autois*) can also be interpreted "judgment was given for them," meaning God judged them righteous and worthy of the reward. The translation followed in the text, however, is based on the Savior's promise to his apostles that they would be the judges of Israel (see Matt. 19:28). John, being one of those, would be acutely aware of this.

Judgment here should signify presiding power or rule.[8] The Doctrine and Covenants supports this context: "Mine apostles, the Twelve which were with me in my ministry at Jerusalem, shall stand at my right hand at the day of my coming in a pillar of fire, being clothed with robes of righteousness, with crowns upon their heads, in glory even as I am, to judge the whole house of Israel, even as many as have loved me and kept my commandments, and none else" (29:12). The Twelve do not determine the eventual station of souls but rather preside over the righteous. Further supporting this definition of judgment is the Lord's promise that "in mine own due time will I come upon the earth in judgment, and my people shall be redeemed and shall reign with me on earth. For the great Millennium, of which I have spoken by the mouth of my servants, shall come" (D&C 43:29–30).

Joseph Smith explained what would happen to both the righteous living and dead at the time of the second coming.

> The saints that are upon the earth, who are alive, shall be quickened and be caught up to meet him. And they who have slept in their graves shall come forth, for their graves shall be opened; and they also shall be caught up to meet him in the midst of the pillar of heaven— they are Christ's, the first fruits, they who shall descend with him first, and they who are on the earth and in their graves, who are first caught up to meet him; and all this by the voice of the sounding of the trump of the angel of God.
> And after this another angel shall sound, which is the second trump; and then cometh the redemption of those who are Christ's at his coming; who have received their part in that prison which is prepared for them, that they might receive the gospel, and be judged according to men in the flesh.
> And again, another trump shall sound, which is the third trump; and then come the spirits of men who are to be judged,

and are found under condemnation; and these are the rest of the dead; and they live not again until the thousand years are ended, neither again, until the end of the earth (D&C 88:96–101).

The first resurrection takes in all those, living and dead, who are Christ's at the moment he comes in glory. These are they who "were sanctified, and their garments were washed white through the blood of the Lamb," who "being [made] pure and spotless before God, could not look upon sin save it were with abhorrence" (Alma 13:11–12), who are "virgins" because "they . . . were not defiled with" sexual immorality, and in whose "mouth was found no guile" (Rev. 14:4–5, KJV). These, the first fruits of Christ, are the ones whom John sees as the rulers during the thousand years when the earth shall rest.

"Wickedness shall not be upon the earth," the Lord declared, "for I will reveal myself from heaven with power and great glory, with all the hosts thereof, and dwell in righteousness with men on earth a thousand years, and the wicked shall not stand" (D&C 29:9, 11). John is the only biblical writer to speak of a thousand-year reign of the Lord. What is significant is that he passes over the period in just three verses. John does not elaborate on details that distract from his primary objectives. He writes with a specific agenda: to prepare the Saints for the Second Coming. Thus, the bulk of his writing focuses on the last days and the great battle to be won. Once he has completed this task, he gives but a quick preview of the result of righteousness.

By mentioning the Millennium, John assures the Saints that they will be rewarded for their struggles. John underscores the personal quality of those who will enjoy it. They are both "blessed and holy" (v. 6, KJV), two attributes belonging to both God and the Lamb. Those who overcome and take upon themselves these attributes need not fear the second death. In other words, having come alive in Christ, their lives, like his, are eternal. Therefore they can share the glory, honor, authority, and majesty with him. They are a kingdom of priests and kings, priestesses and queens who rule and reign with him forever.

The Saints compose the kingdom of God not because he rules over them, but because they reign with him.[9] The Millennium marks the beginning of their eternal dominion.

THE BATTLE OF GOG AND MAGOG (vv. 7–10)

7 And when the thousand years are expired, Satan shall be loosed out of his prison,

8 And shall go out to deceive the nations which are in the four quarters of the earth, Gog and Magog, to gather them together to battle: the number of whom is as the sand of the sea.

9 And they went up on the breadth of the earth, and compassed the camp of the saints about, and the beloved city: and fire came down from God out of heaven, and devoured them.

10 And the devil that deceived them was cast into the lake of fire and brimstone, where the beast and the false prophet are, and shall be tormented day and night for ever and ever.

The era of bliss, however, does not move smoothly into eternal glory. John sees that "when the thousand years are expired, Satan shall be loosed out of his prison" (v. 7, KJV). Since the power of God bound him, only it can loose him. Therefore, his freedom must play an important part in the purposes of deity. John makes this clear. Immediately after being loosed, the old serpent sets about doing mischief, "and shall go out to deceive the nations" (v. 8, KJV). The result will be that "men [shall] again begin to deny their God" (D&C 29:22). Perhaps the best model to help understand how this can happen is the demise of the near millennial society found in 4 Nephi and Mormon 1 in the Book of Mormon.

With saddened heart, the prophet Mormon records how a small group of people revolted from the Church around A.D. 150 (see 4 Ne. 1:20). By that time wealth had became both widespread and abundant. Some could not handle it. Ostentation began to abound, and a materialistic mind-set became prevalent. The effect on the society as a whole was twofold: goods and substance were no longer common within it, and class distinction was initiated and promoted. Ironically, there was a proliferation of churches at this same time. However, the record shows that these were not built up to serve God but to justify getting gain. As the people denied goodness, they feverishly sought security in pseudorighteousness. Thus, they promoted wickedness and drank deep of the pernicious poison of the beast and his false-prophet who were yet on the earth. These churches began not only to deny the true church of the Lamb, but also to fight against it. Persecution of the righteous escalated (see 4 Ne. 1:1–37).

Mormon gets at the crux of their condition. He states clearly that the Nephites "did not dwindle in unbelief, but they did wilfully rebel against the gospel of Christ; and they did teach their children that they should not believe" (4 Ne. 1:38). In their willful rebellion, they taught their children "to hate the children of God" (v. 39). The result was war—a war that destroyed the nation.

Satan, smoldering in his pit for a thousand years, will have plenty of time to plot his plans for deception. Very likely he will follow the same scheme that has worked so well for him before. Seducing certain ones, the devil will eventually cultivate them into slaves. These newly won minions will be his mortal executors. They will gather the nations, symbolized as Gog and Magog, against the Saints. John tells us little of the battle. From modern scripture we know only that Satan "shall be loosed for a little season, that he may gather together his armies" (D&C 88:111). This is illuminating. God frees Satan for a purpose: to gather his armies for the very last battle. Of this battle we know that

> Michael, the seventh angel, even the archangel, shall gather together his armies, even the hosts of heaven. And the devil shall gather together his armies; even the hosts of hell, and shall come up to battle against Michael and his armies. And then cometh the battle of the great God; and the devil and his armies shall be cast away into their own place, that they shall not have power over the saints any more at all. For Michael shall fight their battles, and shall overcome him who seeketh the throne of him who sitteth upon the throne, even the Lamb (D&C 88:112–15).

This latter-day revelation specifically clarifies two important points. First, the Doctrine and Covenants suggests that the "fire

[that] came down from God out of heaven, and devoured" Satan's host (Rev. 20:9, KJV) shall be the glory of Michael and his heavenly hosts marching in power to protect the cities of God. Second, the earthly Saints do not appear to have to fight the battle. They are rescued from such horror by the great archangel and his celestial legions. The result is the total overthrow of all wickedness. The wilfully corrupt are devoured by the fire, while "the devil that deceived them was cast into the lake of fire and brimstone" (v. 10, KJV). The divine inferno, which long before began its ceaseless torment of the beast and the false prophet, now accepts their master.

THE LAST JUDGMENT (vv. 11–15)

11 And I saw a great white throne, and him that sat on it, from whose face the earth and the heaven fled away; and there was found no place for them.

12 And I saw the dead, small and great, stand before God; and the books were opened: and another book was opened, which is the book of life: and the dead were judged out of those things which were written in the books, according to their works.

13 And the sea gave up the dead which were in it; and death and hell delivered up the dead which were in them: and they were judged every man according to their works.

14 And death and hell were cast into the lake of fire. This is the second death.

15 And whosoever was not found written in the book of life was cast into the lake of fire.

Only after Michael destroys Satan does the final judgment commence. With the blindness of satanic delusion gone, men, both small and great, will stand to face Christ. The basis of their judgment will consist of records kept in earth and heaven. John sees two sets of records. The first he refers to as "books"; and the second, as "the book of life" (v. 12, KJV). Speaking of these two sets of records, Joseph Smith wrote: "The dead were judged out of those things which were written in the books, according to their works; consequently, the books spoken of must be the books which contained the record of their works, and refer to the records which are kept on the earth. And the book which was the book of life is the record which is kept in heaven" (D&C

128:7). He went on to explain that John actually had reference to priesthood sealing ordinances:

> Whatsoever you bind on earth shall be bound in heaven, and whatsoever you loose on earth shall be loosed in heaven. Or, in other words, taking a different view of the translation, whatsoever you record on earth shall be recorded in heaven, and whatsoever you do not record on earth shall not be recorded in heaven; for out of the books shall your dead be judged, according to their own works, whether they themselves have attended to the ordinances in their own *propria persona*, or by the means of their own agents, according to the ordinance which God has prepared for their salvation from before the foundation of the world, according to the records which they have kept concerning their dead (D&C 128:8).

All will be "judged out of those things which were written in the books, according to their works" (Rev. 20:12, KJV). In the final analysis, the Lord judges on the basis of works. Those who have accepted the gospel and been sealed by the power of the priesthood will come under his domain and receive everlasting life. But those who have not accepted him, who have not partaken of his grace and power, who have not participated in the sealing ordinances "remain separately and singly, without exaltation, in their saved condition, to all eternity; and from henceforth are not gods, but are angels of God forever and ever" (D&C 132:17).

After the battle, John sees the sea (the old home of chaos and misery), death, and hell, give up the dead that are in them. The moment of universal judgment has come, which none can escape. The Lord declared: "Before the earth shall pass away, Michael, mine archangel, shall sound his trump, and then shall all the dead awake, for their graves shall be opened, and they shall come forth—yea, even all. And the righteous shall be gathered on my right hand unto eternal life; and the wicked on my left hand will I be ashamed to own before the Father; wherefore I will say unto them—Depart from me, ye cursed, into everlasting fire, prepared for the devil and his angels" (D&C 29:26–28).

Though a somber note ends this declaration, for the vast majority of people neither sorrow nor lamentation cast a shadow over the glory of the moment. This judgment does not mark the beginning of torment, but its end. The misery of death and the pain of hell cannot endure the divine flame emanating from grace and love. All who belong to the Lamb, or who have paid the uttermost farthing, shall come out of captivity into a kingdom of glory.

Nonetheless, John concludes this vision with a note of warning: he whose name "was not found written in the book of life was cast into the lake of fire" (v. 15, KJV). There are those who deny grace and reject Christ, who in their rebellion refuse the power of repentance and spurn the love of God. The Savior spoke of the "eternal fire prepared for the devil and his angels" (Matt. 25:41, AT). Gehenna was not prepared for men, only for demons. But those men who become devils and angels to the devil must partake of that punishment.

This is the second death. It is visited only upon the most hardened, those who cannot find humility and acceptance and who remain "filthy still." These are "vessels of wrath, doomed to suffer the wrath of God, with the devil and his angels in eternity" (D&C 76:33). Becoming like Satan, they have no redemption. Any who "breaketh a law, and abideth not by law, but seeketh to become a law unto itself, and willeth to abide in sin, and altogether abideth in sin, cannot be sanctified by law, neither by mercy, justice, nor judgment. Therefore, they must remain filthy still" (D&C 88:35). These are not resurrected until the very end. When they are resurrected, death—spiritual death—immediately reclaims them.

CONCLUSION

This portion of John's vision, though abbreviated, teaches some important principles. Among them, it teaches that the power of the first resurrection reaches only those of the past and present ages who are Christ's at the time of his coming. That moment is critical. Those who must seek a little time while they get their

lives in order will find that the words "I come quickly" indeed
mean "I come suddenly, even before you are ready." These,
like the five foolish virgins, may find, when they finally are
ready, that the door to celestial glory has been shut. Their cry
"Lord, Lord, open unto us," will hear the response, Go away
for, "verily I say unto you, Ye know me not" (Matt. 25:9–11,
JST).

John's vision drives home another point: the binding of Satan
does more than merely give hope for the future. It speaks to
the present. It says that there is no ultimate dualism. The power
of evil, though deadly real now, has no place in the future. It
exists and operates at any time only by permission of God.[10]
When he determines that it will end, it will end. There will be
no argument, no retort, only the irresistible and overpowering
explosion of divine fire in which all corruption will be eternally
consumed and evil forever incarcerated. Not a whisper of re-
buttal will overreach or penetrate through the massive and fro-
zen walls of Gehenna.

CHAPTER 21

THE NEW JERUSALEM

(AN ANALYSIS OF REVELATION 21)

THE PEOPLE OF GOD (vv. 1–4)

1 And I saw a new heaven and a new earth: for the first heaven and the first earth were passed away; and there was no more sea.

2 And I John saw the holy city, new Jerusalem, coming down from God out of heaven, prepared as a bride adorned for her husband.

3 And I heard a great voice out of heaven saying, Behold, the tabernacle of God is with men, and he will dwell with them, and they shall be his people, and God himself shall be with them, and be their God.

4 And God shall wipe away all tears from their eyes; and there shall be no more death, neither sorrow, nor crying, neither shall there be any more pain: for the former things are passed away.

As the vision of the general resurrection closes, a new vision immediately opens. John sees what he describes as a new heaven and a new earth (cf. Isa. 51:6; Ps. 102:26–27; Matt. 24:29; 2 Pet. 3:10). However, the old earth is not so much annihilated as reconstituted to become a new celestial orb. What John reports confirms a long established Judeo-Christian tradition. Salvation, in the biblical sense, is not just for mankind but for all creation (see, e.g., 2 Cor. 5:17; Rom. 8:21). All things are to be saved including the cosmos itself.[1] The Doctrine and Covenants also affirms this view of the earth: "It must needs be sanctified from all unrighteousness, that it may be prepared for the celestial glory; for after it hath filled the measure of its creation, it shall be crowned with glory, even with the presence of God the Father" (D&C 88:18–19). In order to withstand the full glory of God, the earth and its inhabitants will need to be entirely reconstructed.

"The end shall come, and the heaven and the earth shall be consumed and pass away, and there shall be a new heaven and a new earth. For all old things shall pass away, and all things shall become new, even the heaven and the earth, and all the fulness thereof, both men and beasts, the fowls of the air, and the fishes of the sea; and not one hair, neither mote, shall be lost, for it is the workmanship of mine hand" (D&C 29:23–25). That the universe or even the galaxy will pass away when the earth is renewed is unlikely. More likely a new heaven will manifest itself as the earth takes up its new position as a celestial sun.

What strikes John about the new world is that "there [is] no more sea" (v. 1, KJV). The abode of chaos, the home of the satanic beast, the old seat over which the whore held sway, has vanished. Under the force of the Lamb's radiance, the source of Babylon's sea-borne luxuries and what helped feed and sustain her corruption has boiled into oblivion. But the sea and the abyss are one and the same. Therefore, the destruction of the sea represents the annihilation of the primeval deep, the home of malevolence and evil. Up to this point, it has dominated the world. As the stronghold of Satan's supporters, its existence mocked the hope of a complete victory and a complete sovereignty of the Lord. It has no place in the transformed world where all things spontaneously obey their Lord and their God.[2]

Previewing what he will explore more fully later, John introduces the central seat of celestial rule—the New Jerusalem. In this, John follows Zechariah 9:9–10. Many of the Old Testament prophets were well aware of the millennial Jerusalem and the splendor that it will acquire (see Isa. 54:11–14; 60:10–14; Hag. 2:7–9; Zech. 2:1–5. Moses 7:62–63 also focuses on the millennial New Jerusalem). The same theme is picked up by nonbiblical Jewish documents dating from the second century B.C., showing a clear belief in a new Jerusalem associated with the heavenly order.[3] John compares the beauty and purity of the city to that of a bride adorned for her husband. The Seer meticulously paints this picture, careful to catch just the right image. The dazzling whiteness of the bride's gown, mirroring her radiant purity, stands in contrast to the gaudy splendor of Babylon, which was exposed as nothing more than the seductive trappings of a decrepit and raddled whore.[4]

One point needs to be emphasized. At the center of John's new vision lies a city—a real city. John clearly makes this the heart of the vision. Heaven exists as a society. Joseph Smith explained that the "same sociality which exists among us here will exist among us there, only it will be coupled with eternal glory, which glory we do not now enjoy" (D&C 130:2). The celestial kingdom is a community or system of communities presided over by a central city. Celestial beings, the church of the Firstborn, occupy these areas as families, for families make up communities. Thus, the ideal and perfect community is the eternal family of God.[5]

John records that "the tabernacle of God is with men, and he will dwell with them" (v. 3, KJV). His statement echoes Ezekiel 48:35, which notes that the name of the eternal city is "The Lord is there" (KJV). The word John uses for "tabernacle" (Greek *skēnē*) translates the Hebrew *mishkan*. *Mishkan* means "tent." However, in a number of places in the Old Testament, it is used to denote God's personal presence and attention to Israel (see Lev. 26:11; Ezek. 37:27).[6] The Seer's statement thus emphasizes the very personal association that will be set up on the new earth between God and his children.

The reason why such an association can be maintained is clearly stated: "They shall be his [God's] people" (v. 3, KJV). This fulfills the promise that God made with Israel at Sinai, which had been continuously renewed through his prophets (see Lev. 26:12; Jer. 7:23; 11:4; cf. Hosea 1:9. Note how the promise is renewed in Jer. 30:22; Ezek. 36:28; 37:23, 27; Zech. 8:8). The covenant found fulfillment in the Lord (see Rom. 9:25; 1 Pet. 2:10), and it continues today as part of the new and everlasting covenant. Out of heaven, John hears a great voice proclaiming the privileges of those who have sacrificed the things of the old world in hope of obtaining those of the new. While on earth, they felt themselves as little more than strangers and pilgrims seeking "a better country, that is, an heavenly: wherefore God is not ashamed to be called their God: for he hath prepared for them a city" (Heb. 11:16, KJV).[7] The blessing is spoken by none other than God himself.

HE THAT SAT UPON THE THRONE (vv. 5–7)

5 And he that sat upon the throne said, Behold, I make all things new. And he said unto me, Write: for these words are true and faithful.

6 And he said unto me, It is done. I am Alpha and Omega, the beginning and the end. I will give unto him that is athirst of the fountain of the water of life freely.

7 He that overcometh shall inherit all things; and I will be his God, and he shall be my son.

These words mark the point at which God no longer hides behind the passive voice or the oblique reference. Revelation 16:1, 17 refer to a great voice coming out of the temple, while 16:17 and 19:5 speak of the voice coming from the throne. In each instance, God is the one who is likely speaking. "I make all things new," he now declares (21:5, KJV). As he begins to reveal himself, the first fact fully exposed is that this God is the maker, the creator, the director of all things. He holds the power of regeneration. His purposes allow nothing of the old order to remain. All things must become new, not just heaven and the earth, but all things.

God places humankind foremost in his operation. According to Paul, God begins in mortality to transform people into his image. Those with a spark of the light of Christ behold as in a mirror "the glory of the Lord, [and] are changed into the same image from glory to glory, even as by the Spirit of the Lord" (2 Cor. 3:18, KJV). The operation is quiet and subtle and unseen by the natural man. Nonetheless, working through his Spirit, God makes his minute but daily transformation upon those who are his own. Ever so gradually, but ever so surely, his people become as God.

The vision allows John to realize that transformation also occurs on a cosmic scale. The historian and social prophet may see only the natural world moving ever more swiftly through deepening stages of depravity to doom. But John understands that the hand of God moves in all things, slowly refashioning the whole. In this light the suffering of the earth both at the beginning and end of the millennium is but the travail preceding a new order.[8]

God identifies the objective of the refreshing newness so far as man is concerned: "I will be his God, and he shall be my son" (v. 7, KJV). Each man and woman will be fully one with God, their very constitutions being remade so that they are bone of his bone and flesh of his flesh.

The importance of this work is emphasized by the Lord's command to John, "Write: for these words are true and faithful" (v. 5, KJV). By this oath, John understands that God will accomplish his designs toward mankind and creation. Nothing can prevent it. In this context God states, "They are done" (v. 6, AT), not "It is done," as in the KJV. The Greek is literally "They are done" (*gegonan*).[9] The plural stresses that all the events John has seen are made complete through God. God is in charge. In him the future is secure. Those who have trusted him, who have followed his paths, who have overcome "shall inherit all things" (v. 7, KJV).

As the wonderful enthroned majesty speaks, his identity becomes known. He is "Alpha and Omega, the beginning and the end" (v. 6, KJV). The title of the enthroned figure emphasizes his supreme position. He is Alpha—the beginning, the initiator of all things. Everything proceeds from his will. He is also Omega—the end, the finisher, the one in whom all things take meaning and find completeness. Supporting this idea, Joseph Smith taught that God "contemplated the whole of the events connected with the earth, pertaining to the plan of salvation, before it rolled into existence," that he "was acquainted with the situation of all nations and with their destiny," and that he "ordered all things according to the council of His own will."[10] The last statement is arresting. That will determined that the faithful will be blessed, "and God shall wipe away all tears from their eyes; and there shall be no more death, neither sorrow, nor crying, neither shall there be any more pain: for the former things are passed away" (v. 4, KJV).

THE SECOND DEATH (v. 8)

8 But the fearful, and unbelieving, and the abominable, and murderers, and whoremongers, and sorcerers, and idolaters, and all liars, shall have their part in the lake which burneth with fire and brimstone: which is the second death.

Though on the very threshold of incomprehensible joy, God reminds John of those who suffer the horror inflicted by the great dragon. What is surprising is that those who lead the cavalcade of the hell-bound are the cowards and the unfaithful. Though few would ever dismiss these vices as unimportant, fewer yet would place them among the great sins. The reason the Seer may have placed them before all others grows out of the context of the revelation itself. John experienced the latter days in which Christ and the beasts would vie for the souls of men. He understood that opposition to goodness and virtue would constantly increase. The result would put ever greater pressure on people to abandon the ways of God. Under these excruciating conditions, courage and faithfulness would be the supreme virtues. Cowardice and unfaithfulness would become great sins.[11]

John quotes the Lord as saying such sinners "have their part in the lake which burneth with fire and brimstone: which is the second death" (v. 8, KJV). The term second death as used here apparently refers to the punishment of the wicked before they are saved from the fires of hell. Latter-day revelation states that "these are they who are cast down to hell and suffer the wrath of Almighty God, until the fulness of times, when Christ shall have subdued all enemies under his feet, and shall have perfected his work" (D&C 76:106). They "shall not be redeemed from the devil until the last resurrection, until the Lord, even Christ the Lamb, shall have finished his work" (D&C 76:85). Such sinners are Lucifer's but only for a time. While they are under his power, his full wrath will be spent upon them. For a thousand years their tears, their torment, their misery will be his wine, and their scorched souls and burning consciences the butter of his bread.

Note that Doctrine and Covenants 76:31–39 tells us that only those who are sons of Perdition will suffer the second death. The suffering of the telestial souls under the power of Satan, though unimaginable, will not match that of Lucifer's sons. This idea is suggested from the statement that the sons of Perdition will go into "eternal punishment, to reign with the devil and his angels in eternity, where their worm dieth not, and the fire is not quenched, which is their torment—and the end thereof, neither the place thereof, nor their torment, no man knows" (D&C 76:44–45).

THE NEW JERUSALEM (vv. 9–11)

9 And there came unto me one of the seven angels which had the seven vials full of the seven last plagues, and talked with me, saying, Come hither, I will shew thee the bride, the Lamb's wife.

10 And he carried me away in the spirit to a great and high mountain, and shewed me that great city, the holy Jerusalem, descending out of heaven from God,

11 Having the glory of God: and her light was like unto a stone most precious, even like a jasper stone, clear as crystal;

Verse nine introduces a new vision that continues into the next chapter. One of the seven angels that once carried a bowl of wrath commands John, "Come hither, I will shew thee the bride, the Lamb's wife" (v. 9, KJV). The Seer's language is again deliberate. He places the virgin bride in marked contrast with the great whore. Note that in chapter seventeen this angel, or one of his brothers, commanded John, "Come hither; I will shew unto thee the judgment of the great whore" (v. 1, KJV). Then the Seer was taken into the wilderness to view the harlot and her beast. In the present vision he is taken to the top of a high mountain to see the bride.[12] In both instances he sees a city. The former, he knows, will forever lie in ruins, while the latter will everlastingly bathe in celestial glory.

The imagery of the ascension to the mountain top is arresting. The idea conveyed suggests that John received an additional endowment of the Spirit such that his ability to understand was again magnified. Only through that ability and from that vantage point could he really "see" the holy city—a city that shines like jasper. The term *jasper* (Greek *iaspis*) anciently described a broad category of precious and semiprecious gems. The imagery of dazzling and scintillating colors is representative of the glory of the celestial kingdom. Many a Jewish apocalyptist likewise waxed rhapsodic over the splendor of the New Jerusalem, expressing the glory of God's kingdom in terms of a jeweled city with streets of gold and surrounded with splendor (see, e.g., Isa. 54:11–14; Ezek. 28:11–17).[13] In Revelation 21, we get a feel for the resplendent power of God, which shines forth from the city to give life, light, and law to all things.

THE CITY—ITS WALLS AND GATES (vv. 12–27)

12 And had a wall great and high, and had twelve gates, and at the gates twelve angels, and names written thereon, which are the names of the twelve tribes of the children of Israel:

13 On the east three gates; on the north three gates; on the south three gates; and on the west three gates.

14 And the wall of the city had twelve foundations, and in them the names of the twelve apostles of the Lamb.

15 And he that talked with me had a golden reed to measure the city, and the gates thereof, and the wall thereof.

16 And the city lieth foursquare, and the length is as large as the breadth: and he measured the city with the reed, twelve thousand furlongs. The length and the breadth and the height of it are equal.

17 And he measured the wall thereof, an hundred and forty and four cubits, according to the measure of a man, that is, of the angel.

18 And the building of the wall of it was of jasper: and the city was pure gold, like unto clear glass.

19 And the foundations of the wall of the city were garnished with all manner of precious stones. The first foundation was jasper; the second, sapphire; the third, a chalcedony; the fourth, an emerald;

20 The fifth, sardonyx; the sixth, sardius; the seventh, chrysolite; the eighth, beryl; the ninth, a topaz; the tenth, a chrysoprasus; the eleventh, a jacinth; the twelfth, an amethyst.

21 And the twelve gates were twelve pearls; every several gate was of one pearl: and the street of the city was pure gold, as it were transparent glass.

22 And I saw no temple

therein: for the Lord God Almighty and the Lamb are the temple of it.

23 And the city had no need of the sun, neither of the moon, to shine in it: for the glory of God did lighten it, and the Lamb is the light thereof.

24 And the nations of them which are saved shall walk in the light of it: and the kings of the earth do bring their glory and honour into it.

25 And the gates of it shall not be shut at all by day: for there shall be no night there.

26 And they shall bring the glory and honour of the nations into it.

27 And there shall in no wise enter into it any thing that defileth, neither whatsoever worketh abomination, or maketh a lie: but they which are written in the Lamb's book of life.

The great city has twelve gates—three to a side. Each gate is named in honor of one of the twelve tribes of Israel. In this aspect the city resembles the temple of Ezekiel (see 48:31–35). But there are differences. First, at each of John's gates stands an angel as sentinel. The prophet Brigham Young provided insight into the duty of these angels. Defining the endowment, he stated: "Your *endowment* is, to receive all those ordinances in the House of the Lord, which are necessary for you, after you have departed this life, to enable you to walk back to the presence of the Father, passing the angels who stand as sentinels, being enabled to give them the key words, the signs and tokens, pertaining to the Holy Priesthood, and gain your eternal exaltation in spite of earth and hell."[14] Appropriately, these angels are placed at the gates of the celestial city, symbolizing that only those who have made and kept their covenants in God's holy house will enter his kingdom.

The second difference is that in Revelation the whole city is the sanctuary while in Ezekiel the temple alone is holy. Ezekiel's temple wall separated the sacred sanctuary from the profane city. The prophet was explicit in noting who could and could not come into the sanctuary (44:5–7). The wall marked the boundary line over which the unjustified could not pass. But with John, a dividing line would have been improper since all members of the city are holy.[15]

Third, John's city sat on twelve foundation stones named after the apostles of the Lord, while no mention is made of the foundation in Ezekiel. Note that Paul in 1 Corinthians 12:28; Ephesians 2:20; 4:11 stresses that God's kingdom rests upon the quorum of Apostles. The repetition of number twelve in the stones and gates stands as a constant reminder of the priestly power that guards and envelops all aspects and operations of the holy city. This is seen especially in the measurement of the walls. John notes they are 144 cubits, after the measure of an angel. The size of an angelic cubit is unknown. What is important is the number—twelve squared—signifying the fullness of priesthood authority. This is what surrounds and stands as a great bulwark to the city.

John's knowledge of the dimensions of the city and its gates grows out of the measurements taken by an angel. The scene echoes Ezekiel 40:3–5 where an angel also does the measuring. John himself once performed a similar task under angelic direction. He was given a measuring rod to measure the temple (see chapter 11). The Seer's measuring of the temple's area signified that area's protection from judgment. Now he stands back and watches the angel do the work.

The golden rod of the angel, in contrast to John's rod of judgment, acts as a standard that demonstrates the city's purity. The city is four square, the same shape as the holy of holies, an exact cube, symbol of perfection and eternal stability. This suggests why the angel does the measuring. As great as John is, he is yet mortal and imperfect. The task of measuring the height, depth, and breadth of celestial perfection is beyond any mortal man's capability. This is emphasized by the city's size— 12,000 furlongs (just short of 1,400 miles) in length, breadth, and (if it can be imagined) height. The term *furlong* (a distance of 220 yards) is used consistently in the KJV to translate the Greek *stadion* (a distance of 202.3 yards).

John uses the brilliance of precious stones to describe the limitless beauty of the city. The stones represent the twelve tribes of Israel. John's list of stones also corresponds to, but does not match, those found on the high priest's breast plate. Stones listed in Exodus are "first row shall be a sardius, a topaz, and a carbuncle: this shall be the first row. And the second row shall be an emerald, a sapphire, and a diamond. And the third row a ligure, an agate, and an amethyst. And the fourth row a beryl, and an onyx, and a jasper: they shall be set in gold in their inclosings. And the stones shall be with the names of the children of Israel, twelve, according to their names, like the engravings of a signet; every one with his name shall they be according to the twelve tribes" (Ex. 28:17–21; cf. 39:10–14).

The Seer's arrangement is euphonic and emphasizes the division of four sets of three. All the stones end in the "s" sound except three. These all end in the "n" sound and are the last element in the first three sets. Thus the Greek reads, *iaspis* [jasper], *sapphiros* [sapphire], *chalkedon* [agate] (first set ending with an "n"), *smaragdos* [emerald], *sardonux* [onyx], *sardon* [carnelian] (second set ending with an "n"), *chrusolithos* [chrysolite], *berullos* [beryl], *topazion* [topaz] (third set ending with an "n"), *chrusoprasos* [chrysoprase], *huacinthos* [jacinth], *amethystos* [amethyst] (last set ending with an "s").

In his description of the city, the Seer is following a well-established Jewish tradition. Two of his contemporaries, Philo and Josephus, use much of the same language when they write about the divine community and its association with Israel.[16] Both of John's contemporary writers see symbolic meaning within the jewels. For them the gates are the tribal heads of Israel, the jeweled foundation stones represent the community itself, the gemmed pinnacles represent the established leaders. Such descriptions of jeweled cities are not unique with the Jews; they may reach well back into antiquity, touching man's first glimpse of the heavenly community.[17]

An important part of the walls are the twelve gates. John describes these as huge pearls. A perfect pearl in the mediterranean world was worth more than its weight in gold. The Savior's parable about a pearl of such value that a wealthy merchant would have to sell all he had to buy it was not much of an exaggeration.[18] But it was probably the pearlescent luster, rather than the value, that caused the Seer to use it as an example of the portal.

John has not been the only one to see and attempt to describe such a gate. "The heavens were opened upon us," exulted Joseph Smith, "and I beheld the celestial kingdom of God, and the glory thereof, whether in the body or out I cannot tell. I saw the transcendent beauty of the gate through which the heirs of that kingdom will enter, which was like unto circling flames of fire" (D&C 137:1–2). John notes that these gates never shut (v. 25). They do not need to. The city is never in danger for the glory of God is there (cf. Isa. 60:11–13; D&C 45:67). Harmony, peace, security, and joy dominate not only the city, but also the entire sphere in which it dwells.

What is surprising about the heavenly city is the Seer's statement that "I saw no temple therein" (v. 22, KJV). Both the heavenly tabernacle and temple have been center stage in a number of visions up to this point. Now, as John beholds the eternal and celestial realm, the temple is not to be found. Where did it go? Earthly temples will dot the lands during the millennial era preparing men and women for the celestial kingdom. "When that glorious goal is gained," states Elder McConkie, "heaven itself becomes a temple. The holy of holies in the Lord's earthly houses are symbols and types of the Eternal Holy of Holies which is the highest heaven of the celestial world."[19] The lack of a visible temple emphasizes the idea that the work is completed and perfected. Nothing has been left undone.

To this universal seat of government, the exalted priest-kings of the celestial earth will bring honor and glory. From this seat will flow the power in which the heavenly nations will walk.[20] Thus we see that the new earth, one of the imposing celestial suns, will have its own capitol whose glory the whole planet will radiate as a grand stainless mirror for all worlds to see and reverence.

CONCLUSION

John follows an Old Testament theme in which the ideal heaven is local and earthly. The celestial realm is not beyond this earth but is the earth itself in a sanctified state. A misunderstanding of this very principle was what fueled a number of politico-religious uprisings that occurred during and after the time of the Lord. Many of these are chronicled in Josephus' work on the Jewish wars. To this very earth, the Father will come, and from this very earth, the Son will direct the affairs of the cosmos.

Because Gods will dwell here, the whole must be pure. An angel made this point very clear to Enoch: "Teach it unto your children, that all men, everywhere, must repent, or they can in nowise inherit the kingdom of God, for no unclean thing can dwell there, . . . for, in the language of Adam, Man of Holiness is his name" (Moses 6:57). In this light, John's concluding statement can be appreciated: "There shall in no wise enter into it any thing that defileth, neither whatsoever worketh abomination, or maketh a lie: but they which are written in the Lamb's book of life" (v. 27, KJV).

CHAPTER 22

BLESSED ARE THEY THAT DO HIS COMMANDMENTS

(AN ANALYSIS OF REVELATION 22)

THE TREE AND THE WATERS OF LIFE (vv. 1–5)

1 And he shewed me a pure river of water of life, clear as crystal, proceeding out of the throne of God and of the Lamb.

2 In the midst of the street of it, and on either side of the river, was there the tree of life, which bare twelve manner of fruits, and yielded her fruit every month: and the leaves of the tree were for the healing of the nations.

3 And there shall be no more curse: but the throne of God and of the Lamb shall be in it; and his servants shall serve him:

4 And they shall see his face; and his name shall be in their foreheads.

5 And there shall be no night there; and they need no candle, neither light of the sun; for the Lord God giveth them light: and they shall reign for ever and ever.

As the vision of the city continues, John's escort shows him a river of water, pure and crystal clear. The background imagery seems to be taken from Ezekiel 47:1–12 (but cf. Zech. 14:8). There is a close association between the Spirit and the living water in Ezekiel 36:25–26; John 3:5; and 1 John 5:6–8. Psalm 46:4 also speaks of this river that gladdens the city of God.[1] John is given to understand that the stream represents the waters of life.

The source of the water is important. It flows from "the throne of God and of the Lamb" (v. 1, KJV), note, one throne not two. There is but one source of life — God.[2] But sharing in the responsibility is the Son, who ever stands as "the very Eternal Father of heaven and of earth, and all things which in them are" (Alma 11:39). In his gospel, John recorded the Lord's words: "Whosoever drinketh of the water that I shall give him shall never thirst; but the water that I shall give him shall be in him a well of water springing up into everlasting life" (John 4:14, KJV). Thus both God and Christ occupy the same throne, for life flows from God through the Savior to mankind.

But the water has yet another and more significant meaning. Nephi saw that the "waters are a representation of the love of God" (1 Ne. 11:25). Herein lies the power of the water. It bequeaths and sustains life because it is love—pure, and unaffected.

The Seer's attention is drawn next to the tree of life and the avenue in which it stands. The Greek of verse two is difficult. The relationship between river, tree, and street cannot be determined. If the first phrase *in mesō tēs plateias autēs* (literally "In [the] midst of the street of it") belongs to the preceding verse, then the stream divides the avenue. If the phrase belongs to what follows, the river and stream likely run side by side with not just one but many trees of life in between. There are also other possibilities.[3] However, this in no way affects what John wants his readers to understand. The city is the new Eden, and in her midst stands the tree of life. Other prophets have seen that same tree and left descriptions. "I looked and beheld a tree," exclaimed Nephi, "and the beauty thereof was far beyond, yea, exceeding of all beauty; and the whiteness thereof did exceed the whiteness of the driven snow" (1 Ne. 11:8).

Note that the tree stands alone. It has no competition. The tree of good and evil has ceased to exist because the inhabitants of the city, knowing good from evil, have spurned all evil and eternally choose the good. In consequence the cherubim, placed to guard the tree of life, have been removed, allowing God's people to eat freely of the fruit. Jewish thought looked forward to the time when men would be free to partake of the wondrous tree.[4]

Following Ezekiel 47:12, the Seer notes that each month the

tree produces a different type of fruit. John conveys the idea that the tree does not follow the normal course of budding, blossoming, fruit setting, and ripening, with one harvest a year. The crops grow continually. The entire image, as one scholar notes, "expresses the absolute triumph of life over death."[5] The very leaves of the trees hold healing properties. Where it stands, not a single blade of sorrow or pain can be found. All nations are healed, that is, made whole and complete, through the power of the tree.

But one must not overlook the meaning of the tree itself, for "it is the love of God, which sheddeth itself abroad in the hearts of the children of men; . . . [which is] the most joyous to the soul" (1 Ne. 11:22–23). Thus, the tree and the water symbolize the same thing. The continuous flow of the water and the perpetual bearing of the tree emphasize the limitlessness of God's love. It flows from him forever and unconditionally. All who wish to partake may do so.

John sees that "there shall be no night there; and they need no candle, neither light of the sun; for the Lord God giveth them light" (v. 5, KJV). The whole city is alive with the light of love. The omnipresent power of God suffuses all. Isaiah had long ago promised, "The sun shall be no more thy light by day; neither for brightness shall the moon give light unto thee: but the Lord shall be unto thee an everlasting light, and thy God thy glory" (Isa. 60:19, KJV).

John expressed the real blessing for those who, walking in the light, inherit the divine kingdom: "They shall see his face; and his name shall be in their foreheads" (Rev. 22:4, KJV). One of the tasks that Jesus was to accomplish during his mortal ministry was to reveal the power, attributes, and character of God (see John 14:7, 9; 17:3). Men beheld God through Christ. But it was a mediated vision, coming via the Lord through faith. In the eternal city, faith will give way to perfect knowledge, for the sons and daughters of God will know him.[6] That knowledge does not come through the eyes. They know him because they are like him; in every one of their thoughts, in every one of their acts, he is revealed to them.

John shows the realization of Christ's earnest prayer, offered just hours before his death, for the lives of his people. In that prayer he pleaded, "Glorify thou me with thine own self with the glory which I had with thee before the world was." He prayed further that "all may be one; as thou, Father, art in me, and I in thee, that they also may be one in us" (John 17:5, 21, KJV). Those who inhabit the eternal city shall have his name written in their foreheads because, as he is, so are they. John knew that oneness could be realized. He proclaimed: "Beloved, now are we the sons of God, and it doth not yet appear what we shall be: but we know that, when he shall appear, we shall be like him; for we shall see him as he is" (1 Jn. 3:2, KJV).

EPILOGUE (vv. 6–21)

6 And he said unto me, These sayings are faithful and true: and the Lord God of the holy prophets sent his angel to shew unto his servants the things which must shortly be done.

7 Behold, I come quickly: blessed is he that keepeth the sayings of the prophecy of this book.

8 And I John saw these things, and heard them. And when I had heard and seen, I fell down to worship before the feet of the angel which shewed me these things.

9 Then saith he unto me, See thou do it not: for I am thy fellowservant, and of thy brethren the prophets, and of them which keep the sayings of this book: worship God.

10 And he saith unto me, Seal not the sayings of the prophecy of this book: for the time is at hand.

11 He that is unjust, let him be unjust still: and he which is filthy, let him be filthy still: and he that is righteous, let him be righteous still: and he that is holy, let him be holy still.

12 And, behold, I come quickly; and my reward is with me, to give every man according as his work shall be.

13 I am Alpha and Omega, the beginning and the end, the first and the last.

14 Blessed are they that do his commandments, that they may have right to the tree of life, and may enter in through the gates into the city.

15 For without are dogs, and sorcerers, and whoremongers, and murderers, and idolaters, and whosoever loveth and maketh a lie.

16 I Jesus have sent mine angel to testify unto you these things in the churches. I am the root and the offspring of David, and the bright and morning star.

17 And the Spirit and the bride say, Come. And let him that heareth say, Come. And let him that is athirst come. And whosoever

will, let him take the water of life freely.

18 For I testify unto every man that heareth the words of the prophecy of this book, If any man shall add unto these things, God shall add unto him the plagues that are written in this book:

19 And if any man shall take away from the words of the book of this prophecy, God shall take away his part out of the book of life, and out of the holy city, and from the things which are written in this book.

20 He which testifieth these things saith, Surely I come quickly. Amen. Even so, come, Lord Jesus.

21 The grace of our Lord Jesus Christ be with you all. Amen.

With the promise that men and women can truly become as God, the magnificent visions of John close. The sweep of his prophecy has been vast, stretching from the premortal existence to the postmortal worlds. He has placed all history in its cosmic setting and shown its movement to the end of time. But more grand than the historical review stands his powerful and pure testimony of his King and his God, whose power, judgment, and love he has shown none can escape.

The Seer emphasized both the truthfulness of the vision and the assurance of its accomplishment. By testifying of God's responsibility for the message, John legitimized the vision for his readers. God sent "his angel to shew unto his servants the things which must shortly be done" (v. 6, KJV). Doubly accentuating the point is God's own proclamation that "these sayings are faithful and true" (v. 6, KJV). The law of two witnesses has been satisfied: the angel and the Lamb have testified to John (see v. 16). In turn, John and the Lamb testify to the reader (see vv. 18–20). John even identifies another set of two witnesses: the Spirit and the bride, or the Church (see v. 17).

The vision stands true, established in the mouths of divine and mortal witnesses. Therefore, a curse is laid on any who might tamper with the words of the prophecy (see vv. 18–19). But the real thrust of the epilogue is in the beatitude expressed in verse seven: "Blessed is he that keepeth the sayings of the prophecy of this book" (KJV). In powerful, poetic, and prophetic terms, John has spelled out the full measure of that blessing. Now it is up to his readers to actualize it.

CONCLUSION

The prophet Nephi stated, "I beheld that the rod of iron, which my father had seen, was the word of God, which led to the fountain of living waters, or to the tree of life" (1 Ne. 11:25). Note that in Nephi's vision the tree and the water represent the same thing, each image expressing but a different aspect. The same is true in Revelation. The heart of John's city is love — the pure love of Christ. John, as few others, understood the life-power behind that love. "For God so loved the world," he testified, "that he gave his only begotten Son, that whosoever believeth in him should not perish, but have everlasting life" (John 3:16, KJV).

Christ was the Lamb slain before the foundation of the world. He became flesh so that "as many as received him," he could give the "power to become the sons of God, even to them that believe on his name" (John 1:12, KJV). In another epistle the Seer had taught the Saints: "God is love," and "love is of God; and every one that loveth is born of God, and knoweth God" (1 Jn. 4:7–8, KJV). In the eternal city, all are free to partake of that love, which flows out of him and sustains and embraces all who have been transformed into his very image.

CHAPTER 23

CONCLUSION

The book of Revelation contains, as John clearly stated in his introduction, the revelation of Jesus Christ. That revelation was given to him by God the Father. In it the Savior is revealed as the divine and visible Lamb; and the Father, as the omnipotent invisible God. But the invisible God is a God of action. For much of earth's history, he has chosen to act, as it were, behind the scenes. This has made it easy for natural men and women to attribute the course of history to political, social, or other causes. But this will not be the case for long. Already God is beginning to more openly direct the course of history and manifest more directly his control over the destiny of mankind. Soon he will personally disrupt the flow of history and set it upon a completely new course.

In the meantime, John's vision stands as more than a powerful testimony of God's prophetic abilities. It shows not only that the Almighty knew the end from the beginning and contemplated the whole of earth's history, but also that he arranged it. To say it more strongly, before the first soul was ever placed on the earth, God orchestrated the whole of earthly existence. Since that time, all things have moved in concert with his plans.

The issue throughout Revelation centers on sovereignty. Who is the God of this world, the Father or Satan? John's vision, focusing as it does on cosmic reality, clearly shows that it is the

246

God of heaven, not the master of hell. Further, the Seer discloses that there is never a moment when the Father's supremacy comes into question. He has full power over all things, including death and hell. Nothing, though it may seem at times otherwise, moves independent of his designs—not even the host of Satan. Showing that God overmasters all things, John admonishes his reader to faith and patience. In the end, no matter how bad things may appear until then, righteousness will triumph, and the faithful will have their full reward.

In spite of this, there has never been the slightest interference with either human will or satanic machinations. Each individual stands as a separate player, creating his own lines, developing his own character, and freely producing the drama of his own life. Still, God shares the same stage. Further, he is not only the principle actor, but also the director. Though he may not select the cast, he alone has the power to determine when and where each soul will be played. His self-imposed rules dictate that he must use every person, no matter how evil or twisted he may become or how much good he may do. Each must have his chance. Still, God knows what each will do, how each will respond to any given situation and to life as a whole.

Some have asked, "If God knows the end of every soul, why doesn't he just judge people now and place them in their kingdom?" The question makes two false assumptions. The first tries to make a connection between what God knows and how a person behaves. I have used a simple illustration in some of my classes to show that there is no connection between the two. Taking a pencil, eraser-end down, and placing it roughly six inches above the center of a sloping table, I have asked my students to tell me what will happen when I release it. I stress that they may not guess and must tell me what they absolutely know will happen. They are uncanny in their ability to determine its course, predicting, among other things, that it will fall, bounce, produce a noise, roll, and come to rest. When I drop the pencil, everything happens exactly as they say. I then ask them how they get the pencil to do what they know it will. They assure me that they have nothing to do with what the pencil does. This simple exercise demonstrates that foreknowledge does not cause action: no connection exists between what God knows about us as individuals and our behavior.

The second false assumption is that God is a magician who, by the wave of some divine wand, can make us into creatures of celestial, terrestrial, or telestial glory. But God is not a magician, and he cannot make us into anything. He can protect, guide, and empower us. But we are the ones who make us into something, and we do it through the millions of choices, both big and little (but mostly little), that we make during the course of an entire lifetime. Thus, we shape our eternal character, and in the resurrection what we have shaped is what we become (cf. Alma 41:1–8).

Now to the point. God knows how each person will behave at any given time and under any given circumstance. By knowing what each person will do, he knows how the whole of any combination of people will behave. He shapes history by assembling the aggregate while at the same time allowing each individual free reign over his own destiny.

Thus, John's revelation testifies not only to the omniscience of God, but also to his omnipotence. The Seer appeals to both faith and faithfulness as he shows that everything moves in harmony according to the composition orchestrated by God. God even weaves the discord of Satan into the whole movement. The result becomes a magnificent hymn of praise to his power as both God and the Lamb. In the words of the heavenly choir: "Great and marvellous are thy works, Lord God Almighty; just and true are thy ways, thou King of saints. Who shall not fear thee, O Lord, and glorify thy name? for thou only art holy: for all nations shall come and worship before thee; for thy judgments are made manifest" (Rev. 15:3–4, KJV).

THE STRUCTURE
OF REVELATION

The following outline shows the relationship of the parts of Revelation to the whole.

    A.   Chapter 1, introduction to the vision.

    B.   Chapters 2–3, the letter to the seven churches.

    C.   Chapters 4–5, the vision of the future celestial kingdom.

        1.   God in his glory is worshipped by man and animals (4:2–11).

        2.   The testament or will of God for this earth is revealed (5:1–4).

        3.   The Savior, symbolized as the Lamb, executes the will (5:6–14).

    D.   Chapter 6, the vision of the opening of the six seals, in which each seal represents one thousand years of history.

    E.   Chapter 7, the first interlude explaining how the Saints will survive the great destructions described in chapters 8–9.

        1.   The sealing of the Saints of God against the wrath that is to come forth (7:1–8).

        2.   The vision of the great triumphant multitude (7:9–17).

F. Chapters 8–9, the vision of destruction poured out
during the seventh seal, or the period after the Millennium begins but preceding the Second Coming.
1. The first four trumpets: Great plagues that will
encompass the earth (8:1–12).
2. The fifth trumpet or first woe: The great war, with
its designer, warriors, and intent identified (9:1–
11).
3. The sixth trumpet or second woe: The method
and the extent of the destructions (9:12–19).
4. The refusal of the wicked to repent (9:20–21). [Sev-
enth trumpet or third woe does not begin until
chapter 11]

G. Chapter 10, second interlude giving John some specific personal instructions.
1. John seals up certain teachings concerning God's
work in the latter days (10:1–7).
2. John learns the part he is to play in the events
that are to take place (10:8–11).

H. Chapter 11, the vision resumes.
1. The ministry of the two prophets and the fall of
the holy city (11:1–13).
2. The seventh trumpet or third woe: God's triumph
over the wicked proclaimed (11:15–19).

I. Chapters 12–13, the beginning of the repetition of the
scenario, starting from John's day but this time giving
more background.
1. Flashback to John's day; disclosure of Satan's active persecution of the Church (12:1–6).
2. Flashback to the war in heaven where the conflict
began (12:7–12).
3. Flash–forward to John's day, showing the forces
of apostasy working against the Church (12:13–
17).
4. Symbolic representation of later apostate and civil
forces up to the Second Coming of the Lord (13:1–
18).

J. Chapter 14, the restoration of the gospel and its powers during the last days.
   1. Zion to be established (14:1–5).
   2. The gospel to be preached to all the world (14:6–
       7).
   3. Babylon to fall as God gathers out the righteous
       and harvests the wickedness of the earth (14:8–
       20).

K. Chapter 15, the third interlude showing heaven's
preparation for the final assault upon the wicked
(15:1–8).

L. Chapter 16, the vision resumes, the seven plagues
being poured out. The vision of chapters 8, 9, and 11
repeated but from a different perspective.

M. Chapters 17–18, fourth interlude revealing the Satanic
kingdom and its nature.
   1. The nature of Babylon and the cause of her fall
       (17:1–18).
   2. The Saints are called out of Babylon (18:1–5).
   3. Babylon falls and is mourned by her lovers (18:6–
       24).

N. Chapter 19, the fifth interlude celebrating the marriage
supper of the Lamb.

O. Chapters 20–22, the vision resumes, with the Millennium, final judgment, and celestialization of the earth
being shown.
   1. Satan is bound, and a millennium of peace begins
       (20:1–6).
   2. Satan is loosed to wreak havoc for a short season,
       only to be cast out forever (20:7–10).
   3. The great last judgment takes place (20:11–15).
   4. The earth becomes celestial with its capitol, the
       New Jerusalem (21:1–22:1–5).

P. Chapter 22:6–21, commandment to John to send the
vision to the world.

APPENDIX B

SIX ELEMENTS OF JOHN'S WRITING STYLE

Understanding certain elements of John's writing style and methodology is helpful in untangling the work's complexities.[1] These elements are as follows:

1) *Repetition.* The vision emphasizes certain points through repetition; however, it does not necessarily use identical words to express the same ideas. Some of these are found within one verse, others in the structure of the whole. The repetition not only underscores the points God wishes to drive home, but also allows for further insight through the use of different perspectives.

Some examples from single verses are "His head and his hairs were white like wool, as white as snow" (1:14, KJV); "who created heaven, and the things that therein are, and the earth, and the things that therein are, and the sea, and the things which are therein" (10:6, KJV); "victory over the beast, and over his image, and over his mark, and over the number of his name" (15:2, KJV). Examples from the larger unit of the book include the repeated series of seven plagues (associated with seven seals and trumpets), and the seven bowls (see chapters 8, 9, 16); the repeated hymns of praise all containing similar themes (see, e.g., 4:8, 11; 5:9–10, 12, 13; 7:10, 12); and the repeated depictions of the Saints in triumph (see 7:9–11; 14:1–3; 15:2).

2) *Expansion.* John often introduces brief, indefinite expressions or statements, then expands them, sometimes after an interval. A few examples within closely connected clauses are "thy works," i.e., "thy labor, and thy patience" (2:2, KJV); "a stumblingblock," i.e., "to eat things sacrificed unto idols, and to commit fornication" (2:14, KJV); "my two witnesses" (KJV), characterized as standing before God, being able to seal the heavens, and to cause plagues (11:2–6); and "the camp of the saints," i.e., "the beloved city" (20:9, KJV). Examples of phrases made definite after an interval are "The woman fled into the wilderness, where she hath a place prepared" (Rev. 12:6, KJV) and "to the woman were given two wings of a great eagle, that she might fly into the wilderness, into her place, where she is nourished for a time" (v. 14, KJV); the beast in 13:1 is met again in 17:3; and the fall of Babylon noted in 14:8 is expanded in 18:2–19.

3) *Interruptions.* In the course of thought, John often pauses for explanation. Though this does violence at times to logical order, such interruptions are very Hebraic. The Greeks' strict laws of continuity did not bind the Near Eastern mind-set. (For examples, see the Psalms or the longer Pauline epistles.) The interruptions fall into two categories: a) displacement within a single paragraph, or interjections of brief explanations, and b) insertions of longer episodes — called "interludes" herein — disrupting the main scenario.

An example of category A is the reference to the war in heaven (see 12:7–12) sandwiched in the conflict between the Saints and the dragon (see 12:1–6, 13–17). An example of category B is chapter ten, which interrupts the flow between chapters nine and eleven. The previous chapters of this book assist the reader through these.

4) *Prefaces.* John systematically precedes visions or scenes with prefatory passages of varying length. One of John's purposes was to cheer and sustain his readers. Therefore, he often stops to offer reassurance before proceeding into the more disconcerting aspects of his vision. For example, the whole eschatological section of the book is prefaced by chapters 4–5. In these

chapters God's will is shown to be the executing force behind all that happens. He is in charge. Similarly, before introducing the vision of the seven plagues (see chapters 8–9), John reassures his readers that God's people will be brought through in safety (see chapter 7).

5) *Nonrealism.* Readers of Revelation encounter abrupt changes, impossible combinations, and contradictions. Note, however, that a completely logical and clearly understood apocalyptic style is a contradiction in terms—including Revelation.[2] The reader must be prepared for a trip along a surreal landscape. The prophet received his vision through poetic images free of any need for internal consistency and conformity to reality. The vision presents inconsistencies, sudden transitions, and unimaginable conceptions. But, as will be shown in the next section, this is what gives apocalyptic literature its special punch. The style allows God to communicate through the force of the images and movements he creates. He is not shackled with the need to make all things smooth and logical. An inconsistency can underscore a point.

A few examples will illustrate the writer's style. Three examples of contradictions follow: "Immediately I was in the Spirit" (4:2, KJV), when John had been in the Spirit from 1:10 on. The sanctified are to be pillars in the temple in the New Jerusalem (see 3:12), but later the text specifically states that there is no temple in that city (see 21:22). In 8:7 the grass is destroyed, but in 9:4 it is unhurt.

Examples of abrupt changes are the Lord holding seven stars in his right hand (see 1:16) that is then laid reassuringly on the prophet's shoulder (see v. 17); the beast with seven heads (see 13:1) suddenly having but one mouth, then becoming a personal ruler ("his seat" — KJV; v. 2), and finally being identified by but one of his heads (see v. 12). Examples of impossible combinations are viewing the writing inside a sealed scroll, a lamb taking a book and opening its seals, animal creatures playing harps (see 5:1–8), the description of the locusts as fabulous creatures that hurt only men (see 9:3–10), and a city twelve thousand furlongs high—which translates to about fourteen hundred miles straight up (see 21:16).

6) *Symbolism.* John uses symbols as the major means of communicating ideas.[3] Through this means, the writer vividly represents transcendental and spiritual experiences. John employs symbols in almost every sentence of the revelation. But he does not create them ex nihilo; they come from God and are consistent with the Old Testament and Jewish apocalyptic literature. Indeed, in Revelation John uses the words, phrases, images, and patterns of the ancient covenant as a kind of language arsenal that undergirds and propels the message, which the Seer's contemporaries clearly grasped.[4]

However, John does not bring unmodified a single Old Testament symbol (or even a scriptural reference) into his revelation, whole or complete. Shadows and echoes from the Old Testament abound in over half of the verses in Revelation. Images and figures come particularly from Daniel, Isaiah, Ezekiel, and Zechariah. But in the whole book, there is only one explicit reference to an Old Testament passage. Revelation 15:3, referring to the song of triumph sung by those who overcame the beast, states that "they sing the song of Moses the servant of God" (KJV), but what follows is neither the song found in Exodus 15 nor that of Deuteronomy 32. Rather, it is an amalgamation of several Old Testament themes.[5] Old Testament symbols are modified, reworked, and shaped to meet the special needs of the vision.

In doing so the vision becomes a unique literary composition full of wonder and carrying John's special insights. Therefore, an understanding of Old Testament apocalyptic and prophetic material is helpful, but only to a point. For example, John's introduction (chapter 1) has the familiar ring of Daniel, chapters seven and ten. Daniel's four beasts that rise from the sea, two with wings and one with ten horns (see Dan. 7:3–7), bear a similarity to both John's single beast arising from the same place (see Rev. 13:1–2) and his four beasts surrounding the throne of heaven (see Rev. 4:6–9). His plagues shadow those vented against the Egyptians (see Ex. 7–9). The plague of locusts (see

Rev. 9) echoes that found in Joel 1–2. And the little scroll referred to in chapter ten is foreshadowed in Ezekiel 2–3. The preceding chapters show that, while many Old Testament images and allusions show up in John's work, in every case John alters the traditional text for his own purposes.[6] However, those who feel comfortable with the images created in the Old Testament will probably feel at home with John.

Notes

Preface

1. James R. Clark, ed., *Messages of the First Presidency* (Salt Lake City: Bookcraft, 1965), 1:161.
2. Andrew F. Ehat, Lyndon W. Cook, eds., *The Words of Joseph Smith* (Provo, Utah: Religious Studies Center, Brigham Young University, 1980), 186.
3. Emil Bock, *The Apocalypse of Saint John*, trans. Alfred Heidenreich (Edinburgh: Floris Books, 1951), 17.
4. N. G. L. Hammond and H. H. Scullard, *The Oxford Classical Dictionary* (Oxford: The Clarendon Press, 1970), ix-xxii; George A. Buttrick et al, eds., *The Interpreter's Dictionary of the Bible*, 4 vols. (Nashville: Abingdon Press, 1962), 1:xxix–xxxi.

Chapter 1

1. Thuc. 3.33; Strab. 10.5.13.
2. *Nat. Hist.* 4.12.23. See Tac. *Ann.* 3.68; 4.30; 15.71; Juv. *Sat.* 1.73; 6.563–64; 10.170.
3. *Church News*, Dec. 5, 1987, 14.
4. R. H. Charles, *A Critical and Exegetical Commentary on the Revelation of St. John*, 2 vols. (Edinburgh: T. & T. Clark, 1920), 1:22, notes the most important passages from Origen, Clement of Alexandria, Pliny, and Tertullian concerning the cause of John's banishment.
5. Tertullian, a third-century convert to Christianity, was a lawyer and was therefore careful with legal terms. He states that John had incurred the *relegatio* (see *De praescript. haeret.* 36). For a discussion, see F. J. A. Hort, *The Apocalypse of St. John I-III* (London: MacMillan

and Co., 1908), xli; and G. B. Caird, *A Commentary on the Revelation of St. John the Divine* (Peabody, Massachusetts: Hendrickson Publishers, 1966), 21–22.

6. For a detailed discussion, see Robert H. Mounce, *The Book of Revelation* (Grand Rapids, Michigan: Wm. B. Eerdmans Publishing Co., 1977), 32, 36–37.

7. See Dio Chrys. *Or*. 46.6, 10.

8. For a full discussion of these times, see W. H. C. Frend, *Martyrdom and Persecution in the Early Church* (Grand Rapids: Baker Book House, 1965), 173–253.

9. The Greek apocryphal text *Acts of John* by Prochorus states that John was on the island for fifteen years (see Buttrick, *Interpreter's Dictionary*, s.v. John, Acts of, by Prochorus). However, this text is highly suspect.

10. Edgar Hennecke, *New Testament Apocrypha*, 2 vols., ed. Wilhelm Schneemelcher, trans. R. McL. Wilson (Philadelphia: The Westminster Press, 1964), 2:195–97, 623 cites this tradition about John.

11. See Hugh Nibley, *When the Lights Went Out: Three Studies on Ancient Apostasy* (Salt Lake City: Deseret Book Co., 1970), 1–94.

12. G. Kittle et al, eds., *Theological Dictionary of the New Testament*, trans. Geoffery W. Bromily, 10 vols. (Grand Rapids: Eerdmans, 1964), s.v. *aphistēmi* (cited hereafter as *TDNT*); Stephen E. Robinson, "Warring against the Saints of God," *Ensign*, January 1988, 34.

13. This statement is based on conditions that clearly existed a few decades later. The letters of Ignatius, a Syrian bishop, emphasize the need of a nonprophetic Church order based on the authority of bishops. However, he does claim in one instance prophetic power for the bishops. To the Philadelphians he wrote, "When I was with you I cried out, I spoke with a loud voice, God's own voice: 'Pay attention to the bishop and the presbytery and deacons.' . . . The Spirit made proclamation, saying this: 'Do nothing apart from the bishop' " (7.1). Such a stand suggests that the office and function of the bishop had not yet replaced those of the prophet. The prophetic gift was still recognized as essential by many within the Christian community. Thus, it was necessary to legitimize the central authority of the bishop by claiming the power of prophecy (see Elizabeth Schussler Fiorenza, *The Book of Revelation: Justice and Judgment* [Philadelphia: Fortress Press, 1985], 142–43).

14. See also Robert A. Spivey and D. Moody Smith, *Anatomy of the New Testament*, 4th ed. (New York: Macmillan Publishing Company, 1989), 405.

15. Didachē 11:7–13.

16. Andre Feuillet, *The Apocalypse*, trans. Thomas E. Crane (New York: Alba House, 1965), 75–76.

17. John R. May, "The Judaeo-Christian Apocalypse," in *The Revelation of St. John the Divine*, ed. Harold Bloom (New York: Chelsea House Publishers, 1988), 39.

18. Ibid., 39–41.

Chapter 2

1. Northrop Frye, "Typology: Apocalypse," in Bloom, *Revelation*, 71.

2. Joseph Fielding Smith, comp., *Teachings of the Prophet Joseph Smith* (Salt Lake City: Deseret Book, 1976), 290.

3. Bruce R. McConkie, "Understanding the Book of Revelation," *Ensign*, September 1975, 87. In his *Doctrinal New Testament Commentary*, 3 vols. (Salt Lake City: Bookcraft, 1973), 3:431, Elder McConkie further stated, "We are in a much better position to understand those portions of Revelation which we are expected to understand than we generally realize. Thanks be to the interpretive material found in sections 29, 77, 88, and others of the revelations in the Doctrine and Covenants [and other latter-day scriptures], . . . we have a marvelously comprehensive and correct understanding of this otherwise hidden book."

4. Cited in Robert J. Matthews, *"A Plainer Translation"—Joseph Smith's Translation of the Bible: A History and Commentary* (Provo: Brigham Young University Press, 1985), 25; italics added.

5. *Messenger and Advocate*, February 1835, 80. The sealed portion has been described as consisting of about two-thirds the volume of the golden plates. If that is the case, then the vision of Jared's brother would occupy a substantial portion of over one thousand pages of translated text. This dwarfs John's mere twenty-five pages. However, John devoted only a few lines to six thousand years of earth's history in order to concentrate on the period just before the Second Coming.

6. See also McConkie, "Understanding Revelation," 86.

7. Smith, *Teachings*, 84.

8. See Isbon T. Beckwith, *The Apocalypse of John* (New York: Macmillan Co., 1919; reprint, Grand Rapids: Baker Book House, 1967), 411.

9. For examples in classical Greek, see Pl. *Prt.* 352d; *Grg.* 460a; Plut. *Vit., Cat. Mai.* 20. This is the sense in which the word is frequently used in the Septuagint.

10. Hort, *Apocalypse*, 3.

11. It does appear in the title of 2 Baruch—"The Book of the Apocalypse of Baruch the Son of Neriah"—published shortly after the Revelation of John but not in any documents that antedate John's work. See Charles, *Commentary*, 4–5.

12. A number of studies have been completed on apocalyptic as a literary genre. See for example D. S. Russell, *The Method and Message of Jewish Apocalyptic: 200 B.C.-A.D. 100* (Philadelphia: Westminster, 1964); P. D. Hanson, *The Dawn of Apocalyptic: The Historical and Sociological Roots of Jewish Apocalyptic Eschatology*, rev. ed. (Philadelphia: Fortress, 1979); C. Rowland, *The Open Heaven: A Study of Apocalyptic in Judaism and Early Christianity* (New York: Crossroad, 1982). Some major apocalypses bearing some resemblance to Revelation are Psalms of Solomon (written ca. 50 B.C.), Odes of Solomon (collected between ca. 50 B.C. and A.D. 50), the Testament of the XII Patriarchs (copied between ca.

100 B.C. and A.D. 50), Book of Jubilees (written between ca. 50 B.C. and A.D. 50), Second Esdras or Fourth Ezra (written ca. A.D. 75), the Apocalypse of Baruch (written ca. A.D. 75), the Apocalypse of Abraham (written ca. A.D. 50). There are a number of works (e.g., the Ascension of Isaiah, and the Life of Adam and Eve) that have small apocalyptic sections and add some detail but are much later than Revelation. For analysis, see Beckwith, *Apocalypse*, 186–197.

13. Beckwith, *Apocalypse*, vi. Relevant texts and insights will be brought to bear in the analyses of the chapters.

14. The elements discussed here pertain to Christian apocalyptic in general. Note that a definition of apocalypticism and of the literature as a genre is problematical. Participants at the Uppsala colloquium on apocalypticism refrained from even suggesting a definition. (For a discussion see Fiorenza, *Revelation*, 1.) It is not my purpose to enter into the debate. The elements chosen here are accepted by a wide range of conservative Christian scholars, meet with my own observations, and conform to LDS theology. The outline followed is that of Mounce, *Revelation*, 19–21.

15. May, "Christian Apocalypse," in Bloom, *Revelation*, 37.

16. M. H. Abrams, "Apocalypse: Theme and Romantic Variations," in Bloom, *Revelation*, 9; Fiorenza, *Revelation*, 5.

17. For collections, see Hennecke, *Apocrypha*, 2:578–803, and James H. Charlesworth, ed., *Old Testament Pseudepigrapha*, 2 vols. (Garden City: Doubleday, 1983). Volume 1 deals excusively with apocalyptic literature.

18. Charles R. Erdman, *The Revelation of John* (Philadelphia: The Westminster Press, 1966), 16–18; Beckwith, *Apocalypse*, p. vi.

19. *Ensign*, September 1975, 87; see Gerald N. Lund, "Seeing the Book of Revelation as a Book of Revelation," *Ensign*, December 1987, 46–52 where four keys are provided, and "Three Keys Help Understanding of Revelation," *Church News*, December 12, 1987, 7.

20. For a good discussion of various interpretation, see Beckwith, *Apocalypse*, 320–336.

21. Smith, *Teachings*, 289, 247; cf. Ehat, *Words*, 184–85.

22. The analytical sections will cite allusions to and similarities between John and the Old Testament scriptures.

23. Abrams, "Apocalypse," in Bloom, *Revelation*, 9.

24. Ibid., 12–13.

25. Feuillet, *Apocalypse*, 77.

26. Some believe that the structure of Revelation was determined by the number seven. Not counting the prologue and epilogue, they argue, the book has seven divisions, and most of these are again subdivided by seven (see Erdman, *Revelation*, 27–28 for analysis). Though the argument is arresting, there is not enough evidence for consensus. All such schematics seem somewhat forced and arbitrary, and so are not used in this study.

27. Feuillet, *Apocalypse*, 36.

28. Smith, *Teachings,* pp. 290–91.

29. Beckwith, *Apocalypse,* vii, 214–15.

30. Examples are the seven stars of Revelation 1:16 explained in v. 20; the waters in 17:1 are defined in v. 15; and seven heads in 17:3 are interpreted in v. 9. See also 4:5; 5:6; 11:8; 12:9; 19:8.

31. Erdman, *Revelation,* 15.

32. See for example Revelation 8:1; 9:14–15; 10:3–4; 12:15–16; 13:3, 18.

33. Austin Farrer, *A Rebirth of Images: The Making of St. John's Apocalypse* (Boston: Beacon, 1963), 19.

34. Erdman, *Revelation,* 14.

35. Fiorenza, *Revelation,* 22.

36. Homer Hailey, *Revelation, An Introduction and Commentary* (Grand Rapids: Baker Book House, 1979), 41; Erdman, *Revelation,* 15. The analytical chapters draw out the meaning of the numbers in their various contexts.

Chapter 3

1. Joseph Fielding Smith, *Doctrines of Salvation,* 3 vols. (Salt Lake City: Bookcraft, 1955), 1: 27.

2. Erdman, *Revelation,* 35–36.

3. The words *sign, mark,* and *token* share the meaning of some discernible indication of what is not itself directly perceptible. But each term denotes a specific aspect of the indication. A *sign* is any indication to be perceived by the senses or reason. A *mark* is something impressed on something or inherently characteristic of a thing. A *token* serves as a proof of something intangible (*Webster's Ninth New Collegiate Dictionary,* s.v. sign).

4. Charlton T. Lewis, *A Latin Dictionary* (Oxford: Clarendon Press, 1890), s.v. *signaculum, signo,* and *signum.*

5. Mounce, *Revelation,* 65.

6. Originally, the worship service of the Christians followed closely the pattern of the synagogue. Scripture reading played a major role in the service. Initially, readings seem to have been only from the Old Testament. Later, the Gospels and Epistles were included. For the Jewish background, see Nehemiah 8:2; Exodus 24:7; Luke 4:16; Acts 13:15; 2 Corinthians 3:15. For the adoption of the practice by Christians, see Just. *Apol.* 1.67; Charles, *Commentary,* 1: 7.

7. James E. Talmage, *The Great Apostasy* (Salt Lake City: Deseret Book Co., 1958), 44–45.

8. For discussion, see Mounce, *Revelation,* pp. 67–68.

9. Josephine Massyngberde Ford, tr., *The Anchor Bible: Revelation* (Garden City, New York: Doubleday & Company, Inc., 1975), 376. The Song of the Doves at Dodona speaks of "Zeus who was, Zeus who is, and Zeus who will be" (Paus. *Asin.* 10.12.10). At Sais the shrine of Minerva boasted, "I am all that hath been and is and shall be" (Plut.

Mor., De Is. et Os 9; see Mounce, *Revelation,* 68; for a technical discussion of the title, see Charles, *Commentary,* 1:10).

10. Caird, *Revelation,* 16.
11. Mounce, *Revelation,* 68.
12. In Zechariah 4:1–10 the seven lamps represent the omniscience of the Lord. The source of the imagery may specifically have been Zechariah 4:2, 10, where the seven lamps "are the eyes of the Lord, which run to and fro through the whole earth."
13. Joseph Smith was permitted to see the future celestial kingdom where, along with past prophets, he saw his then living mother and father along with his dead brother Alvin (Smith, *Teachings,* 107).
14. Mounce, *Revelation,* 70–71.
15. The JST states that Christ "hath made us kings and priests unto God, his Father" (v. 6). The omission of the "and" between "God" and "Father" clarifies to whom men become kings and priests. However, some years later Joseph Smith reinterpreted the verse insisting that the "and" should be used (see Smith, *Teachings,* 370).
16. McConkie, *Commentary,* 3:436. For a discussion of the phrase "kings and priests," see Charles, *Commentary,* 1:16.
17. Joseph. *AJ.* 3.290, 310.
18. The idea that all will see him together comes out of Zechariah 12:10, 12; Job 19:24–27; see also Doctrine and Covenants 45:51–52.
19. Hort, *Apocalypse,* 14.
20. *TDNT,* s.v. *biblion.*
21. See, e.g., Ex. 28:4; 29:5, Septuagint, where it is connected with the attire of the high priest. The girdle of the high priest was made of fine-twined linen and embroidered with needlework (see Ex. 39:29), while the clasp or girdle that gathered together the long robe of the Lord was of gold. Josephus, however, notes that during his time the high priest's girdle was interwoven with gold (*AJ* 3.7.2). The golden clasp or *porpē* was worn by the king and his associates (1 Macc. 10:89; 11:58) and so served as the mark of an important office (for discussion, see Charles, *Commentary,* 1: 28; Mounce, *Revelation,* 77–78).
22. McConkie, *Commentary,* 3:443.
23. McConkie, *Commentary,* 3:442.
24. *TDNT,* s.v. *machaira* and *rhomphaia.*
25. In the Old Testament, Hades was the world of departed spirits. By John's day the meaning of the term was in transition and came to stand in contrast to paradise, the realm of the blessed. Hades lies within the earth—one goes down into it (see Matt. 11:23; Luke 10:15; cf. Rev. 10:7). John calls it the *phulakē,* or "keep," meaning an underground prison (cf. Rev. 20:2–3 with 20:7). Souls are held there only temporarily. Thus, it stands in contrast to Gehenna (Greek *geenna*), the place of eternal torment of the devil and his angels (see Rev. 20:10, 14; see *TDNT,* s.v. *hadēs* and *geenna*).
26. Charles, *Commentary,* 1:32.
27. W. M. Ramsay, *Letters to the Seven Churches* (Grand Rapids: Baker Book, 1963), 183–92.

28. For argument, see Charles, *Commentary,* 1:24–25; Caird, *Revelation,* 15.

29. For argument, see Fiorenza, *Revelation,* 144.

30. Bock, *Apocalypse,* 33.

31. Fiorenza, *Revelation,* 116.

Chapter 4

1. Charles, *Commentary,* 1:102.

2. It or its equivalent is fairly standard fare in apocalyptic literature for this purpose (see, e.g., Dan. 7:6–7; 1 Enoch 86:2; Test. Jos. 19:3; 4 Ezra 11:22, 33; 13:5, 8. In a shortened form, see Ezek. 1:4; 2:9; 8:2, 7, 10; 10:1; Zech. 1:8; 6:1; 1 Enoch 14:14–15; 2 Bar. 36:1–2, 7, 37:1). In each of the above, the phrase introduces an ecstatic condition in which a vision or a new aspect was opened.

3. In the Testament of Levi 2:6, the heavens open to admit that prophet. Note the contrast with John's open door, for all its size, to time depicted in Revelation 19:11 when the whole of heaven is opened so that its legions can march forth in the train of the Son of God.

4. Smith, *Teachings,* 220.

5. See Mounce, *Revelation,* 134.

6. See 1 Enoch 14:18–19; Testament of Levi 5:1; 2 Enoch 22:2. For discussion, see Ford, *Revelation,* 70–71.

7. See Charles, *Commentary,* 1:114–15; Bock, *Apocalypse,* 41. Walter Scott, *Exposition of the Revelation of Jesus Christ,* 4th ed. (Grand Rapids: Kregel Publications, n.d.), 121, notes that these stones appeared on the High Priests breast plate, the sardis being first, and the jasper last (see Ex. 28:17–20).

8. Caird, *Revelation,* 63.

9. 2 Baruch 21:6 notes that there are "holy beings . . . [of] flame and fire, who stand around your throne." Thus, the idea of God being surrounded by beings glorious in their own right was current in John's day.

10. The term was used in Greek-speaking areas to designate a civic official such as a senator. Among the Jews the term applied to the chief officer of a synagogue and to a member of the Sanhedrin. Among the Christians, the term seems to have designated any Church officer. The Septuagint uses the term in this way in Isaiah 24:23; 63:9.

11. Joseph Smith had the same experience on 21 January 1836. In vision he saw his mother and father—who were still living—in the celestial kingdom (*Teachings,* 107).

12. Charles, *Commentary,* 1: 132–33; Scott, *Exposition,* 122.

13. Joseph., *AJ.* 7.365–67; Ford, *Revelation,* 72–73.

14. Hailey, *Revelation,* 168.

15. Mounce, *Revelation,* 135–36. In apocalyptic literature the idea of royal priestly authority as the reward for righteousness is very common (see, e.g., Asc. Isa. 7:22; 8:26; 9:10–13, 18, 24, 25; 11:40).

16. Charles, *Commentary*, 1:132–33.

17. Bock, *Apocalypse*, 41–42.

18. Scott, *Exposition*, 124–25.

19. In 1 Enoch 71:7 and 39:12, the cherubim praise God day and night, saying "Holy, Holy, Holy, Lord of the Spirits."

20. Joseph Smith, *History of the Church*, 7 vols. (Salt Lake City: Deseret Book, 1973), 5:324; Ehat, *Words*, 171.

21. Smith, *History*, 3:325; see also Ehat, *Words*, 189.

22. In 2 Enoch 19:6; 21:1 the seraphim and cherubim have six wings and many eyes and are found standing before God's throne singing: "Holy, holy, holy is the Lord God of Sabaoth: heavens and earth are full of Thy glory." John's description, therefore, appears to follow Jewish apocalyptic motifs (Charles, *Commentary*, 1:120–21).

23. See 1 Enoch 71:7, where they are described as "the sleepless ones who guard the throne of [God's] glory."

24. For a discussion of this law, see Hyrum L. Andrus, *Doctrines of the Kingdom* (Salt Lake City: Bookcraft, 1973), 223–59.

Chapter 5

1. The Greek *biblion* can mean book, scroll, or document. However, at this early date books were uncommon. What John saw, therefore, was probably a scroll in the hand of God.

2. Mounce, *Revelation*, 142–43. The idea of a book containing the history of the earth was not new with John. Psalm 139:16 suggests the idea, and in 1 Enoch 81:1–2 there is mention of heavenly tablets that contain "all the deeds of men . . . that will be upon the earth to the remotest generations" (see also 47:3; 106:19; 107:1).

3. Ford, *Revelation*, 92–93. The scroll was found by Yigael Yadin in the Judean desert. It was bound by seven threads, each of which was locked with a seal on which was the name of a witness. The document dated from the late first century. That would make it contemporary with Revelation.

4. Charles, *Commentary*, 1:137–38.

5. McConkie, *Commentary*, 3:471.

6. Ford, *Revelation*, p. 85. For discussion, see chapter ten.

7. Hailey, *Revelation*, p. 175.

8. The Greek word *klaiō*, literally "wailing," denotes deep mourning. Its biblical use frequently refers to the wailing of professional mourners hired for the purpose.

9. The figure of the Messiah as a lion is seen in 2 Esdras 12:31 and elsewhere.

10. Fiorenza, *Revelation*, 73.

11. Testament of Joseph 19:8; 1 Enoch 90:38; Ford, *Revelation*, 30–31.

12. Mounce, *Revelation*, 144.

13. Hailey, *Revelation*, 176–77.

14. Fiorenza, *Revelation*, 73–74.
15. In 1 Enoch 90:9, the Maccabees are stylized as "horned lambs."
See Charles, *Commentary*, 1:141–43.
16. Caird, *Revelation*, 75.
17. Smith, *Teachings*, 158.
18. See *TDNT*, s.v. *apostolos*.
19. Mounce, *Revelation*, 147.
20. Charles, *Commentary*, 1:146.
21. Elder McConkie states that John saw 100,000,000 plus thousands of thousands of saved souls. "The expansion of world population being what it is, we can suppose that the billions who live on earth during the Millennium—and who 'grow up without sin unto salvation' (D&C 45:58)—shall far exceed in number the total hosts of men who have lived during the preceding six thousand years. Truly, in the aggregate, there are many who shall be saved" (*Commentary*, 3:475).

Chapter 6

1. The concept of definite divisions of the world's history appears for the first time in Daniel 7, 9, the prophecies dealing respectively with the four kingdoms and the seventy weeks. Various modes were adopted in other apocalyptic writings. The most common break is into four, seven, ten, or twelve periods (for a full bibliography, see Beckwith, *Apocalypse*, 78–79).
2. Caird, *Revelation*, 79–80.
3. Mounce, *Revelation*, 152.
4. The KJV follows the major manuscript tradition with the words: "I heard . . . one of the four beasts saying, Come and see," as though it were directed to the Seer himself. However, there is another strong tradition in which the command is a summons to each horse and rider to execute their power on the earth. A major point this tradition has going for it is that the imperative form of the Greek here is *erchou*, as it is with each of the other seals. In those instances where the Seer is specifically summoned (see Rev. 17:1; 21:9), the imperative is *deuro* (Charles, *Commentary*, 1:161; Beckwith, *Apocalypse*, 516). Thus, a better translation of the text would be, "I heard one of the four living creatures say, . . . 'Come!' And I saw, and behold . . . " I have chosen to follow the majority tradition in the text.
5. See, e.g., Herod. 7:40; 9:63; Philostr. *V. A.* 1:30; Charles, *Commentary*, 1:162.
6. By the time John was writing the distinction between the two words was beginning to blur (see James H. Moulton and George Milligan, *The Vocabulary of the Greek Testament* [Grand Rapids: Eerdmans, 1952], s.v. *stephanos*). However, their use in Revelation suggests that the distinction was important to John.
7. McConkie, *Commentary*, 3:477.
8. Cf. Zechariah 1:8; 6:2; 2 Kings 3:22, Septuagint, on the color

applied to horses; and 1 Clement 8:3 and Ford, *Revelation,* 98, on its symbolic meaning.

9. See chapter three, pp. 25–42, for a discussion of the term.

10. Ford, *Revelation,* 106.

11. McConkie, *Commentary,* 3:478–79.

12. Ibid., 479–80.

13. On prices, see Cic. *Verr.* 3:81, 84.; Beckwith, *Apocalypse,* 520; Charles, *Commentary,* 1:166–67.

14. McConkie, *Commentary,* 3:480.

15. Beckwith, *Apocalypse,* 521.

16. *BJ.* 5:565.

17. Ford, *Revelation,* 98–99.

18. The Greek word *thanatos,* death, should probably not be taken literally here, but rather be translated as "pestilence." The Septuagint often uses *thanatos* as a translation of the Hebrew word meaning "pestilence" when a specific kind of death is meant (see, e.g., Lev. 26:25; Jer. 14:12; 24:10; Ezek. 5:12, 17; 14:21; 33:27). Since it is coupled with famine, the choice seems sound (Beckwith, *Apocalypse,* 523; Hailey, *Revelation,* 193).

19. Beckwith, *Apocalypse,* 524–25; Charles, *Commentary,* 1: 174.

20. A saying of Rabbi Akiba, *Aboth,* R.N. 26; see Charles, *Commentary,* 1:173.

21. Beckwith, *Apocalypse,* 526.

22. McConkie, *Commentary,* 3:483–84.

23. Apocalyptic literature was full of the belief that the consummation would not occur until the predestined number of the elect had been filled (cf. 2 Es. 4:36; App. Bar. 30:2).

24. See, e.g., Testament of Naphtali, 3:2–5; Ford, *Revelation,* 111.

25. Mounce, *Revelation,* 161–62.

26. In apocalyptic literature, see Assumption of Moses 10:4; 2 Esdras 5:8; 2 Baruch 70:8.

27. Beckwith, *Apocalypse,* 528.

28. McConkie, *Commentary,* 3:486.

29. Ford, *Revelation,* 112.

Chapter 7

1. John is not the only apocalyptist to use interludes. Such are found in the Old Testament just before the deluge (see Gen. 6–7) and in apocalyptic literature before the building of the ark (1 Enoch 66:1–2, 67) and before the destruction of the temple (2 Bar. 6:4–7:1).

2. See Matthew 14:30, 32; Mark 6:51; John 6:18; Acts 27:14. *Anemos* stands in contrast to *pneō,* "wind" or "breeze," in Acts 27:40 and *pnoē,* "wind," in Acts 2:2.

3. Ford, *Revelation,* 121. The Greek equivalent was the *kauma,* or "hot wind." 1 Enoch 76 speaks of noxious winds that brought drought, heat, destruction, and cold, as well as locusts and other pests. In this

chapter Enoch was shown the secrets of the winds, how they both bless and curse.

4. Joseph Fielding Smith, *Church History and Modern Revelation* (Salt Lake City: Deseret Book, 1953), 1:300–301.

5. McConkie, *Commentary,* 3:490.

6. If the number four is to be taken literally, these angels could symbolize John the Baptist and Peter, James, and John, who restored the priesthood keys to the dispensation of the fullness of times (see D&C 27:12–14).

7. McConkie, *Commentary,* 3:491–92. See also Smith, *Doctrines of Salvation,* 1:170–174.

8. Branding slaves and soldiers, especially those in the emperor's service, was a common practice in certain parts of the Roman empire. Guild members also bore tatoos as a means of identification. Among those religions that came out of the east, it was not uncommon for devotees of a certain god to wear his mark upon their heads as a sign of their consecration to that God (see Ford, *Revelation,* 116–17 for discussion).

9. Smith, *Teachings,* 321.

10. For an excellent discussion of this doctrine, see McConkie, *Commentary,* 3: 323–350.

11. Smith, *History,* 6:365; Ehat, *Words,* 368.

12. McConkie, *Commentary,* 3:491.

13. Iren. *Haer.* 5.30.2. The argument is based on the interpretation of Genesis 49:17 and Jeremiah 8:16 and expressed in the Testament of Dan 6:1.

14. The Testament of Dan 5:6 states that the prince of the tribe of Dan is Satan. However, not too much should be made from this since omitting tribal names from various lists was not uncommon: for example, Simeon in Deuteronomy 33, Judah in Judges 5, and Gad and Asher in 1 Chronicles 27.

15. Ford, *Revelation,* 118.

16. Caird, *Revelation,* 100.

17. Scott, *Exposition,* 171.

18. Mounce, *Revelation,* 173.

Chapter 8

1. In 1 Enoch 20:2–8 the names of the seven archangels are given as Suru'el, Raphael, Raguel, Michael, Saraqa'el, Gabriel, and Remiel. Seven angels are also mentioned in 1 Enoch 81:5; 90:21–22. The "angel of his presence," coming out of Isaiah 63:9, is mentioned repeatedly in Jubilees 1:27, 29; 2:1–2, 18; 15:27; 31:14. The idea of seven angels who administer the will of God was not foreign to John. However, John probably used the number to symbolize totality. All of heaven is mobilized to move at God's command.

2. John's erratic grammar causes some doubt as to the relation-

ship between the incense and the prayers of the Saints. The phrase *hina dōsei tais proseuchais* translates literally "in order that he will give [the incense] with the prayers." Here "with" translates the simple dative of the Greek. But in 5:8 the Seer has already specified that the incense and the prayers are one. Therefore, it is reasonable to assume that the same correlation exists here. The incense represents the prayers of the Saints making the dative a dative of reference (for discussion, see Mounce, *Revelation*, 182).

3. Bock, *Apocalypse*, 68.

4. The silence has been represented as a symbol of eternal rest, as a necessity so that God can hear the prayers of the Saints, as a military silence just before battle, and as the silence of creation (see Ford, *Revelation*, 134–35, for discussion). None of these seem to fit John's context.

5. Smith, *Teachings*, 157–58, 167–69.

6. Bock, *Apocalypse*, 71.

7. *The Way to Perfection* (Salt Lake City: Genealogical Society of Utah, 1931), 291. See also Bruce R. McConkie, *The Millennial Messiah* (Salt Lake City: Deseret Book, 1982), 578–88.

8. Mounce, *Revelation*, 184.

9. Charles, *Commentary*, 1:234.

10. Reference to the burning mountain is found in 1 Enoch 18:13 with a clear parallel to Revelation in 21:3, but cf. 1 Enoch 108:4.

11. McConkie, *Millennial Messiah*, 379–88.

12. The *dendron* of Matthew 7:17 is a fruit bearer, as is that of Jude 1:12. The *Baba Metzia* 59b states that when the world was smitten, a third of the olive crop, a third of the wheat crop, and a third of the barley crop were destroyed (on this, see Ford, *Revelation*, 132–33).

13. The idea current in John's time of God's judgments being in part a strike against the waters, which would turn them useless, is found in 4 Ezra 5:9. The thought may have come out of Jeremiah 9:15 and 23:15 and Proverbs 5:3–4. It is the reverse of the miracle recorded in Exodus 15:25 in which God healed the bitter waters. Wormwood (Hebrew *la'nah* and Greek *apsinthion*) is not itself poison, but in a number of Old Testament passages it is found parallel to a plant (*ra'ash*) that is (see Deut. 29:18; Lam. 3:19; Amos 5:7; 6:12). The connection may result from the fact that the bitterness of wormwood would make the water as undrinkable as if it were poisoned.

14. Hugh W. Nibley, *Since Cumorah* (Salt Lake City: Deseret Book, 1967), 384–87. Elder McConkie has written that these destructions "are of such a nature that they (speculatively!) could be brought to pass in large part through atomic warfare" (McConkie, *Commentary*, 3:499).

15. Caird, *Revelation*, 113.

16. The KJV, which uses *aggelos*, "angel," apparently is of the segment that follows Andreas's commentary on Revelation.

17. Mounce, *Revelation*, 189.

Chapter 9

1. The Greek for the KJV phrase "the key to the bottomless pit" is *hē kleis tou phreatos tēs abussou*, literally, "the key to the shaft of the abyss." The *phrear* is the shaft that leads down to hell.

2. See Amos 9:3; Job 41:31–32, Septuagint; 1 Enoch 17:7–8. These verses indicate that initially the abyss was the ocean, but it came to be viewed as a chasm in the earth, perhaps influenced by Isaiah 24:21–22. This latter idea prevailed in later literature. It was viewed as the place of intermediate punishment (cf. Luke 8:31; Charles, *Commentary*, 1: 240).

3. Hailey, *Revelation*, 225–26.

4. Ibid.

5. See Mounce, *Revelation*, 193–94.

6. Ford, *Revelation*, 148.

7. 1 Enoch 76 shows this same influence having the locusts invade primarily out of the north.

8. Mounce, *Revelation*, 195.

9. Hailey, *Revelation*, 230.

10. For discussion, see Ford, *Revelation*, 151; Mounce, *Revelation*, 196–97.

11. The term *abad* refers both to destruction (see Job 31:12) and to the place of destruction (see Job 26:6; Prov. 15:11; 27:20). The personification of Destruction along with Death in Job 28:22 could give rise to the name being associated with the prince of the underworld. The name of the Greek god Apollo comes from the same stock as Apolluōn. The sign of Apollo was the locust, and the god was called the "far darter" (referring to the darts he cast against his enemies) because he was the god of plague (for an example of his work, see Hom. *Il.* 1:43–52; for discussion, see Mounce, *Revelation*, 198).

12. Ford, *Revelation*, 145. The idea of angels of punishment is a popular motif in apocalyptic literature (see e.g. 1 Enoch 40:7; 53:3; 56:1; 62:11; 63:1; Test. Lev. 3:3; 2 Enoch 10:3). An example of destroying angels instigating a great host to move against Israel is found in 1 Enoch 56:5–6.

13. Charles, *Commentary*, 1:248.

14. The JST seems to underscore the idea that the numbers are not literal. John "sees" a vast host, which he symbolizes as myriads.

15. The source of the number could be Psalm 68:17 where the Septuagint has myriads of myriads (cf. Dan. 7:10; Rev. 5:11).

16. Scott, *Exposition*, 211.

17. Scott, *Exposition*, 213.

18. Mounce, *Revelation*, 204.

19. Smith, *Teachings*, 157; McConkie, *Millennial Messiah*, 578–80.

Chapter 10

1. Ford, *Revelation*, 161.

2. See ibid., 162.

3. Ibid.
4. McConkie, *Commentary*, 3:505.
5. Smith, *History*, 1:176.

Chapter 11

1. Ford, *Revelation*, 168.
2. On Solomon's temple, see 1 Kings 6; Ezekiel 10:5; 40:17, 20. If John had meant the temple complex of Herod with its courts, buildings, and porches, he would have probably used the word *hieron*, "temple" (cf. John 2:14).
3. The verb carries the meaning of being cast out by force, removed from favor, or left out of consideration.
4. 1 Enoch 61:1–5 mentions an angel with a measuring cord surveying the righteous for the purpose of preservation (cf. Zech. 12:2–3).
5. McConkie, *Commentary*, 3:509.
6. One cannot help but be reminded of the time Nephi was so filled with the power of God that had Laman or Lemuel touched him they would have been consumed. Even after a few days the residual power of the Spirit remained so strong that Nephi's touch shocked them (see 1 Ne. 17:48, 53–54).
7. The Qumran and other Jewish sects used a thirty-day solar calendar (Ford, *Revelation*, 171).
8. Ibid., 170.
9. Mounce, *Revelation*, 221.
10. Ibid., 221.
11. Charles, *Commentary*, 1:289, argues on the basis of an alternate interpretation of the phrase *hoi katoikountes epi tēs gēs* that the term does not mean those who dwell upon the earth, but those dwelling in the land of Palestine.
12. This is according to Clement of Alexandria, *Stromateis* 6.15 quoting a missing portion of the Assumption of Moses.
13. Scott, *Exposition*, 237.
14. Ibid., 238.
15. The words in the Elders' song echo Psalm 2:1–5.
16. McConkie, *Commentary*, 3:513; Mounce, *Revelation*, 233.
17. Caird, *Revelation*, 145.
18. There is some confusion on this verse. Malachi 4:1 reads, "The day that cometh shall burn them up," and this same phrase has been preserved in some accounts of the First Vision. However, since the most recent edition retains the phrase "They that come shall burn them," the official version is followed here.

Chapter 12

1. See endnote 21 following.
2. The full texts can be found in Ehat, *Words*, 168–90.

3. *TDNT*, s.v., *sēmeion*. See Moulton, *Vocabulary*, s.v. *sēmeion* where the word is used for a "sign," "seal," or "distinguishing mark" that is visible to the eye.

4. Ford, *Revelation*, 188; Scott, *Exposition*, 247.

5. Ford, *Revelation*, 188. Zion herself in 4 Ezra 9:43–45 and 10:43–45 also bears a child.

6. Hyrum L. Andrus, "Joseph Smith, Social Philosopher, Theorist and Prophet" (unpublished D.S.S. thesis, Syracuse University, 1955), 569. For discussions of the political kingdom of God, see James R. Clark, "Church and State Relationships in Education in Utah" (unpublished Ed.D. dissertation, Utah State University, 1958); Hyrum L. Andrus, *Foundations of the Millennial Kingdom of Christ*, vol. 3 in *Doctrines of the Kingdom* (Salt Lake City: Deseret Book, 1973); and the unsympathetic version by Klaus Hansen, *Quest for Empire: The Political Kingdom of God and the Council of Fifty in Mormon History* (Michigan: Michigan State University, 1959).

7. Smith, *History*, 7:381–82, where Brigham Young states: "As observed by one of the speakers this morning that kingdom [i.e. the kingdom of God] grows out of the Church of Jesus Christ of Latter-day Saints, but it is not the church."

8. Brigham Young, *The Kingdom of God* (n.p.: n.p., n.d.), 13. This is a pamphlet containing a speech given by the prophet July 1855 in Salt Lake City. A copy is located in the Harold B. Lee library at Brigham Young University.

9. Smith, *Doctrines*, 1:229; italics in original.

10. This was not the only thing that failed during the period of the meridian church. Joseph Smith noted that the Savior wished to gather Israel that they might "build unto the Lord a house whereby He could reveal unto His people the ordinances of His house and the glories of His kingdom. . . . Jesus did everything to gather the people, and they would not be gathered, and He therefore poured out curses upon them" (*Teachings*, 307–8). Part of that cursing was to take the kingdom away.

11. *TDNT*, s.v., *drakōn*. The symbol reaches way back in antiquity, being found among the Mesopotamians as both Tiamat and Labbu and among the Egyptians as Apophis, the main symbol of the Typhon along with the crocodile. In the Old Testament, it has the name of Rahab (see Isa. 51:9–10; Ps. 89:10), Leviathan (see Ps. 74:12–19; Isa. 27:1), and as the dragon of the sea (see Job 7:12; Ezek. 29:3–6; 32:2–8; see Charles, *Commentary*, 1:318–19).

12. For discussion, see John Day, *God's Conflict with the Dragon and the Sea* (Cambridge: Cambridge University Press, 1985), 62–87.

13. Scott, *Exposition*, 249–50.

14. Joseph Smith noted that when the prophets speak of beasts, they mean images, "they being types to represent certain things. At the same time they received the interpretation as to what those images or types were designed to represent" (*Teachings*, 291). He stated, fur-

ther, that the word "dragon" is actually a mistranslation and should be rendered "devil" (see Ehat, *Words*, 187).

15. Some variant readings replace red (*purrhos*) with fire (*pur*). The color may be derived from tradition. The serpent Set-Typhon of Egypt is red, as is that of Homer, *Iliad* 2.308.

16. Of interest is that the Ugaritic sea monster Leviathan possessed seven heads (see A. Herdner, *Corpus des tablettes en cuneiformes alphabétiques*, 2 vols. [Paris: University of Paris, 1963], 3.IIID.39; 5.I.3); and the idea is repeated in the Odes of Solomon 22:5 and *Pis. Soph.* 66.

17. Hailey, *Revelation*, 270.

18. Mounce, *Revelation*, 237–38.

19. The Greek is *surei*, the present indicative active third person singular form of the verb.

20. Adela Yarbro Collins, "The Power of Apocalyptic Rhetoric Catharsis," in Bloom, *Revelation*, 80–81.

21. Mounce, *Revelation*, 245.

22. Robinson, "Warring Against the Saints," 36.

23. For details and bibliography, see Day, *God's Conflict*, 101–4, 182–83.

24. Collins, "Power of Apocalyptic Rhetoric," in *Modern Critical Interpretations of the Revelation of St. John the Divine*, 80.

25. This incident is referred to a number of times in the Old Testament (see Num. 26:10; Deut. 11:6; Ps. 106:16–18).

Chapter 13

1. See Ehat, *Words*, 184–87.

2. Smith, *Teachings*, 294.

3. Ehat, *Words*, 184. See the beginning of chapter twelve. The record of Joseph Smith's talk by William Clayton shows that the beasts in chapter thirteen do not represent *all* the kingdoms of the world, but either the prophet did not explain what they did mean or the recorders missed it.

4. McConkie, *Commentary*, 3:520–21. Joseph Smith commented: "I make this broad declaration, that whenever God gives a vision of an image or beast, or figure of any kind, He always holds Himself responsible to give a revelation or interpretation of the meaning thereof, otherwise we are not responsible or accountable for our belief in it. Don't be afraid of being damned for not knowing the meaning of a vision or figure, if God has not given a revelation or interpretation of the subject" (*History*, 5:343; cf. Ehat, *Words*, 185).

5. Smith, *Teachings*, 293; cf. Ehat, *Words*, 187.

6. Collins, "Power," 80.

7. Hailey, *Revelation*, 283–84.

8. *TDNT*, s.v., *zōon; thērion; ktēnos*.

9. Mounce, *Revelation*, 250.

10. Hailey, *Revelation*, 283–84.

11. For a discussion of theories, see Hailey, *Revelation,* 285–86.

12. For an argument against the popular view, see A. Minear, "The Wounded Beast," *Journal of Biblical Literature,* 72 (1953): 97.

13. Ford, *Revelation,* 219. Joseph Smith's explanation of verses 2–3 has been poorly transmitted, making it difficult if not impossible to understand what he taught on the subject. According to the Clayton diary: "The beast John saw [crossed out at this point are the words 'as spoken of in the 13th chapter'] was an actual beast to whom power was to be given. An actual intelligent being in heaven and this beast was to have power given him" (Ehat, *Words,* 186). The crossed-out portion suggests that a correction was made because the reference was not to the beast in chapter thirteen. What Joseph did refer to seems to have been lost in transmission.

14. Charles, *Commentary,* 1:351.

15. Caird, *Revelation,* 166–67.

16. Ibid., 167; Mounce, *Revelation,* 254.

17. This is my translation. The passage is difficult. The NIV reads, "If anyone is to go into captivity, into captivity he will go. If anyone is to be killed with the sword, with the sword he will be killed." The RSV reads, "If anyone is to be taken captive, to captivity he goes; if any one slays with the sword, with the sword must he be slain."

18. Mounce, *Revelation,* 257.

19. Ibid., 248.

20. The tradition of the Antichrist held that miracles would be his mark (cf. 2 Esd. 5:4; Sib. Or. 3:63–67).

21. Mounce, *Revelation,* 258–59.

22. Bock, *Apocalypse,* 106–7.

23. *Commentary,* 3:523.

24. Mounce, *Revelation,* 259.

25. Mounce, *Revelation,* 260.

26. Charles, *Commentary,* 1:360.

27. *TDNT,* s.v., *Charagma.*

28. Adolf Deissmann, *Light from the Ancient East,* 277.

29. In a Christian example, the Sibylline Oracles 1:342–44 give the number of the name of the Savior in Greek as 888 (I = 10, A = 8, S = 200, O = 70, Y = 400, S = 200; for discussion, see Mounce, *Revelation,* 263).

30. For methodology, bibliography, and a list on many of the proposed solutions, see Ford, *Revelation,* 215–17; and Charles, *Commentary,* 1:366–68.

31. On these, see Irenaeus, *Against Heresies* 5.30.3.

32. For a broad spectrum of views on the subject, see Erdman, *Revelation,* 114–15; Hailey, *Revelation,* 297–99; Mounce, *Revelation,* 264–65.

33. Ezra Taft Benson, "Beware of Pride," *Ensign,* May 1989, 4–7.

34. Cf. C. S. Lewis, *Mere Christianity* (New York: Macmillan Publishing Company, 1960), 94–99.

Chapter 14

1. Erdman, *Revelation,* 116–17.
2. Caird, *Revelation,* 179; Mounce, *Revelation,* 270.
3. *TDNT,* s.v. *pseudos.*
4. Ford, *Revelation,* 243–44.
5. McConkie, *Commentary,* 3:529–30.
6. Bock, *Apocalypse,* 118.
7. Caird, *Revelation,* 184.
8. The idea of the Greek phrase (*kekerasmenou akratou*) translates literally "having been mixed undiluted." The participle denotes wine prepared with the addition of spices. The terms used stress that the wine is carefully prepared in its full strength (see Mounce, *Revelation,* 275.)
9. Cf. Mounce, *Revelation,* 274, and Caird, *Revelation,* 185.
10. See Matthews, *"A Plainer Translation,"* 210.
11. Mounce, *Revelation,* 281.
12. Ibid., 280–81.
13. Zechariah 14:1–4 sets the scene of the final battle near Jerusalem, while 1 Enoch 53:1 describes a deep valley near the city as the place of judgment.
14. Mounce, *Revelation,* 283.

Chapter 15

1. Hailey, *Revelation,* 319.
2. Caird, *Revelation,* 198.
3. Mounce, *Revelation,* 287.
4. Caird, *Revelation,* 199–200.
5. Scott, *Exposition,* 318.
6. Ibid., 323–24.

Chapter 16

1. Hailey, *Revelation,* 325. The scene painted here is not that of the final judgment, but that of the recompense of the Son of Man upon the wicked. The final judgment does not come into view until chapter twenty.
2. See, e.g., Mounce, *Revelation,* 291–92.
3. Ibid., 293–94.
4. See Moulton, *Vocabulary,* s.v. *kakos,* for this usage.
5. Hailey, *Revelation,* 327.
6. Ibid., 328.
7. Belief that angels were given direct responsibility over parts of the earth and the forces of nature grew during the postexilic period. By John's day, they were divided in ranks and orders culminating in an imposing hierarchy (see 1 Enoch 60:17, 19, 21; 61:10 for examples).

8. Caird, *Revelation*, 202.

9. For apocryphal literature, see 4 Ezra 13:43–47.

10. See Doctrine and Covenants 5:19; 29:16; 88:85 for just a few references showing the historical reality of Revelation.

11. Mounce, *Revelation*, 299. Frogs were regarded by the Zend religion as the source of plagues and death. Over much of the Near East, they were viewed as the agents of evil (see Charles, *Commentary*, 2:47).

12. Hailey, *Revelation*, 333–34.

13. Charles, *Commentary*, 2:48. According to 1 Enoch 15:8–11; 16:1; 19; and 99:7, the demoniac spirits made league with the antediluvian giants but abandoned them upon their destruction. They then went forth to afflict and seduce men through false signs. These demons, subject to Satan, were exempted from divine wrath until the final judgment (see Matt. 8:29; 1 Enoch 16:1).

14. See also 1 Enoch 56:5–8; 90:13–19.

15. Mounce, *Revelation*, 300.

16. Ibid., 300–301.

17. The Hebrew *bath* used in the scripture references designates a small unwalled town usually occupying the top of a hillock.

18. A good summary of thoughts can be found in J. Jeremias, "Har Magedon (Apc. 16:16)," *Zeitschrift für die neutestammentliche Wissenschaft*, 31 (1932): 73–77. Though this article is dated, it remains one of the best discussions on the subject. See also Charles, *Commentary*, 2:50–51.

19. For discussion, see Bruce R. McConkie, *Millennial Messiah*, 476–94.

20. The disappearance of the mountains is associated with the last days in apocalyptic literature (see Asmp. Mos. 10:4; 1 Enoch 1:6; cf. Sib. Or. 8:234, 236). The reason for the earth's smoothness is to make communication easier during the millennial era (cf. Sib. Or. 3:778–79).

Chapter 17

1. Hailey, *Revelation*, 345.

2. Bock, *Apocalypse*, 165–66.

3. Alfred Edersheim, *The Temple: Its Ministry and Services As They Were at the Time of Jesus Christ* (Grand Rapids: Eerdmans, 1975 reprint ed.), 312.

4. Ford, *Revelation*, 287.

5. Sir. 50:14–15 notes specifically that the cup of libation used by Simon the high priest was made of pure gold and filled with "the blood of grapes."

6. Ford, *Revelation*, 288.

7. For discussion, see Steven E. Robinson, "Early Christianity and 1 Nephi 13–14," in Monte S. Nyman and Charles D. Tate, Jr., eds., *The Book of Mormon: First Nephi, The Doctrinal Foundation* (Provo,

Utah: Religious Studies Center, Brigham Young University, 1988), 177–91.

8. For an excellent discussion of the great and abominable church in this guise, see Robinson, "Early Christianity," 182–84.

9. Bock, *Apocalypse*, 146.

10. Fiorenza, *Revelation*, 7.

11. Robinson, "Early Christianity," 180.

12. See Moulton, *Vocabulary*, s.v., *thaumazō*, for such usage.

13. The tense is future but the construction is paraphrastic (*kai mellei anabainein ek tēs abussou*). The beast is about to come out of the abyss; its arising is close at hand.

14. Caird, *Revelation*, 215–16.

15. From the days of Servius Tullius, Rome's sixth king, the city was known as *urbs septicollis*, the city of seven hills. The *Septimontium*, a holiday in December, celebrated the enclosure of the seven hills with Rome's walls (see Suet *Dom.* 4). Latin literature abounds in references to the city of seven hills (see Verg. *G.* 2.535; *Aen.* 6.783; Hor. *Carm.* 7; Ov. *Tr.* 1.5, just as examples).

16. Mounce, *Revelation*, 315.

17. For a sampling, see Charles, *Commentary*, 2:71–72; and especially Ford, *Revelation*, 289–90.

18. See Charles, *Commentary*, 2:67, 70, 76–87.

19. Mounce, *Revelation*, 316–17.

20. See also 1 Enoch 9:4; 2 Maccabees 13:4. The title is old and can be traced back to early Babylonian times when the god Marduk was designated by this title. Further, Babylonian and Persian kings claimed the title, maintaining that they were rulers by divine right (see Ezra 7:12; Daniel 2:37). Thus, the title designates deity or one empowered by deity.

21. Cf. 1 Enoch 38:5; 90:19; 91:12. See Charles, *Commentary*, 2:74.

Chapter 18

1. Caird, *Revelation*, 222.

2. Mounce, *Revelation*, 330–31.

3. Caird, *Revelation*, 224.

4. Ibid., 223.

5. Ford, *Revelation*, 303.

6. This whole passage appears to have been modeled after Ezekiel 27. There the fall of Tyre is described in much the same way as that of Babylon.

7. The last phrase (*hoti ekrinen ho theos to krima humōn eks autēs*) is difficult to translate. It says literally "because God judged the judgment of you from her." Since *krinō* carries the idea to decide cases or pass judgment upon, I have translated it in the sense "to pass judgment upon." *Krima* is used three ways in the New Testament: the right to act as judge (see Rev. 20:4), the judicial act of passing sentence (see

NOTES TO PAGES 203–28 277

John 9:39; Rom. 5:16), and most frequently the sentence passed by a judge. Only the last definition fits the context as "your judgment."

Chapter 19

1. Moulton, *Vocabulary*, s.v. *althēs*.
2. In apocalytic literature, cf. 2 Baruch 29:3–7.
3. Scott, *Exposition*, 382.
4. *Teachings*, 119.
5. Exodus 15:3 depicts Jehovah as a man of war. The idea persists in 2 Maccabees 3:22–30 and in the Qumran scrolls 1QM 12.10–11; 19.2–4.
6. McConkie, *Commentary*, 3:566.
7. Caird, *Revelation*, 241.
8. McConkie, *Commentary*, 3:567.
9. Mounce, *Revelation*, 345–46.
10. Ibid., 345–46.
11. Caird, *Revelation*, 245.

Chapter 20

1. Erdman, *Revelation*, 153.
2. In 1 Enoch 53:4–54:5, the binding powers are exercised against the dark angels and the kings of the earth, and both are judged together. In 1 Enoch 28:12–16; 19:1–2; 21:1–6, the angels of the devil are held in temporary punishment until the final judgment. Azazael, however, is bound separately from the rest and in the end is cast into everlasting punishment (Charles, *Commentary*, 2:141–42).
3. Scott, *Exposition*, 396.
4. McConkie, *Commentary*, 570–71.
5. George Eldon Ladd, *Revelation* (Grand Rapids: Eerdmans, 1972), 263.
6. Smith, *Doctrines*, 2:29; 3:63–64.
7. The Greek of Revelation is sufficiently irregular that it is hard to determine if John had in mind one, two, or even three groups.
8. *TDNT*, s.v. *krinō* and *krima*, where it is noted that the Greek words refer to judgment in legal matters but that when they are used to translate Old Testament concepts, they take on the idea of rule.
9. Ladd, *Revelation*, 264.
10. M. Eugene Boring, *Revelation* (Louisville: John Knox Press, 1989), 202.

Chapter 21

1. Ladd, *Revelation*, 278.
2. The idea appears in Sibylline Oracles 5:447 and the Assumption of Moses 10:6 (Caird, *Revelation*, 262).

3. See 2 Baruch 4:2–4; 1 Enoch 7:26; 13:36. Charles, *Commentary*, 2:161.

4. Caird, *Revelation*, 262.

5. Mounce, *Revelation*, 370.

6. For discussion, see Caird, *Revelation*, 264–65.

7. Ibid., 264–65.

8. Ibid., 266.

9. Some mauscripts have *gegona* and seem to refer to those things spoken to John.

10. Smith, *Teachings*, 220.

11. Caird, *Revelation*, 267.

12. Ford, *Revelation*, 339.

13. Beckwith, *Apocalypse*, 54–55. See also Tobit 13:16–18; Sibylline Oracles 3:743–45; Apocalypse of Baruch 73:2–4; 1 Enoch 10:17–21; 25:6.

14. Brigham Young, *Journal of Discourses*, 26 vols. (Liverpool: Albert Carrington, 1869), 2:31.

15. Boring, *Revelation*, 218.

16. Joseph. *AJ* 3.7.7; Philo *De Mon.* 2.5. These authors bring something into play that is worthy of at least a note. They connect the twelve Israelite gems with the twelve signs of the Zodiac. Ancient Arabian and Egyptian belief ascribed godly power to these because heaven was the home of the gods. But John lists the stones in exactly the reverse order in which the sun actually moves through them. This seems more than coincidental. John may well have been aware of various speculations about the home of the gods and was stating that the reality had nothing to do with earthly conjectures on the subject (Charles, *Commentary*, 2:166–67).

17. For discussion, see Boring, *Revelation*, 214; Charles, *Commentary*, 2:158–59.

18. Ford, *Revelation*, 336. The only systematic treatments of the nature of stones coming out of the ancient world are Theophrastus's *On Stones* and Pliny's *Natural History*, book 27.

19. McConkie, *Commentary*, 3:588.

20. Both 2 Esdras 13:35–38; Apocalypse of Baruch 40:1 paint a similar picture.

Chapter 22

1. Ford, *Revelation*, 338 notes a tradition in which there are two springs, one of milk and the other of honey, which flow out of the city.

2. God himself appears to be the fountain of living waters in Jeremiah 2:13 and 1 Enoch 96:6.

3. For discussion, see Mounce, *Revelation*, 386–87.

4. See, for example, 1 Enoch 25:2–7; 2 Enoch 8:3.

5. Ladd, *Revelation,* 288.
6. Ibid.

Appendix B

1. The ideas used here follow Beckwith, *Apocalypse,* 241–42.
2. Feuillet, *Apocalypse,* 34.
3. For a discussion, see Eugene H. Peterson, "Apocalypse: The Medium Is the Message," *Theology Today,* 26 (1969): 133–41.
4. G. R. Beasley-Murray in "The Contribution of the Book of Revelation to the Christian Belief in Immortality," *Scottish Journal of Theology,* 27 (1974): 76–93, writes about the recent recognition by scholars that John's symbolic images were drawn extensively from an ancient tradition. His language would have seemed clear to his contemporary audience.
5. Fiorenza, *Revelation,* 135; Beckwith, *Apocalypse,* 221.
6. Fiorenza, *Revelation,* 22; Hailey, *Revelation,* 36; Beckwith, *Apocalypse,* 221. For a complete study, see Charles, *Commentary,* 1:lxv–lxxxvi.

SCRIPTURE INDEX

SUBJECT INDEX

Abomination, biblical meaning of, 189

Adam, 92–93, 95, 110

Adam-ondi-Ahman, 110

Agency, 53, 247–48

Alexander the coppersmith, 6

Almighty, Jesus Christ as, 31

Alpha and Omega, 231

Altar, imagery of, 69, 175–76

Amos, 97

Angel(s): "signifies" vision of John, 26; strong, searches for one to open scroll, 54–55; four, holding winds in check, 77; carrying seal of living God, 80–81; with censer containing prayers of Saints, 90, 92–93; release of destroying, 107–8, 269 n. 12; "another," preceding seventh trumpet, 112–15; with everlasting gospel to preach throughout earth, 157–59; proclaims fall of Babylon, 159, 199; harvesting of earth by, 161–64; seven, with seven last plagues, 166, 169; hurls millstone into sea, 204; rebukes John for worshipping him, 210; summons

birds of prey, 212–13; casts Satan into bottomless pit, 215–17; takes John to see bride, 233; positioned at gates of heavenly city, 235; names of, in apocryphal book, 267 n. 1; hierarchy of, 274 n. 7 (ch. 16)

Antichrists, 6, 38, 146, 190

Apocalyptic literature, 14–17, 259–60 nn. 12 and 14

Apostasy: threat of, to early church, 5–6, 37–40; described in Book of Mormon, 41–42, 221–22

Apostles, 57–58, 219, 235–36; false, 6–7

Ark of the covenant, 125

Armageddon, 179–80

Armies, 108, 179, 222–23

Authority, divine, 5–8, 35, 37–38, 181

Babel, tower of, 204

Babylon: angel proclaims fall of, 159–60, 199; harlot identified as, 189–90; power of, grounded in wealth, 199–200, 204–5; Saints are warned to come out